TEACHING DRAMA 11–18

Related titles:

Martin Blocksidge (ed.): *Teaching Literature 11–18*
Sue Cowley: *Starting Teaching*
Colin Durrant and Graham Welch: *Making Sense of Music: Foundations for Music Education*
Duncan Grey: *The Internet in School*
Richard Hickman (ed.): *Art Education 11–18*
J.G. Lloyd: *How Exams Really Work*
Roy Prentice (ed.): *Teaching Art and Design*

Teaching Drama 11–18

Edited by
Helen Nicholson

continuum

Continuum

The Tower Building
11 York Road
London SE1 7NX, UK

80 Maiden Lane
Suite 704
New York, NY 10038

www.continuumbooks.com

First published 2000
Reprinted 2003, 2004, 2007

British Library Cataloguing-in-Publication Data
A catalogue record for this book is available from the British Library.

ISBN-10: 0-8264-4805-4 (paperback)
ISBN-13: 978-0-8264-4805-7 (paperback)

Typeset by Paston Prepress Ltd, Beccles, Suffolk
Printed in Great Britain by Biddles Ltd, *www.biddles.co.uk*

Contents

The Contributors

Merrilyn Evans has taught students on literacy schemes, adults in continuing education and young people in secondary schools. Currently head of English and drama in a girls' school, where she regularly directs productions, Merry is keen to promote enjoyable encounters with Shakespeare. Following work with the Royal Shakespeare Company, she is researching into 'active' teaching methods.

Jane M. Gangi is an assistant professor in the teacher education programme at Sacred Heart University in Fairfield, Connecticut. Her research interests include responding to literature and drama in the context of a mass-media communication environment. Her published work includes a chapter in David Hornbrook's edited collection *On the Subject of Drama*.

Sharon Grady is an assistant professor in the Department of Theatre and Dance at the University of Texas at Austin (USA) and an Associate Fellow at The Central School of Speech and Drama in London. Her areas of specialization include the practice and theory of drama and theatre in education as well as qualitative research methods.

Shane Irwin has worked as a scenic artist, performer, writer, director and teacher. In 1992 Shane co-founded Colourise Theatre Company, creating performance, educational and community-based work. He currently lectures on the BA Theatre Arts, Education, and Deaf Studies course at the University of Reading, and teaches drama at Hamilton Lodge school for deaf children.

Melissa Jones is currently co-ordinator for expressive arts and teacher of drama at Saffron Walden County High School in Essex. She has also worked as an examiner for drama at many different levels. In 1988 she spent a year in New Zealand where she ran courses for drama teachers. Melissa is closely involved with initial teacher training in drama and arts education.

Andy Kempe leads the postgraduate certificate of education (PGCE) drama course at the University of Reading, where he trains teachers of drama in secondary schools, and is assistant director of the whole initial teacher training course. He has written many practical handbooks and curriculum guides for drama teachers, and has also researched and written on a wide range of issues in drama education.

Denise Margetts is currently working in Hackney, London, as a literacy consultant. She was formerly an advisory teacher for English in Oxfordshire with a particular interest in whole-school literacy. She taught English and drama at Peers School, Oxford, where she was the co-ordinator of one of the pilot summer literacy schools.

Helen Nicholson is director of drama studies at Homerton College, Cambridge. She teaches undergraduate courses in drama production and contemporary theatre, and PGCE courses in drama education. Formerly head of arts in a secondary school, Helen has research interests in many different aspects of arts education.

Jennifer Simons is a senior lecturer in drama education at the University of Sydney, Australia. She has taught in primary and secondary schools, and has been involved in pre-service and postgraduate teacher education for about 20 years. Jennifer has also worked with teachers in Europe, New Zealand, Canada, USA, Mexico and Africa.

Robert D. Taylor is associate professor of interdisciplinary arts and performance at Arizona State University West. Primarily a teacher of acting and directing for multimedia performance, Rob is also a strong advocate for arts education. He is co-author of the award-winning high school textbook, *Theatre-Art in Action*, published by NTC/Contemporary.

Steve Waters is a playwright and teacher. Until recently, he was head of performing arts at Hills Road Sixth Form College, Cambridge. He is currently playwright in residence at the Hampstead Theatre, London, where his play *English Journeys* was recently performed. He also teaches undergraduates at Homerton College, Cambridge, and on an MA in playwriting at Goldsmiths College, University of London.

Bryony Williamson is currently drama co-ordinator at the Priory School, Hitchin, Herts. Prior to this she founded three drama companies, most notably Artsmeet which worked to bring the expressive arts to young people with learning difficulties. Her proudest achievement is her son Rowan, who was born while she was working on her contribution to this book.

Bruce Wooding is a lecturer in drama education at The Central School of Speech and Drama, London. Formerly head of drama at an inner London comprehensive school, he has a particular interest in world theatre. Bruce holds an MA from the Open University, and has worked in the Netherlands, Switzerland, India and Ghana.

Acknowledgements

I am sure that all the contributors to this book would wish to join with me in paying tribute to the energy, enthusiasm and lively criticism of all the students we have taught, in many different contexts, and from whom we continue to learn. For my part, I should like to thank those who have worked with me on this book, who have shared their ideas and experiences so generously, and have responded to my questions and editorial comments with enormous thoughtfulness and patience.

Helen Nicholson

Introduction: Dramatic Practices and Pedagogic Principles

Helen Nicholson

This collection of writings is about how students learn to explore and communicate ideas, thoughts and feelings in a diversity of dramatic languages. In this book, drama teachers and practitioners share their experiences of working with students in the 11–18 age range, offer practical ideas for teaching, and reflect on how the concepts, skills and knowledge described in their practice contribute to students' drama education. Using a range of dramatic practices and teaching strategies, the contributors to this book record and discuss how students might combine thought, language and feeling in a range of energetic and creative ways.

Whatever differences of approach are illustrated in this book, there is general agreement that drama education is centrally concerned with encouraging students to reach new understandings by shaping and developing ideas in the process of making and performing drama, and gaining insights into diverse dramatic, theatrical and performative practices, histories and traditions. As a creative subject, however, it is clearly too simplistic to talk about students gaining 'understandings' and 'insights' as if it were a simple matter of transmitting a well-defined body of knowledge which the teacher knows and the students must memorize. On the contrary, although there are recognizable practices in drama which students might acquire, reaching new understandings implies a creative and personal involvement with the work. In relation to drama education, this form of understanding is a difficult concept to describe, so I shall borrow from Timberlake Wertenbaker's play, *Our Country's Good*, where it is particularly well illustrated. The play charts the experiences of a group of eighteenth-century convicts who, on arrival at Sydney cove, prepare to perform the first Australian production of Farquhar's *The Recruiting Officer*. As they rehearse, one of the characters, Wisehammer, reflects on the significance and purpose of drama. Drawing on his experience of working on the play, he suggests that 'a play should make you understand something new'.[1] Unlike many of the officers in the play, for whom drama is, at best, a means of civilizing the 'savages' and at worst an irrelevant frippery, the convicts have come to recognize that drama and theatre can be a powerful way to create a sense of community, to develop shared understandings, to resist oppression and to become active participants in a culture. In this context, Wisehammer's line implies that it is through the process of engagement with drama, through actively creating and exploring ideas, thoughts and feelings in dramatic form, that they temporarily escape the harsh realities of their everyday lives and learn to imagine something different.

It seems appropriate to begin this book by invoking Wisehammer's words because the idea that drama should 'make you understand something new' is deeply embedded in a whole range of practices in drama education. Drama education is not, of course, solely concerned with performing scripted plays, nor does it necessarily create a better world, but it does enable and invite students to reach new understandings by working in a variety of dramatic contexts. In common with many art forms, drama is in itself often regarded as an educative medium; it is a particular way of creating, inventing, symbolizing and representing values, ideas and feelings. The semi-fictional convicts in Wertenbaker's play recognized the ways in which drama might engage the imagination, enabling them to think, feel and see things differently; young people similarly need imaginative forms with which to explore the ambiguities and contradictions of the world within which they are growing up.

Drama education, at its most inclusive, invites students not only to engage with the dramatic narratives of others, but also to find ways to communicate their own ideas. In drama, intellectual and emotional involvement with the narratives of others is integral to the learning, wherein moral, political and cultural values are open, temporarily and contingently, to renegotiation and interpretation.[2] In this context, making drama, as all drama teachers are well aware, involves a rather messy process of discussion, questioning, speculation, experimentation and reflection; it requires students both to explore their own ideas and values and to interpret those with which they are less familiar. From this point of view, drama education is a living art form in which students might 'understand something new' both about their own lives and those of others.

This book reflects the diverse interests and experiences of the contributors, and the very different educational contexts and artistic practices within which they work. It does not represent a manifesto for drama teaching nor does it articulate a standard ideology or single approach to drama education. What does emerge from this book, however, is a shared view that drama offers students the space and time to develop new ideas and insights in a range of contexts, and that by working in the medium they may learn how to use different dramatic conventions, genres, forms and structures to communicate with others. In this way, the practice of drama is regarded both as a discipline and as a journey; it involves a synthesis of student-centred and subject-centred educational approaches. At its richest, the drama curriculum embraces a range of cultural forms, includes a variety of aesthetic and artistic practices and introduces students to new ways of thinking and feeling. It is an uncertain, creative and sometimes haphazard process in which, to borrow words attributed to Brecht, 'One thinks feelings and one feels thoughtfully.'[3]

A MAGIC MACHINE: THE LANGUAGES OF DRAMA

One of the special qualities of drama is that participants are able to 'think feelings and feel thoughtfully' in a variety of different ways. Unlike many traditional education practices which are dominated by the written word, drama is a 'multi-modal' art form, and necessarily requires students to use visual images, movement and sound as well as words. This means, in practice, that participants in drama use its visual, kinaesthetic, aural and verbal qualities to shape, symbolize and represent thoughts and feelings into dramatic structures, genres and forms which are recognizable to others. With the educational implications of this in mind, I have chosen to unite the various techniques, skills, devices, conventions, crafts, traditions, genres and styles, which constitute and describe drama practices under a single metaphor and conceptual term: the *languages* of drama.[4]

To apply the term 'languages' to drama is perhaps surprising to those of us who work in an educational climate where language and literacy have become associated with correctness and accuracy rather than creativity. However, by looking beyond this narrow definition of language learning, a more interesting picture emerges. Understanding language is not simply a case of decoding isolated images, of defining individual words, or rote learning. Rather, acquiring a language is a process which involves both emotion and cognition; language enables us to think, to describe emotions, to participate in a culture and to practise drama. Writing specifically about drama education, Michael Fleming suggests that 'to use language effectively is to learn to live with uncertain boundaries'.[5]

In identifying the physical, dynamic and creative qualities of language, Merleau-Ponty describes it as a 'magic machine', which lies at the heart of all social interaction.[6] Ian Frowe, who discusses the significance of language in the secondary school curriculum, argues that language is not only a means of social communication, but also integral to emotional and conceptual development.

> Language enables us to operate in a world which is no longer tied to the physical and the concrete, to the here and now ... To comprehend the idea of something meaning something else – a gesture or grunt as symbolic – is to be operating in a linguistic domain.[7]

Seen in this light, it seems logical to extend the term 'language' to the complex physical, aural, visual and verbal sign-systems which constitute drama. Drama has many functions but, in common with verbal languages, it has a particular power to conceptualize, represent and interpret the social world. As such, all language, including the multi-modal languages of drama, is a symbolic system which is part of the collective fabric of social interaction, cultural exchange and dialogue; it is a living, vibrant and creative mode of communication and thought, which changes with use. This means, importantly, that language is central to creative learning; it is in language that concepts are formulated because we use language, including the artistic and multi-modal languages of drama, to think and to bring feelings to cognition.[8]

By calling these different modes of representation and ways of working in drama 'languages', I am attempting to draw attention to a theory of knowing and understanding which does not separate the mind from the body, cognition from the emotions, the intellectual from the physical. What drama demonstrates is the interrelationship between the two, where the gaps and silences, the stillness and the movement speak as loudly as words. In drama, there is a special interconnectedness between the mind and the body, thought and action. Simon McBurney, artistic director of Théâtre de Complicité, suggests that successful practice relies on a shared and constantly evolving theatre language which he describes as 'physical, vocal, musical and architectural'.[9] As such, in the practice of drama, it is through the body that thought, emotions and experiences are created, materialized, symbolized and represented in ways that are interactive, enactive and energetic. This is what Merleau-Ponty calls 'body-knowing', a term he uses to suggest that the body is not merely the instrument of the mind nor a 'chunk of space or a bundle of functions'. It is very literally how we experience and interact with the world.[10]

Understanding the physical languages of drama, and using them to think as well as to feel, enables students to interpret and question the particular mix of personal, social, artistic and cultural narratives which they carry with them. Because drama necessarily includes a range of artistic languages – the visual, verbal, aural, kinaesthetic – drama opens up different ways of exploring experiences and communicating with others. In this book, practitioners and teachers reflect on how they have encouraged students to combine the artistic languages of drama in interesting and creative ways. In balancing student-centred and subject-centred approaches to drama education, they demonstrate how students' creative and intellectual horizons might be extended by introducing a diversity of cultural forms and dramatic practices into their teaching, while also recognizing the different ways in which individual students feel, think and learn.

STRUCTURE AND FLEXIBILITY

In the drama classroom, one of the challenges which confronts teachers who work with students in the 11–18 age range is how to balance the need for clearly structured learning objectives with the kind of flexibility which leads to innovative and creative drama. It is a case of how to introduce students to a range of cultural forms and dramatic practices, and encourage them to feel physically, intellectually and emotionally involved with the work. Further-more, for many teachers of drama in secondary schools and colleges there is a potential tension between, on the one hand, the demands of an education system driven by standardization and measurable learning outcomes and, on the other, the processes of working in drama which are often most interesting when the unexpected or unforeseen is accommodated and accepted.

Finding a balance, rather than a compromise, between these two apparently conflicting positions requires a theory of learning which not only recognizes the open, dialogic and 'unfixed' qualities of drama but also acknowledges that students are often supported and challenged by approaches to learning which are clearly structured. This is a recurring theme throughout this book, where different practitioners demonstrate a range of ideas about how this issue might be addressed. In an attempt to recognize what John O'Toole calls the 'unpredicted meanings' of drama, and to provide a structured learning environment, many of the writers draw directly or indirectly on the work of Vygotsky and Bruner, whose theories about the relationship between thought, language and learning have been long embedded in educational theory and in drama education.[11] However, as it is the key concept of 'scaffolding' which provides many authors in this book with the bridge between structured learning and creative flexibility, it is worth revisiting.

The metaphor of 'scaffolding' is particularly helpful in drama education because it suggests both the kind of active, creative and exploratory learning which is central to the subject, and the kind of structured intervention which enables the students to move forward. In practice, what this means is that the rationale, starting point and learning objectives for the drama are carefully planned in advance, although, unlike science where the results of experiments are predicted and predictable, in drama it is the particular area of learning which is planned, and not the shape or outcome of the practical work. For example, in Chapter 2 by Shane Irwin about physical theatre, the students know that they are working within a particular style and genre, and the dramatic form itself gives students a particular framework which they can interpret and adapt for themselves. By contrast, in Chapter 5 Andy Kempe describes ways of devising drama which are potentially more eclectic in dramatic style, but the starting point for the drama – a character, a space, image or dramatic idea – is clearly delineated. In both cases, the drama begins with a structure, and because the focus for the work is well established – physical theatre and devised drama – there are artistic constraints imposed. It is, perhaps paradoxically, because there are constraints on the work that students are prompted to find creative solutions to artistic problems; they gain new insights into how drama works as an art form as they explore their own ideas. To use an analogy from the visual arts, students in this age range are usually able to work more creatively with paint if they have learnt how to mix colours.

The ability to offer 'scaffolding' for students' learning is particularly relevant for a drama curriculum which aims to encourage students to try out new ideas during the process of working. As the drama develops, original intentions are revised, material rejected or changed, and alternative ideas take shape. Art-making, as Richard Wollheim has pointed out, is a process of speculation, improvisation and invention within the medium itself, where ideas and intentions are revised and changed as the artwork takes shape.[12] In educational terms, however spontaneous this may look on the surface, it requires meticulous planning and subject-knowledge on the part of the teacher. It involves an analysis of the relationship between dramatic form and content, and an understanding of what particular knowledge, skills and understanding students require when, for example, they develop a devised play, improvise in role or create a piece of physical theatre. As the contributors to this book demonstrate, this detailed preparation provides the focus for the work; it enables them to intervene with purpose, to define clear assessment criteria, to encourage students to interpret ideas flexibly and use the medium creatively.[13]

In the drama practices described in this book, the role of the teacher is not one of didactic instruction, but of guided intervention. Guidance is almost invariably embedded in the practical activity of the classroom, where teachers monitor and evaluate student progress, and introduce appropriate resources, information and materials to consolidate and challenge their learning as the work develops. In drama, as a physical and ephemeral art form, one of the ways to introduce new ideas and ways of working is through modelling practice and providing clearly identified frames for their work. Both processes – modelling and framing – are forms of 'scaffolding'; they enable students to recognize and understand the structures and conventions of the dramatic form within which they are working. By responding to, and interacting with, the work of others, the students learn how to use a particular aspect of drama for themselves. Jennifer Simons in Chapter 1 gives a careful analysis of the place of modelling in role play, and the particular ways in which the device of teacher-in-role can encourage younger students to engage in dramatic story-telling. In Chapter 3, Denise Margetts, with her class of 14-year-olds, frames their dramatic writing by asking them to enact physically, deconstruct and interpret a playscript, while Sharon Grady (Chapter 11) offers her group of 17-year-old students a structure to help them 'read' and interpret the language of *kathakali* dance drama with which they were unfamiliar. In all cases, the students' learning is purposefully mediated by structured teaching, and is also embedded in the practice of drama as a physical, active and reflective process.

Finding a balance between structure and flexibility in drama education ought not to be a matter of squeezing pedagogic aims into a rigidly audited curriculum. On the contrary, drama practitioners have adopted processes of learning which are appropriate to the form itself. Neither the creative practice of making and performing drama, nor the educational practice of 'scaffolding' is a linear process; concepts, ideas and feelings are revisited, revised, contested, reinterpreted and renegotiated. As such, learning to make, perform and respond to drama is a cyclical process, where a well-structured curriculum will allow for reflection and experimentation. Part of the magic of teaching drama lies not only in introducing students to a diversity of dramatic languages, but also in giving them space and time to find the gaps and silences where meaning is made.

LEARNING IN CONTEXT

Taken as a whole, this book includes a range of approaches to teaching drama. It does not, however, in any way represent an attempt to map an entire drama curriculum; there are obvious omissions and inevitable gaps. Indeed, one of the pleasures of teaching drama is that, despite an increasing emphasis on standardization in education, there is often considerable flexibility to choose which aspects of drama are included in any particular curriculum framework or educational programme. Drama is, by its nature, a healthy hybrid and an eclectic art form; it spans the literary traditions of Western theatre, new technologies of film, television and live art, performative events such as ritual, carnival and street theatre, and the spontaneity of improvisation and role-play. Indeed, theatre anthropology has expanded the description of what constitutes drama and performance and new practices continually emerge as traditions are juxtaposed, revisited and reinterpreted. In practice, this means that any drama curriculum is necessarily selective, and the practices and pedagogies included in the drama classroom reflect the values of the teachers, the needs and interests of the students and the particular local contexts in which they work.

Despite differences in curriculum content, there is widespread agreement, both between the contributors to this book and elsewhere, that learning takes place most appropriately when dramatic practices are contextualized. It is a point made by Michael Fleming who, in his discussion of progression in drama, recognizes the risks of superficiality in a skills-led drama curriculum which does not ground the work in appropriate contexts.[14] Learning in drama takes place most successfully in the context of practical exploration, where theoretical understandings and technical skills are acquired as an integral part of the students' creative work. Reciprocally, creativity is enhanced by explicit knowledge of dramatic forms, developed as a result of research, practical experimentation and focused reading. Sharon Bailin describes this approach to drama education as 'creativity in context', in which students are encouraged to make connections between their own work and that of other practitioners.[15] In this way, creativity is both inventive and reflexive; it is a process in which students are engaged in critical interrogation of both the dramatic form and the ideas, feelings and values which they seek to symbolize and represent.

The idea that critical and creative practices are intimately connected, and that all drama is culturally specific, places a renewed emphasis on the context of dramatic production and reception. Informed by various versions of reader-response theory, this position rejects the traditional liberal humanist notion which assumes that all individuals share similar emotions, values and cultural reference points, and recognizes that all aspects of cultural praxis, including drama, may be interpreted in a multiplicity of ways. This recognition of difference, as a feature of equality, entails critical reflection on one's own inherited values and beliefs, and an understanding of the social and cultural contexts of others. Writing about critical reception as a creative act, Pierre Bourdieu suggests that there is a reciprocal relationship between self-reflexivity and other-understanding. In order to establish a popular aesthetic, he argues, which is based on active participation in the arts and engaged readership, there is a need both to recognize and interrogate one's own assumptions and understand the social contexts in which works of art were produced. Bourdieu regards this as one way in which individuals might extend their cultural horizons; through contrasting one's own values with others, he argues, it becomes possible to escape the kind of self-contemplation which he regards as narcissistic.[16]

Acknowledging the contexts of dramatic production and reception is one way to avoid the pitfalls of exoticism and the superficiality of cultural tourism which sometimes accompany the study and practice of non-Western dramatic forms. However, a sharp division between 'self' and 'other', particularly when related to cultural practice, risks sustaining old inequalities where anything other than dominant values and mainstream dramatic forms are effectively marginalized.[17] Furthermore, in our globalized and culturally diverse societies, any attempt to categorize either individual identity or social practices as belonging exclusively to one culture, community or tradition is likely, at the very least, to run into problems. None the less, as many of the contributors to this book argue, drama education does provide an active and dynamic forum for debate, self-interpretation and cultural exchange. In this way, a diversity of voices, dramatic forms, cultural languages and experiences might be recognized, interrogated and valued.

A CULTURE OF PARTICIPATION

As all the contributors to this book illustrate, at the core of our subject lies the familiar Deweyan notion that students learn best by doing. However, what is particular about drama is that experiential learning is not just a pedagogic tool, it is intrinsic to the art form itself. Unlike many other subjects in the curriculum, drama requires physical action and collaboration; the processes of creative, critical and lively engagement with ideas and practices are not prefaces to more sober forms of learning, but integral to the subject. Furthermore, as a collaborative art form, drama does not rely on individualized learning, but on group work; students are obliged to work together to reach shared understandings and agreed interpretations, albeit temporarily, if their work is to have artistic coherence.

Achieving a culture of participation in drama, where students might engage in robust debate and share thoughtful practice, is not, however, solely dependent on students' co-operative behaviour, although this is obviously important. Students are also supported as collaborative learners when they have a precise understanding of the aims and scope of the drama, and when the teaching strategies included in the lessons accommodate different ways of learning. This is where a concept of dramatic languages, when combined with theories of learning styles, is particularly helpful. Recent research into how students learn confirms, unsurprisingly, that they learn differently. Michael Fielding suggests that some students are primarily visual learners, preferring to learn through the written word, diagrams, pictures and other visual images; some are mainly auditory learners, who find it easier to learn through talk, discussion and listening to others, and some students, frequently the most neglected by traditional teaching methods, are kinaesthetic learners, who remember what they do and experience, who like to move around the classroom and work through problems physically.[18]

What is striking about this description of differentiated learning styles is how closely it mirrors the practice of drama, which often synthesizes aural, visual, kinaesthetic and verbal languages. Interestingly, therefore, drama necessarily includes a range of learning styles within the art form itself. For example, kinaesthetic learners may be most immediately engaged when they are able to explore ideas in movement, and when they are able to use choreography as a form of dialogue; aural learners may feel most comfortable with the dynamics of sound and the spoken word; visual learners may have particular insights into the visual imagery and the use of space. The strength of working in drama is that these skills can be pooled, and that all are necessary to lively creative practice. In terms of the practicalities of the classroom, what this means is that a culture of participation does not rely primarily on the good intentions of the students to co-operate with each other; they are also supported by working in a range of dramatic forms and practices. Indeed, it has long been recognized that drama is a powerful learning medium, and this is in part explained by the fact that its multi-modality enables students to find different points of entry into the work and, once involved, they can develop a wider repertoire of learning styles.

Developing a culture of participation in drama, where students are actively engaged in their own learning, is one way to challenge the kind of passivity which is sometimes associated with a consumer culture. As teachers, it also enables us to demonstrate to students that their ideas matter. In this context, drama education provides a public forum for dialogue, discussion, debate and dissent; it is a place where difference, and the limits of difference, might be negotiated and explored. In drama, however, students can explore ideas in sound, negotiate in movement, and debate in visual images; an active culture of participation in the drama classroom invites students to communicate with their bodies as well as in words.

It is worth reiterating that active and physical engagement in drama enables students to develop new understandings and forms of knowing which may not be so accessible in other, more traditional, ways of learning. What is special about the drama curriculum is that the students are also expected to communicate their ideas, however abstract or complex, using kinaesthetic, aural and visual languages as well as the written word. In this way, drama education offers one way to encourage all students to become active makers, doers and thinkers. Indeed, it is the interrelationship between critical thinking, cultural praxis and creative practice, however differently emphasized, which characterizes much forward-thinking drama teaching. In the practice of drama, dialogic interaction allows students to 'unfix', interrogate and interpret cultural meanings rather than becoming inert and passive consumers of second-hand knowledge.

THINKING PRACTITIONERS

In drama education, the move, according to Michael Fleming, from 'tacit to explicit knowledge of dramatic forms' is an important element of progression.[19] Linking progression to assessment, he argues that students are supported when they understand the learning objectives of the work, and when these objectives relate to subject-specific assessment criteria. The emphasis on assessment criteria which are firmly rooted in the substance of dramatic practice is important; as drama teachers we undoubtedly encourage students to explore, reinterpret, represent and symbolize values, feelings and ideas but to *assess* the specific beliefs and attitudes held by students seems uncomfortably invasive. In effect, what I am suggesting is that a fully differentiated drama curriculum finds ways to value the students' cognitive and affective engagement with the work. Equally, it recognizes that, in the 11–18 age range, students' progression in drama is informed by their ability to explore, create and communicate meanings using their knowledge, skills and understanding of dramatic process and form. In this context, learning is, of course, not linear but spiral; students will frequently revisit areas of learning, and consolidate, deepen and extend their experience of drama as they progress.

The chapters that follow are written by experienced in-service teachers and practitioners, all of whom work regularly with young people. In this book, they share experiences of teaching drama, either as a subject in its own right or as part of the English curriculum, and consider the educational implications of the particular aspects of drama they are discussing. In so doing, they offer much sound, practical advice and, although I have outlined some practices and principles in this introduction, the book as a whole is not intended to offer a set of instructions into how 'we' think drama should be taught. Indeed, although there is some consensus between contributors, there are also some implicit disagreements and lively differences between us. This energetic mix of shared practice and amicable discourse is, I hope, good for the continuing intellectual and creative health of our subject. And, as all educational practices are revitalized by periodic review, I would like to think that the ideas contained in this book not only will encourage drama teachers to try out new ways of working, but also will stimulate debate and discussion.

The book is organized into three parts, each of which focuses on specific aspects of drama practice undertaken with a particular age group. It is arranged according to the chronological ages of the students with whom each contributor has worked, but this is not meant to imply that the practices discussed relate only to that particular moment in young people's development. Indeed, there are many aspects of drama, of which devised work is a good example, which are likely to form part of the curriculum at many different levels. But as the students move from tacit to explicit knowledge of dramatic forms, as their dramatic repertoires are extended, they are able to make increasingly independent and informed choices. It is by knowing more about the languages of drama that students become, in Sharon Grady's words, 'thinking practitioners'.

NOTES

1 Wertenbaker, T. (1998) *Our Country's Good* (London: Methuen), p. 74.
2 For an excellent discussion of how this aspect of drama education might be explored in the primary school curriculum, see Winston, J. (1998) *Drama, Narrative and Moral Education* (London: Falmer Press).
3 Quoted in Eagleton, T. (1976) *Marxism and Literature* (London: Methuen), p. 67.
4 The idea that the arts are 'languages' was related to education by the writers of the National Curriculum Council Arts in Schools project of the 1980s; see the National Curriculum Council (1990) *The Arts 5–16: Policy and Practice* (London: Oliver & Boyd). I am specifically using the term here in a Wittgensteinian sense; in demolishing the idea that language has an 'essence', Wittgenstein argued that language is the instrument of thought and understanding. See Wittgenstein, L. (1963) *Philosophical Investigations* (Oxford: Basil Blackwell), pp. 31–9.
5 Fleming, M. (1994) *Starting Drama Teaching* (London: David Fulton), p. 22.
6 Merleau-Ponty, M. (1973) *The Prose of the World* (trans. J. O'Neill) (London: Heinemann), p. 17.
7 Frowe, I. (1999) ' "Sticks and stones . . .": the power of language', in E. Bearne (ed.) *Use of Language across the Secondary Curriculum* (London: Routledge), p. 17.
8 Wittgenstein argues that language is a 'vehicle of thought', and I am applying this premise to a broad conception of language. See Wittgenstein, L. (1963) *op. cit.*, p. 107.
9 Quoted in Giannachi, G. and Luckhurst, M. (eds) (1999) *On Directing· Interviews with Directors* (London: Faber & Faber), p. 75.
10 O'Neill, J. (ed.) (1974) *Phenomenology, Language and Sociology· Selected Essays of Maurice Merleau-Ponty* (London: Heinemann), p. 283.
11 See O'Toole, J. (1992) *The Process of Drama: Negotiating Art and Meaning* (London: Routledge), pp. 226–7; Vygotsky, L. (1978) *Interaction between Learning and Development in Mind and Society* (Cambridge, MA: Harvard University Press); Bruner, J. (1986) *Actual Minds, Possible Worlds* (Cambridge, MA: Harvard University Press). For a very clear explanation of Vygotsky's theory Zone of Proximal Development in relation to drama education, see Kempe, A. (ed.) (1996) *Drama Education and Special Needs* (Cheltenham: Stanley Thornes), p. 5.
12 Wollheim, R. (1987) *Painting as an Art* (Princeton, NJ: Princeton University Press), pp. 16–25.
13 This point is made very clearly and thoughtfully by Robin Pascoe. Working with a teacher in this age range, he identified that it was her lack of knowledge and understanding about drama as an art form which meant that she was ill prepared to offer her students appropriate 'scaffolding'. See Pascoe, R. (1997) 'Research and the arts in schools: a two-way dialogue'. *NADIE Journal*, **21**(2), 33–48.
14 Fleming, M. (1994) *op. cit.*, p. 143.
15 Bailin, S. (1998) 'Creativity in context', in D. Hornbrook (ed.) *On the Subject of Drama* (London: Routledge), pp. 36–50.
16 Bourdieu, P. (1996) *The Rules of Art* (trans. S. Emanuel) (Cambridge: Polity Press), p. 302.
17 For a more detailed discussion of the politics of race and culture in relation to drama education, see Sita Brahmachari's influential chapter 'Stages of the world', in D. Hornbrook (ed.) (1998) *On the Subject of Drama* (London: Routledge), pp. 18–35.
18 Fielding, M. (1996) 'How and why learning styles matter: valuing difference in teachers and learners', in S. Hart (ed.) *Differentiation and the Secondary Curriculum* (London: Routledge), pp. 81–103.
19 Fleming, M. (1994) *op. cit.*, p. 143.

Part One

Teaching Drama 11–14

PROCESSES OF LEARNING

The first part of this book presents four different approaches to teaching drama in the 11–14 age range. It is not intended to offer a complete overview of a drama curriculum; on the contrary, the contributors to this part have selected particular aspects of their work to discuss rather than offering an entire pedagogical framework. However, taken as a whole, this part does raise some interesting questions about the kinds of learning that students undertake in drama: how do they progress from an integrated curriculum to a curriculum organized around discrete subjects? Where might drama be placed in the curriculum? What is the value of extra-curricular drama? How might we encourage students to work collaboratively? How should we assess their work?

All these questions are, of course, value laden and all have implications for the teaching of drama. As Jerome Bruner has pointed out, nothing is 'culture-free'; this includes both drama teaching and, more broadly, the culture of education.[1] However, rather than trying to find definitive answers to these difficult questions, the contributors have reflected on the different contexts in which they teach, shared their own dramatic interests and areas of expertise, and have taken account of the individual needs and experiences of their students. Furthermore, there is an acknowledgement that drama takes place in a range of educational contexts; Jennifer Simons and Shane Irwin specifically discuss ways of working in the drama curriculum, Denise Margetts applies her knowledge and understanding of the practice of drama to the English class-room, and Bryony Williamson describes and discusses processes of working in drama and theatre as an extra-curricular activity.

Jennifer Simons explores the relationship between drama, narrative, story-telling and role-play. Her work is particularly focused on the younger students in this age group, many of whom are at the point of transition from primary to secondary schools. She suggests ways in which we, as teachers, might build on their experiences of working in role in primary schools. In the early years of secondary education, she suggests, students are often supported when the work is carefully structured and crafted by teachers, who are able to slow down the action and thus encourage them to learn, think, and feel more deeply. Working in the context of an English classroom, Denise Margetts also finds ways to help her 14-year-old students reflect on their work by encouraging them to understand how meanings are made and represented in dramatic form. She asks students to slow down the process of working by capturing and framing dramatic moments using various forms of computer information technology such as video and digital cameras. Although the educational contexts are different, both processes stress the importance of collaborative working practices; drama requires students not only to share ideas and insights, but also to embody them.

The emphasis on the body in drama education is not exactly new, but it is newly recognized. It provides a bridge between verbal language, feeling and cognition; the physical is, as Denise Margetts points out, an important element of literacy which is often ignored. Shane Irwin, in his chapter on physical theatre, makes similar connections between language, movement and abstract thought. In pointing out that 'an intellectual concept is often clarified by physical action', he recognizes the importance of somatic learning and the inseparability between the mind and body in cognitive development. It is an aspect of learning which Bryony Williamson also explored when she combined the roles of teacher of drama and director of a play; she implicitly rejects the idea that performance is solely concerned with technical skills or entertainment, and offers many valuable insights into how performing plays offers creative and intellectual challenges to students as they learn how to interpret and realize a dramatic script.

THE PROVISIONALITY OF DRAMA AND FORMS OF ASSESSMENT

All the practitioners who have contributed to this part of the book raise questions about the dynamic, unfixed and provisional qualities of drama. Indeed, it is suggested that, in order for students to understand the processes of working in drama, they are aided when they have a conceptual understanding that all dramatic texts are always in some way 'unfinished' and open for reinterpretation. However, there is a potential tension between forms of assessment, in which criteria are necessarily predetermined, and the open-endedness of drama as a creative practice.

Jennifer Simons provides a helpful description of the significance of the relationship between formative and summative assessments. In linking student-centred and subject-centred approaches to teaching, she recognizes that teachers use their knowledge of both drama and of their students in assessment procedures. Assessment is really helpful only if it provides new information about individual students' learning, when it clarifies the relationship between teaching and learning, and where it enables teachers to help students to progress. However, as Denise Margetts points out, a dramatic vocabulary helps students to evaluate their learning. It would appear that when assessment criteria are explicitly framed in subject-specific terms, and communicated to the students, they learn to recognize how new or unexpected ideas were developed. Indeed, in his discussion of learning processes, Vygotsky uses specifically dramatic terms to point out that students who are motivated in their work, and understand why they are working in a particular way, are able to contribute appropriately and inventively to the work.[2] In practice, this means that students are not assessed on their private values, beliefs or attitudes, but on their actual and visible contributions to the development and realization of the drama.

Throughout this part of the book, there is an awareness of how to encourage students to learn by balancing clearly identified objectives with well-defined assessment procedures. However, as the contributors also recognize, in the reality of classrooms there is sometimes a gap between the real and the ideal, between neatly invoked educational theories and day-to-day classroom practices. It is this gap, however, which is often inventive and productive, enabling students to work creatively for themselves.

NOTES

1 Bruner, J. (1996) *The Culture of Education* (Cambridge, MA: Harvard University Press), p. 14.
2 See, for example, how Vygotsky recognizes the importance of motivation in Vygotsky, L. (1962) *Thought and Language* (trans. E. Hanfmann and G. Vakar) (Cambridge, MA: MIT Press), pp. 149–50.

Chapter 1

Walking in Another Person's Shoes: Storytelling and Role-play

Jennifer Simons

As Macbeth's world collapses towards the end of Shakespeare's play, he registers his utter despair by describing life as

> a tale
> Told by an idiot, full of sound and fury,
> Signifying nothing.[1]

This image is shocking partly because it simultaneously evokes and denies the belief that stories are told to make sense of life. Barbara Hardy called narrative 'a primary act of mind transferred to art from life'. Bruner tempered this, but agreed that 'no one questions that learning the subtleties of narrative is one of the prime routes to thinking about life'.[2]

Every culture has a history of oral stories and, contrary to Macbeth's image, a traditional tale is usually told by a highly respected figure to teach important history, laws and customs. In the oldest living culture, Australian Aboriginal Dreaming, most clans tell stories related to the creation myth *The Rainbow Serpent*. From such stories, understood literally by children and metaphorically by the Elders, people learn how they should relate to each other and to the land. Stories are created when we survey people, places and events, selecting and connecting significant moments in such a way as to make sense out of otherwise chaotic experiences. Usually a story has an orientation, a complication and a resolution, though sometimes we are plunged in with little introduction, and not all complications are happily resolved. Sometimes the way that events are connected does not fit a pattern of logic we are used to (as in Magic Realism). Stories vary with the author's culture and creativity.

Audiences are also active and creative when they apply stories to their own lives. Britton suggests that 'we improvise upon our world representation ... either to enrich it, to embroider it, to fill in its gaps and extend its frontiers, or to iron out its inconsistencies'.[3] Because ultimately meaning is made at the level of reception, stories offer multiple meanings and one interpretation does not rule out other possibilities. Sometimes, as in stories which assert the dominant culture, it is only through finding and exploring gaps and inconsistencies that students are able to see how the story relates to them, and drama is an effective way to do this.

In this chapter I shall explore some of the ways that storytelling and role-play can be used both to increase students' understanding of themselves and their lives, and developing an aesthetic appreciation of the techniques themselves.

DRAMA AND STORYTELLING

For the layperson, 'drama' and 'story' may seem interchangeable terms; indeed hearing a story and watching drama may seem to produce the same result. However, dramatists and storytellers construct their artworks differently and their audiences process them in different ways. For example, storytellers use words and voice to evoke a fictional world in the imagination of each listener, but dramatists present actual three-dimensional representations to a mass audience. Dramatists construct signs, simultaneously using multiple channels of communication, from which audiences deduce the story, much as they do in everyday life. In classroom drama if there is no external audience students may sign at a more intimate level of understanding, not attempting to communicate beyond the group itself. They work in complicated metaphor, engaging in *metaxis*, that is simultaneously in the fictional world and in reality. They manipulate time differently, focusing moment by moment on the present, and the narrative viewpoints that they adopt may shift as they create.

Role-play is a collaborative art form, and is most effective when it draws upon the cumulative experiences of the group, producing stories with which they all can engage. Teachers scaffold learning around the elements of the art form, such as finding a *focus* or theme; creating or playing with different forms of dramatic *tension*, and finding ways to create *symbol*. The defining element of role-play is *role* and deciding whose point of view is to be adopted is one of the crucial planning decisions. Morgan and Saxton usefully explain that students can choose from five different levels of role:

- *dramatic playing* (students are themselves in a fictional context)
- *mantle of the expert* (the students' status is as 'the ones who know')
- *role-playing* (students sustain a point of view not necessarily their own)
- *characterization* (students adopt attributes of a specific person)
- *acting* (students adopt an external appearance, voice movement, etc. in order to create a role for an audience).[4]

Each level of role has its own appropriate place in the students' arsenal of techniques for developing and presenting a story. Gavin Bolton has pointed out that students mix 'modelling' and 'managing' in role-play, sometimes duplicating behaviour they have seen, but at other times resolving emerging dilemmas as they occur.[5] Students gradually become more conscious of the role level they are using, and more able to manipulate role-playing to create their own collaborative stories.

Through the technique of *teacher-in-role* improvisational skills may be enhanced. Students are assisted to develop their roles when the teacher is inside the drama with them, modelling what it means to sustain belief, and judiciously using questions which inform the drama. In role, teachers may suggest possible actions, make offers and challenge thinking. For example, 'They told me that I'd find you people, the Volunteer Brigade, useful in preparing for bushfires. My farmhouse is isolated and a fair distance from the dam. There are water tanks on the roof, though. What should I do?'

SCAFFOLDING ROLE-PLAY TO CREATE OR EXPLORE STORIES

Making meanings from story has always meant connecting it with lived experience. In reading or listening these connections are usually made privately but drama students make their understandings public, risking rejection by the group. Because of this, role-playing may challenge self-esteem, so we teachers need to create a secure environment for students. In practice, we can help students move from the private world of stories to the public realm of role-playing by planning carefully. This involves three interrelated elements:

- the choice of stimulus or content of the role-play
- the dramatic structure of the role-play
- the implications of the students' roles.

Although role-play often looks as if it develops spontaneously, for it to work successfully the lesson needs to be carefully crafted. It is really only when we as teachers recognize the opportunities presented by the topic, anticipate the potential risks in the roles and define a structure for the drama that we set up conditions where collaborative creativity can occur.

The choice of stimulus may depend on the students' background knowledge of language or culture or stories. Information may need to be fed into the drama or students may like time to prepare by pooling ideas. If the topic contains difficult or disturbing material, the chosen stance may need to be a distanced one. In a story where a young person commits suicide, the students may be framed as archaeologists unearthing the bones, reflecting from a distance in time. It is also important that drama students have their real world strongly in place, and do not become lost in the fiction. An imaginary or symbolic knife works better for role-play than a real one.

The choice of topic often suggests how the lesson might be structured. Theatre audiences watch a story unfold moment by moment, deducing meaning from people in action. In the early years of secondary school it is usually the teacher who chooses and sets up these significant moments around which students create their drama. Students tend to focus on plot and rush into action but teachers can slow the process with different techniques and structures. For example students can begin with a story's ending, and work backwards, exploring why it happened or they can adopt role within role – students being Clark Kent being Superman – to deepen the exploration of meaning. Focus can be shifted from *what* happened to *why* or *how* it happened.

The initial steps of the lesson should lure or edge students into the drama world. They become imaginatively engaged, and are positioned to use their lived experiences in the role-play. One effective starting point is what Cecily O'Neill has called a *pretext* – a stimulus which implies a strong context and characters, and plants clues for the creation of an enticing drama world.[6] As in life, students link the significant events and characters of their emerging fictional world in a meaningful way, making sense of events.

The choice of topic, the structure of the lesson and the techniques chosen all have implications for the roles that the students adopt. They may begin in different ways: from outside (for example with a still image) or from inside the character (for example after hot-seating). Students might consider the *function*, the *status* and the *attitude* of the role. Sometimes in issues-based drama the role function is enough: the 'Bulldozer Man' is of interest only because he threatens the trees that the 'greenies' are trying to save. Knowing the status of the role will affect the way others relate – the vocabulary and tone of voice adopted. The role's attitude or emotional stance may help create mood. Sometimes the real intentions are revealed only through *subtext*, presented through body stance or tone of voice.

These three aspects of role-play (the chosen pretext or topic, the techniques and structure, and the development of role) all require teachers and students to work together with craft and skill. They engage with other roles by making them *offers of action* – statements with embedded cues for action that the others can either accept or reject. It is important that these offers are not negatively blocked with a denial of the fiction. In response to the offer, 'Is it hard to be an only child?' a good reply could be, 'Oh, I'm not an only child but we don't talk much about my sister' rather than the blocking response, 'I'm not!' Groups of students can be given a few moments to prepare or sketch out what they will do, or they can be sprung into immediate improvisation. In both cases, they have to draw upon their experiences and understandings of the real world in order to create the fictional one.

The next section of this chapter will explore two examples of drama classes where teachers and students worked together to explore the boundaries between lived experience and fiction, role and narration, role-play and story-telling.

STRUCTURED LEARNING AND FLEXIBLE NARRATIVES USING A PICTURE AS PRETEXT

In 1996 as part of the NADIE Phoenix Project in Australia, Tiina Moore used as her pretext a picture chosen by her students from several alternatives that she offered them.[7] This picture shows a girl in shadows, lying in bed. Her arm has dropped from holding a book, out of which a vine is growing. The picture is subtitled, 'MR. LINDEN'S LIBRARY He had warned her about the book. Now it was too late'. From this starting point her class built an original story in their chosen genre (the supernatural), based on one student's suggestion that 'Tess' (as they named the character in the bed) had somehow entered the book. In order to develop the story, the class drew upon their knowledge of pop culture, using jargon from *The X Files*, describing Tess as in a state of 'forever sleep'. As teacher-in-role Moore facilitated them into expert roles: doctors trying to suspend their scientific disbelief in the paranormal and bring Tess back to life and out of the book.

As in all good teaching, the drama evolved within a structure set in place by the teacher, but filled out in unexpected ways by the students. Moore describes her intentions for the lessons:

> My own practice is rooted in drama for literacy whereby narrative becomes the basis for speculation about story outcomes and for embedding drama skills and structures. Form and content are intertwined in improvisational work in order that children first have something to say and secondly have choices as to how best to say it ... I wanted every student to feel he/she had an investment in the story and I wanted the experience to be a strong and memorable end to their primary years. I foresaw a synthesising of many learned drama structures and forms within what I hoped would be a good story.[8]

Reflecting on the lesson, Moore describes the behaviour of some students at the beginning of the lesson as an 'unexpected gift' that set the tone for the lesson. Moore's plan included specific resources, but allowed for flexibility; she duplicated the picture on the overhead projector, and 'just in case', also provided a rostrum, white sheets, book and a trailing vine similar to those in the picture. Three girls entered the classroom before the teacher and, undirected, 'with aesthetic attention to detail ... proceeded to give an almost ritualistic quality in the setting up of the bedroom scene'. They re-created the image, and then one of the girls climbed into the bed, taking on the role of Tess.

> The fact that we had a main character, a strong focus for our discussion as doctors, and a serious attitude to the story which was not imposed by the teacher, meant that we could enter straight into the positive tensions of the situations rather than the sometimes tedious detail of setting up. It is perhaps embarrassing to admit, therefore, that although our story moved forward I am not convinced that we again equalled the lovely awe of those first minutes of class.[9]

Moore's 'embarrassment' is merely a recognition that in drama lessons students often achieve beyond the teacher's expectation; good scaffolding allows them to enter what Vygotsky called the *zone of proximal development*.

To help the class create their story, Moore used a range of drama strategies such as mantle of the expert, chant, thought tracking, hot-seating and writing in role. She had planned to use still images to express some of Tess's adventures when she was inside the book but acceded to the students' request for a less controlled technique, and allowed them to choose their own means of dramatic expression. Kate Donelan, present in the class as an observer, comments on Moore's reflection-in-action decision to alter her plans.

> Watching the purposeful and joyous group work proceed simultaneously way beyond Tiina's initial time constraint, it occurs to me that her judgement is absolutely sound. These students need this extended time; although the room is noisy and seemingly unfocused the group process is engaging most of these students in quite complex and demanding problem solving. Up to this point the lesson tasks have required controlled reflection, watching, listening and restricted language responses. This group task has now released them ... They are manipulating dramatic elements to express what has intrigued them in this unfolding narrative. They seem to need this phase of exploring their sense of the possibilities of 'dual worlds' before they can focus again as a class on the unconscious side of Tess in order to bring her back to the 'real world'.[10]

In the course of their role-play the students created a highly complex dramatic story. The group with whom Moore worked were at the end of primary school and, in terms of continuity and progression, her work provides a suitable model for drama which might be developed with students in the early years of secondary education.

CREATING A ROLE-PLAY FROM GAPS IN A REAL STORY

One useful source of real-life pretexts which allows for role distance is to be found in 'squibs', the little fillers in newspapers which give the dry bones of a story which will be given more fully in the next day's paper. It is best to find reasonably ambiguous stories, where gaps are present or possible, and which has the potential to link with the students' experience. One that I have used is 'The Baby on the Train', which taps into the fact that most Sydney students come to school by train.

> On Friday 20th August at 5.30 p.m. a group of school children found an eighteen-month-old baby, apparently abandoned on the train between Maintown and Greystanes. The baby was in good health, apparently well cared for. They took the baby to the stationmaster, who handed it to the police.

Using this fragment the class explores the text and creates an original story. This topic is as old as *Oedipus* and as metaphoric as a fairytale – the myth of the abandoned child. What makes this pretext palatable for use with young students is the possibility of a happy ending and the (perhaps strange) fact that it is the children, not adults, who save the baby. Although the work needs to be adapted according to context, here is an outline of the planning of a unit of work that I have used several times with different classes and with different results.

Step 1 The *teacher-in-role*, as a representative of the Transport Ministry, conducts a 'Trains Summit' inquiry into problems encountered by city commuters. The students can choose roles related to train travel, such as guards, passengers, station officials. In the course of the summit the teacher elicits a real description of peak-hour trains from several points of view. Who is likely to be on board? Which groups of children might be on an evening peak-hour train? How safe is it?

Step 2 Out of role the class is asked to negotiate the *arrangement of the space*, moving chairs to construct a peak-hour train. Students position themselves as someone on that train. Each is invited to step momentarily out of the picture and view the total *frozen image*. Then the teacher *'taps in'* to hear the thoughts of each person on this peak-hour train.

Step 3 The students are asked to come *out of role*. The teacher reads the squib, and the pretext is launched: this is the train; this is where the baby was found. What questions occur to you? What are the gaps in this story? Their questions are written on the blackboard and remain there throughout the drama.

Step 4 In groups of four the students are asked to *prepare role-plays* set back in time one year, when the baby was 6 months old. Each group can decide its own family circumstances but they are given a built-in *tension* – to choose a moment which is happy but which contains the seeds of a future problem. The baby is to be present in each role-play as a bundle in a blanket. Each group shares its presentation; the spectators are asked to identify the seeds of the future problem buried in each role-play.

Step 5 It is six months later; the problem has escalated and the baby is a year old. Each group is to decide who would now be the chief carer of their child and one person in each group is to enact this carer. The representatives of each group are simultaneously *hot-seated* as a panel on a TV show hosted by the teacher-in-role, discussing childcare, its joys and difficulties. They may choose to talk about their difficulties or reveal them in subtext.

Step 6 One of these stories is pursued as a *gestalt*. Each group now takes on roles related to the chosen baby, and each is allotted a particular time to explore on the day on which the baby was lost. (There is no need to make these flow as a connected story; they could be thought of as rumours.) Students prepare and present in chronological order, and several possible explanations emerge. The class decides on one story – perhaps the most interesting or most likely version.

Step 7 Half the class *sculpts* a volunteer as the central character in the baby's life. The other half become people in the story who helped, or made life more difficult. They are placed in the space, relative to their impact on the central character. Symbolic props can be added (e.g. a stool to elevate the social climber; a school bag for the weighed-down student). The image is *animated*, with sound-effects or single words. The groups swap places, mirroring and repeating the image, so both halves see the picture from the outside. Students then reflect out of role on the process.

I have taught this unit to students at many different levels. The sculptured image, where the social forces on the carer of the child were represented, always emerged as a powerful symbolic representation, summarizing the understandings of the group as each symbolic character is placed.

ASSESSMENT

An important part of lesson planning is to match planned outcomes with suitable evaluation techniques. In drama this is problematic as the content of the lesson often deviates from the plan because of spontaneous input from the students and on-the-spot changes in direction by the teacher. Therefore the planned assessment tasks need to be fairly flexible. What the teacher assesses may be skills such as the ability to sustain a role, or to manipulate an element of drama, such as mood or tension. Group processes or the ability to connect with an outside audience may have been important objectives.

Assessment can be *formative*, used to determine how the learning is progressing, and what the next lesson should be, or *summative*, measuring the intended learning at the end point. The type of assessment that a teacher uses partly depends on the planned outcomes. Bill Spady describes three kinds of outcomes: technical, transitional and transformational, which vary according to differing time frames. Technical outcomes pursue immediately observable changes in learning. With transitional outcomes change becomes observable after a longer time, perhaps the end of a unit of work. Transformational outcomes seek to bring about new understandings; they 'are the "bigger picture" outcomes. For example, what do you really hope the students in your class will achieve by being in your class? What do you want them to take with them at the end of the year?'[11]

An important assessment tool is the teacher's observation of the class. Using Eisner's concept of the *connoisseur*, John Thompson has argued that experienced teachers can use this tool effectively because of their professional knowledge of drama and of their students.[12] Sometimes teachers feel insecure about using such apparently 'intuitive' appraisal, but as Ben Shahn observed:

> intuition in art is actually the result of prolonged tuition. The so-called innocent eye does not exist. The eye at birth cannot perceive at all, and it is only through training that it learns to recognise what it sees.[13]

In the first unit of work – the story of Tess – Moore's description of her intentions indicates that she was pursuing transitional and transformational outcomes, difficult to evaluate at the time of the lesson. Because she was researching the whole teaching-learning process for the Phoenix Project, Moore had more potential sources of assessment than is usual in teaching. She kept video records, an oral taping of the class, and reflective notes on her own practice. She observed the students and also had an outside observer. The students' written work was also a means by which to assess. They reflected in journals, and wrote in and out of role. As is the case with many drama lessons, the pressure of time meant that Moore had to end more abruptly than she wished. As a final task she asked students to write in role addressing the story's ending and was pleasantly surprised by the responses.

> In several instances students who were very self-conscious and seemingly minimally involved ... had written poignantly in role. It is always worth checking shifts in understanding in more ways than simply through teacher observation. Insights often come out of discussions ... allotted significance by the luxury of time.[14]

In the second unit, 'The Baby on the Train', although my original intention had been to explore the failure of the adults to save the baby, generally the students were more interested in the circumstances of the baby's life. The assessment therefore needed to be adjusted to the reality of the class. Rather than rigidly adhering to the planned task (writing in role as one of the adults on the train) this was adapted to writing an explanation to the grown-up baby of why he or she was taken into care. Students also rewrote the squib as a full media story including the created details. Students could be assessed (by teacher observation) for their contribution to the group processes leading to the performance. Prior to each lesson the teacher could note pertinent criteria for summative assessment, such as 'offered ideas to the group' or 'accepted and built on ideas' or 'fulfilled one of the group tasks, e.g. kept notes on the group work', and place individuals under these criteria. Individual students can be tracked over several lessons, with appropriate intervention to make sure that the students are developing well.

IN CONCLUSION: WALKING IN ANOTHER PERSON'S SHOES

Storytelling and role-playing are basic skills in drama, and probably form the strongest bridge between the teaching and learning of drama in primary school and secondary education. Through constructing collaborative stories, especially when expressed through role-play, students are able to develop meaning-making skills as they create original artworks.

Tiina Moore, reflecting on the ways that each teacher across Australia in the Phoenix Project had used role-play to create drama stories, comments:

> as in the teaching of story writing, there will be times that the emphasis may shift to style or grammar rather than topic but when form and content are effectively married, both are strengthened. The teacher's particular

emphasis will be determined by the children's needs, administrative agendas, his or her own educational philosophy, skills and timetables.[15]

Stories can connect us in metaphor to people around the world, in the past and in the future, helping us to explore what it means to be human. It is in respecting difference as well as finding similarities that humanity can develop its full potential. In becoming aware of perspectives left out or submerged by a story students may be taught to question the taken for granted. Because drama uses specific contexts as well as common themes, students are able to reflect on their own position in a range of possibilities, and become aware of the values embedded in particular constructions of events. Trying these out in role-play takes students a good way along the road to walking in another person's shoes, aware of the affective dimensions of the learning.

NOTES

1 Shakespeare, *Macbeth*, Act 5, sc. v, lines 26–8.
2 Hardy, B. (1977) 'Narrative as primary act of the mind', in M. Meek, A. Warlow and G. Barton (eds) *The Cool Web: The Pattern of Children's Reading* (London: Bodley Head), p. 12; Bruner, J. (1996) *The Culture of Education* (Cambridge, MA: Harvard University Press), p. 94.
3 Britton, J. (1970) *Language and Learning* (London: Penguin), p. 8.
4 Morgan, N. and Saxton, J. (1987) *Teaching Drama: A Mind of Many Wonders* (London: Hutchinson), p. 30.
5 Bolton, G. (1989) 'Drama', in D. Hargreaves (ed.) *Children and the Arts* (Milton Keynes: Open University Press), p. 126.
6 O'Neill, C. (1995) *Drama Worlds: A Framework for Process Drama* (London: Heinemann), p. 33.
7 Moore, T. (ed.) (1998) *Phoenix Texts: A Window on Drama Practice in Australian Primary Schools*, NADIE Research Monograph no. 5 (Melbourne: NADIE), p. 72. This project is recorded in full in this monograph. In 1996 teachers in each state of Australia created drama units using the same pretext *The Mysteries of Harris Burdick* by Chris van Allsburg.
8 Moore, T. (1998) *ibid.*, p. 73.
9 Moore, T. (1998) *ibid.*, p. 81.
10 Moore, T. (1998) *ibid.*, p. 80.
11 See Spady, B. (1992) *Outcomes-based Education: Australian Curriculum Studies* (Belconnen: ACT); Cusworth, R. and Simons, J. (1997) *Beyond the Script: Drama in the Classroom* (Sydney: PETA), p. 31.
12 Thompson, J. (1991) 'Assessing drama: allowing for meaningful interpretation' in J. Hughes (ed.) *Drama in Education: The State of the Art* (Sydney: Educational Drama Association).
13 Best, D. (1980) 'The objectivity of artistic appreciation'. *British Journal of Aesthetics*, **20**(2), 124.
14 Moore, T. (1998) *op cit.*, p. 84.
15 Moore, T. (1998) *ibid.*, p. 85.

Chapter 2

Physical Theatre

Shane Irwin

WHAT IS PHYSICAL THEATRE?

Physical theatre is a renaissance of humanism. It explores human anxieties, passions, aspirations and sensitivity through the languages of theatre. It is inclusive as opposed to exclusive in that it embraces all systems of theatrical communication. It emphasizes the plastic, kinaesthetic and aesthetic sensuality of the human figure. It is not about delivery of the written or spoken word, although this may play a part, nor is it singularly concerned with the physical body. It explores the human figure in space, colour and light as its own protagonist. Physical theatre is an eclectic adventure into the human spirit which is accessible to all and concerns all – theatre that combines and touches mind and heart. Perfect for 11–14-year-old students and beyond!

During the 1980s and 1990s there has been a growing propensity to employ the term 'physical' when describing contemporary theatre. Companies as diverse as DV8, Tag Teatro, Trestle, Théâtre de Complicité and Derevo have all been described as leading exponents of visual theatre, movement theatre or new mime. All these terms emphasize the physicality of theatrical language and may be included in the generic term, physical theatre.

As part of the 1999 International Mime Festival 'Total Theatre' (the UK umbrella organization for mime, physical and visual performance) hosted a debate at the Royal Festival Hall entitled 'What is the new mime?' In the follow-up article Jon Potter defines new mime as

> work that comes from a training of the body, that draws on the imitation of the natural and the human world, work that often uses sensual means rather than cerebral means in its conception and execution; work that can celebrate complexity and difference, that exists between cultures, and that can touch our human spirits.[1]

In the same article Joseph Seelig, a director of the festival, states:

new mime begins to locate itself not as a rigidly characterised way of working that offers a stock of traits and readily classifiable ideas, but more as an art form in flux, a literal body of works in which physicality and feeling are increasingly highlighted and fore-ground, but in which other disciplines, multiple perspectives, and even (dare I say it?) the spoken word will happily find a place.[2]

These statements suggest a sensual and physical approach to working forms the foundation of physical theatre and that its inclusive nature encourages theatrical exploration.

PHYSICAL THEATRE IN YOUR DRAMA SPACE

By introducing physical theatre into our drama curriculum in the 11–14 age range, we expand the creative options open to our pupils. Alternative and accessible methods of performance, improvisation, script-writing, devising and design become available, all of which are important in the drama courses they may take later.

Just as every respected theatre practitioner has in some way contributed to contemporary physical theatre, so every teacher of drama teaches aspects of its style and techniques. This means that we can dispense with needless anxiety and focus on the joy. We all have a body, we all move, we all feel and think. In my experience children of this age feel and think a great deal; through physical theatre we can find a way to explore, contextualize and give form to these thoughts and feelings.

Due to the eclectic nature of theatre, children are offered a wide range of paths on which to access and experience learning. It has a vocabulary accessible to all. Through a combination of movement, gesture, image, sound and colour they can be encouraged to create their own dramatic syntax. For me this is probably the best reason for employing physical theatre techniques; children learn to structure their own approach to and presentation of work, creating a real sense of ownership. Working from the sensual perspective children are able to introduce personal interpretation. In this way physical theatre is very similar to abstract art in that there is no right or wrong way to define what one sees; it is a personal response and as such not wrong. Having said that, there is a wonderful opportunity to question and begin to understand why we respond to certain images, gestures, movement and colour enabling us to build upon this knowledge and create consensual understanding. This examination of personal perspectives encourages children to recognize difference through the acceptance of alternative readings, and challenge stereotypes through close examination of the intricacies of physical language.

As with all drama, discussion is a key element in both the actual process and in response to the product. Language development occurs as a natural, ongoing process. I have found that by working physically I am able to introduce abstract concepts which enhance language acquisition. For example, 'Water's Journey' is a scheme of work I use with 11-, 12- and 13-year-old pupils. We begin by physically exploring the movement of water and its different states – *ice, steam, river, sea*, etc. We then explore transitions – *water to steam, river to sea* – creating movement sequences that examine the processes of condensation or precipitation; eventually this leads to a physical consideration of the water cycle. I find ample opportunity to introduce vocabulary and elements of language structure in class, group and individual discussion. Movement becomes words, words become movement – somatic learning.

The use of symbols as part of the physical and visual vocabulary enables children to engage with language in a direct and active manner making linguistic ideas concrete. There are moments when the children recognize that they themselves have become the language and learn to modify meaning through action. While working with the symbol of the moon I watched an 11-year-old pupil explaining to her group how, 'if we all run away quickly, except the Moon, and crouch down we can make it look lonely' ... the moon responded with, 'and I can look up and hold my hands'. The group were obviously very keen to explore language construction as they tried several suggestions. By developing physical theatre techniques, children develop a deeper understanding of how to use language and, perhaps more importantly, how to appreciate the beauty of language as it becomes a physical presence.

Being accessible, physical theatre enables all children to experience the benefits attributed to educational drama so there is no need to list them here. There is, however, one important value that working with physical theatre especially inspires – a sense of competency.[3] This includes a competence in their own physical skills, in interpreting and understanding language, and a competence in their own ability to determine meaning and to express feelings and perspectives in a creative and stylized manner. This sense of competence becomes apparent as they observe their own physical interaction and development; they watch themselves create language and meaning to communicate and express. We can in fact all have a go!

PROGRESSION AND DIFFERENTIATION

My philosophy regarding progression in the 11–14 age group is simply to awaken 11-year-old pupils to basic techniques. In the following year these are explored in more depth, paying attention to their aesthetic potential and the communication of meaning. Finally, with 14-year-old pupils I aim to consolidate techniques into a working form that the children recognize and apply to social and moral issues. My intention is to prepare the foundations for a deeper understanding of the styles of theatre they will explore in the courses followed by 14–16-year-olds, and to realize alternative methods of working.

With such a prolific and readily accessible vocabulary to work with, I find differentiation an almost effortless process. The option is always available to adjust the level of task through alternative methods of working which incorporate and facilitate understanding. It is also through the progressive introduction of exercises that differentiation is considered and accounted for.

The acquisition of physical skills is a continuous and progressive process and it is our responsibility to ensure that pupils gain knowledge and understanding at every stage. When setting up a task I believe it is extremely helpful if you are able to demonstrate with a physical example. For some strange reason when I am prepared to show physically what I think water looks like, it appears to encourage their own experimentation and occasionally raises a smile. An intellectual concept is often clarified through physical action.

ASSESSMENT

For the work I am describing here the following elements would be my assessment criteria:

- Is there creative involvement in the process and creative imagination in the product?
- In group discussions do they proffer relevant and imaginative suggestions?
- Are they able to execute the work with a degree of commitment and reflect a full use of the languages of movement, image, gesture, sound and colour?
- Are they able to engage with the work of others and offer opinions as to its effectiveness and value?
- Are they able to work in groups of varying sizes and do they contribute to the overall effectiveness of ensemble or group work?

PRACTICAL IDEAS

Drama in the 11–14 age range is for me primarily about process; I aim to continually stimulate the children's imagination by introducing a wide variety of stimuli and working with a substantial range of exercises. I hope in this way to encourage a considered and adaptable approach to their work.

Atmosphere

Physical theatre is an exciting topic; it actively encourages us to re-examine our humanly response to each other and the world at large. Through exploring individual interpretations of experience, thought, action and sense we confront ourselves. It is therefore essential that the drama space radiates an atmosphere of mutual respect and acceptance. When introducing concepts of physical theatre make a little magic in your space, create an atmosphere with some lighting, sound or burning an incense stick/oil burner (lavender oil sets the scene perfectly). This creates a sense of mystery and brings a little of the unordinary into an ordinary lesson; it is also a useful starting point for discussing how our senses stimulate feelings.

Warm-up

As teachers we are all aware of just how flexible and full of energy children at this stage can be; however, it is a useful strategy to begin with a warm-up. These need not be carefully planned routines full of complicated stretching exercises: favourite 'tag' games are equally suitable and at times preferable. One alternative method is to lead the children through a series of movements yourself. This is particularly useful when working on pace and rhythm as you are able to direct specific qualities. I have found that leading my own form of Tai Chi improves concentration and adds a certain energy to subsequent work.

Tension is an area often overlooked in the warm-up and yet it is extremely relevant to this type of work. Always introduce it at the close of the warm-up to ensure that muscles are ready and do stress the importance of doing only what is comfortable for them. One exercise I use is the 'cold but happy flying penguin'. Ask the children to become penguins, which requires them to stiffen, and follow you around the room, ensuring that the whole body is involved. As you move explain how the penguin is at first cold which naturally makes it shiver and tighten – then out comes the sun and we all relax a little, but oh dear the sun goes in again (get the point?). As the penguin's finale we begin to fly, flapping our arms as we go. Great fun, useful and inspires some unusual conversations. Water slowly freezing, volcanic lava forming mountains and thunderbolts hitting the earth are all themes which can be employed to focus on body tension.

Focus

Warm-ups tend to excite and raise energy levels, so it is now important to harness and direct that energy. The best way I have found is to focus attention imaginatively. This I do by asking the children to find a space on the floor, lie down comfortably, close their eyes and become silent and still. At this point I may ask the children to use their imagination like a beam of light to scan their bodies from the top of their head to the tips of their toes. I might ask them to note the weight of each part of their body and its distance from the floor. This is an excellent introduction to body awareness and does help focus energy. Alternatively I ask them to imagine their favourite colour and bring this to rest just behind the eyes; the colour is then slowly moved down through the body to the toes and back again. I may lead them with my voice on an imaginative journey or ask them to picture their own journey to a fantastic land full of fantastical things. I may ask them to imagine themselves as a feather or leaf that is being lifted and carried by a gentle breeze and finally comes to rest. Whatever form this takes, it is a beneficial way to create an appropriate atmosphere, centre energy and encourage imaginative focus. Discussion of the colours or journeys imagined can stimulate further work through enactment and depiction.

EXERCISES

In this section I have outlined exercises related to depiction, movement, dynamics and symbols with the intention of providing you, the teacher, with a platform for your own imagination to mix and integrate exercises into your work.

Expressive depiction

Expressive depiction is for me the first objective, understanding how we portray and read emotion and attitude within still images. A good starting point is, having spread out, simply ask everyone to look *happy, sad, proud, lonely, shy* ... etc. Having run through your prepared list of emotions discuss what makes us look as if we are experiencing these emotions. Initially everyone tends to focus upon facial expression. After discussion and forum examples begin to draw their attention to how the arms are carried, their posture and position of feet, ask about bodily tension and how the eyes affect what we show. When answering your questions, ask the students to show, rather than say, what they mean, and check to see if everyone agrees or not. Explore as many alternatives as possible, look at levels of sitting, kneeling and lying down, encourage them to question why they think certain physical shapes relay certain feelings. Having gone through the list it is worthwhile just recapping. One method is to ask the children to move around the space. On a given signal they freeze, portraying the expression that is written on a card and held aloft. This again provides opportunity for discussion and registers the word in written form.

There are many ways to progress this work. For example, working in pairs ask them to present four different ways of showing each emotion, match the images of feeling with sound (introduce the concept of onomatopoeia) or create a sentence that describes the feeling. Moving into group work ask the children to present a series of three images which show someone becoming *happy*, etc. Depict a progression into the final image. Working in unison, ask them to explore changing from one expression to another, begin quite simply with *happy to sad* and end with more complicated combinations like *dreaming to lonely*. Ask them to think about pace and how they might use speed or slow motion when changing to emphasize the feelings, allow them to select their own expressions to work with.

Expressive depiction can be a useful method of physicalizing text, in particular poetry; it enables the children to distil the emotional essence of stories or poetry and physicalize this through expressive imagery. Lewis Carroll's *Jabberwocky* provides an excellent opportunity to combine abstract and concrete images allowing children to create their own physical interpretation.[4] Read and discuss the poem selecting lines you feel will encourage visual and physical interpretation: 'The Jabberwock, with eyes of flame'. How will they depict the Jabberwock? Very useful for highlighting the importance of eyes. 'O frabjous day! Callooh! Callay!' Could this be three depictions? Investigate the meaning in each line and through forum work distil consensual meaning and depict.

Expressive depiction is strengthened by using imaginative focus. Ask them where they might be when in that expression or what they might be seeing. Introduce colour – which do they associate with proud or dreaming? An exercise useful for colour association is to lay pieces of large coloured paper or card over the floor. Ask them to select a colour and take up an expression they feel matches this. Better still if you have access to lighting and sound equipment, set up a series of coloured spotlights and use these as the stimulus; this leads to further work combining colours and shades of expression to one particular feeling, while shades of coloured card or lighting can be linked to progressing states of an expression.

Having worked extensively with emotions it is useful to look at attitudes, expressions such as: '*I don't care*' – '*I'm better than you*' – '*I don't want to*' – '*I'm always right*' – '*I'm really sorry*' can be explored in the same manner. This enables the concept of status to be introduced and if you prepare these on cards can make an excellent exercise for paired or group work. Examine occupations and types of people, how might an older person appear *happy*, etc., what's different? Is that really the way older people appear when *sad*, etc.? Abstract concepts may also be depicted, which allow a greater freedom of interpretation and encourage creative thought. I have included a list of abstract themes in the appendix to this chapter. With abstract ideas such as *Heaven's Gate* or *The Feeling of a Reflection* I begin by discussing what sensations and feelings are inspired. I then work with varying volunteers to shape the images that we all feel portray something of its essence. We build pictures and consider movement and text. The children then work in small groups constructing their own expressive depictions; these may be enhanced by the inclusion of colour in the form of card, confetti-like paper or material.

When working in this particular way it is important to continually seek the students' responses and with sensitive questioning allow them room to explore and justify their own work.

Expressive movement

Expressive movement may be introduced through exercises used to explore depiction. Once again, beginning with a free association of feelings and movement, examine the specific physical details that convey an expression. An interesting way to open up discussion is to have a choice of moods and attitudes on display. Ask the children to select one and begin to move around the space, then on a given cue ask them to join others who appear to be expressing the same feeling or attitude. This often leads to the realization that some expressions are similar and that small movements alter our reading.

Explore simple physical actions such as sitting down, shaking hands, eating, and so on. Change the feeling or attitude and discuss the results: how does a *shy* person sit down, eat or shake the hand of a *lonely* person? Extend this by beginning simple actions in one feeling and changing the feeling midway. Exercises that examine the progression from one feeling to another may be contextualized by the children themselves. When might a person change from being *sad to happy, proud to embarrassed*, and so on? Who are they? Where are they? Alternatively you may wish to focus on the pace and quality of movement used to show changes in expression. Do we feel the same when we move in different ways? If we do something a lot slower does it make us feel old?

Reactions and responses can also be worked upon. Set up a space and ask the children to enter expressing one feeling; upon seeing something in this space their feeling changes and consequently their movement. You see something you like – that scares you – angers you – makes you laugh ... ask the children to explore situations where feelings drastically change.

Music or sound can be introduced to enhance movement and explore different qualities such as *heavy – light – fast – slow – big – small*. Ask the children to put together short movement sequences using two or three qualities and one feeling. Working in pairs and using a variety of expressions create sounds to match movement and/or expression, if possible borrow some instruments from the music department. Introduce a variety of recorded music and explore how this makes us feel and move. Music provides atmosphere and a sense of place which affects movement. Discover which styles of music are appropriate to certain sensations or situations.

Expressive movement animates descriptive language, combining opposites like *accept–reject, strong–weak, aggressive–passive, blatant–secretive*, highlighting the qualities that convey meaning. Working in groups of four, ask the children to explore these opposites, focus on pace and use of levels and discuss the different qualities that emerge. Is it possible to move in the same manner with different feelings and attitudes? Do we have to change the pace or quality of movement to emphasize the difference? Set up exercises that allow the children to explore these possibilities in terms of movement without context; working in this way enriches future work that includes characters and situations. In later improvisations always refer the children back to their work on expressive movement.

Working with movement can encourage children to portray abstract ideas with confidence and imagination. An introductory exercise is to ask small groups to spontaneously create movement that portrays: *sea – flying – fire – wind – planets forming – dawn breaking*. Again quality and pace can be discussed before progressing to more complex themes such as *darkness – light – taste – touch – moon – sky*. Word-chains can also be used to devise small movement pieces: provide a list of words (not necessarily connected – very easy to construct) and ask the children to create movement that draws upon the words given: *new – touch – joy – forget, awake – follow – push – sad, surprise – loss – listen – sleep, grow – hold – hide – dream*.

Creating movement directly from text follows the same principles as for depiction: distil the expression in a word, line or verse and use that as the catalyst to movement. Lewis Carroll's *Jabberwocky*, as with depiction work, is an ideal text as it is full of movement opportunities: 'Long time the manxsome foe he sought ... Did gyre and gimble in the wabe.'[5]

Expressive movement is concerned with improving physical skills and stretching the imagination. As with the expressive depiction work, ensure that responses are fully discussed and valued.

Expressive dynamics

Expressive dynamics is the combination of movement and depiction. It is here that we explore the integration of tableaux, movement, gesture, colour and sound. Ensemble work and concepts of structuring presentation are approached. To begin dynamics, refer back to individual depiction work upon feelings and attitudes. Ask the children to add one gesture that they feel conveys this feeling. After discussion of the different results explore if changing the speed or repetition of a gesture alters meaning. Having worked individually, ask them to work in small groups creating an image of the same expression. Begin by using one gesture and examine this, then ask for two or three gestures to be included. It soon becomes apparent how meaning and relationships emerge. Experiment with two or three children repeating their selected gesture on the formation of the image – '*lost and lonely*' (hands move to the sky) – what does this do?

Physical interaction brings movement and depiction together. What may be understood by someone kneeling down before you, stroking your hair, holding your hand, pulling you along, leading or pushing you forward. Moments such as these happen to us all. Explore one action such as *holding a hand* in different situations. In discussion ask for suggestions to be shown and always seek alternatives: the aim is to fully explore how we can create clear expression. Physical interaction is often best highlighted when performed en masse: one person *holding a hand* makes a statement, while several in unison exaggerates and emphasizes the expression. To achieve this we need to work as an ensemble.

Ensemble work brings the whole group together in the creative process and may be used to reinforce expressive movement work. It does not necessarily mean that everyone moves identically or at the same time; sections and individuals can be still while others move. The emphasis is upon the sum of its parts forming the whole. There are a number of exercises designed to introduce ensemble work; one that I particularly favour is to ask the group to move around and find a point where they all face the same way at the same time. Alternatively have one member continually running while the others remain still and when that child comes to a stop another takes over. These exercises aim to construct a cohesive group response and reaction. Once some semblance of unity is achieved select an image, for example *sea*. Discuss and agree movement and perform this, paying attention to rhythm, pace and expression. Ask the group to portray the *sea* individually and discuss the difference in affect. In a similar fashion ask the ensemble to create expressive depictions, work on portraying atmospheres, or thought-provoking words such as *equal, time, attack, balance, together, protect*. It is very important to allow individuals the opportunity to step out of the ensemble to evaluate and modify the overall effect being communicated.

Another simple way of combining depiction and movement is to use the image as either a starting or finishing point. This provides a good opportunity for detailed group discussion. Ask four volunteers to step forward, arrange three standing together on one side of the space and the remaining one sitting on the other side. What does this convey? If the three standing turn their backs, what does this suggest? Add a gesture to change the meaning, or simply improvise the scene to life. What happened before or next? Having worked through some ideas, ask the children to depict an expression and bring this to life. Extend this by asking them to find two or three important moments and hold the image for a count of five before continuing. By interspersing movement, depiction and ensemble work we begin to build our *product* and so can turn our attention to the aesthetics through discussion and forum work.

Symbols

Symbols provide another language and are well worth exploring. Begin by examining different shapes. What can a circle represent or mean? What if we place it on the floor or hold it aloft? Move on to discuss and incorporate *leaves, stones, flowers, sand, stars, feathers, branches* and so on. Ask the children to devise a series of progressive ensemble expressions based on a sensation – *joy.* When this has been rehearsed, ask them to identify the moments of change and incorporate different symbols – *a key or piece of coloured material* – into the movement or composite image. What do the symbols begin to tell us? What could they represent? Taking on board the results of the exploration of symbols, incorporate them into depiction, movement and ensemble work. This sounds very complicated but in actual practice is easily explained and achieved. The inspirational value of working with symbols is inestimable and I believe encourages the children to interact physically with language and themes.

CONCLUSION

You should now possess enough ingredients to create physical theatre in your drama space with students in this age group. I have not been able to cover all the techniques that I feel contribute to a comprehensive approach to physical theatre. Working with mask, techniques of clowning and aspects of *commedia dell'arte* are extremely valuable and I would urge you to explore these yourselves.

In this chapter I have explained my guiding philosophy of introduction, aesthetics, creative use, and finally the application of techniques and concepts. There is a natural progression from stillness to movement to ensemble dynamics and exercises should progress accordingly. However, only the teacher who knows the individuals in the class can select a progressive route suitable and accessible to everyone. As drama teachers or specialists I am sure you will have many exercises and creative extensions to add and I hope that you are able to select and mix ideas presented here with your own to create physical theatre. In written form many of these suggestions may appear complex, but I strongly believe that with the right energy, enthusiasm and patient explanation you will be amazed at what can be achieved. Children at this age have an immense ability to make abstract ideas concrete in the most imaginative way. As Jodie, a 14-year-old student told me, 'drama helps me see people and the world better'.

ACKNOWLEDGEMENTS

I am extremely grateful to Melanie Holman, my partner in Colourise Theatre Company and current drama co-ordinator at Salisbury School, London, and to the children and staff at Hamilton Lodge school for deaf children, Brighton.

APPENDIX: ABSTRACT THEMES FOR PHYSICAL THEATRE

The dream of a leaf as it falls from a tree
A lonely bird in a summer's sky
A swan on a lonely lake
The heart of a tree as it grows old
The happiness in the eyes of an older person
The shadow of love
A baby's first dream
The dream of night
Heaven's Gate
The smile of a mountain
The thoughts of sand on a beach
The warmth of the sun on your face
The first sight of a new day
The heart of a lion
The song of a river
The hope in a prayer
The breath of a tree swaying in the wind
Light dancing on the ripples of a lake
The touch of sunset on a meadow
The slow breath of winter

NOTES

1 Harradine, D. (1999) 'What is the new mime?' *Total Theatre*, **11**(1), 18–19.
2 Harradine, D. (1999) *ibid.*, pp. 18–19.
3 I was introduced to the concept of competence by Andy Kempe in his keynote address, entitled 'Kissing with confidence', at the National Drama Conference, 14–17 April 1998. I am indebted to Andy for this insightful concept. See Kempe, A. (1999) in C. Lawrence (ed.) *The Canterbury Keynotes* (London: National Drama Publications), pp. 27–36.
4 Berry, J. (1997) *Classic Poems to Read Aloud* (London: Kingfisher), p. 106.
5 Berry, J. (1997) *ibid.*

Chapter 3

Reading and Writing Plays in an Electronic Classroom

Denise Margetts

One of the characters in Liz Lochhead's play *Cuba*, on which the work described in this chapter was based, is an English teacher called Mr Shaw. When he tells his class to write down Keats' line 'Beauty is truth, truth beauty', he is told 'Sir, we did that last week'. 'Write it down again then,' he replies. Unlike Mr Shaw, who expected his students to appreciate 'great' writers of literature by copying, we are now more committed to a model of English teaching which aims to encourage students to develop their own abilities as writers by recognizing, deconstructing and analysing the craft of a wide range of authors. There are, however, issues which confront students and their teachers when they engage in dramatic writing, which are particular to the form. In my own teaching, I have been interested in how I might scaffold or frame my students' dramatic writing in order to encourage them to work as playwrights. How might I help them to understand the role of the script in dramatic performance as a more provisional and dynamic entity than the lines of poetry copied repeatedly in this play? This chapter describes a possible solution to this complex problem.

My decision to base most of this work on Liz Lochhead's *Cuba* came from a desire to find a text written for young people which used a variety of dramatic conventions.[1] The play uses a range of conventions such as narrator, chorus and tableau which are non-naturalistic and therefore highly visible. In practice, the students moved between the English classroom and the drama studio, weighed down with cameras, copies of Lochhead's play and their own emergent scripts. I was interested throughout in the question of how, within the context of the English classroom and curriculum, I might enable students to conceptualize plays as essentially physical texts, changing shape in the context of rehearsal, and recognize and experiment with their unique conventions.

THE PROBLEM OF FRAMING AND FRAMING THE PROBLEM

My mixed-ability English class of 14-year-olds were familiar with writing frames, which they used to support their understanding of the shape of written text. When they began their own writing, we usually read an example of the particular written form together, noting the function and features of text, investigating and deconstructing an appropriate model. It was a process that seemed to work well; the students understood how the texts worked, and were able to recognize how they might experiment creatively with the model for themselves. However, when I began to think about how I might apply this method to writing dramatic texts, it dawned on me that a writing frame which, as Wray and Lewis suggest, 'simply gives the basic structure for a piece of writing by setting out a sequence of cohesive ties to which the writer supplies the content', was a more problematic tool.[2] An understanding of the function of conventions, such as stage directions and dialogue, involves a sense of the text as something which is not in itself finished, but anticipates physical enactment in rehearsal or performance. The cohesive ties in a dramatic text are those that direct physicality, and this would provide my students with a particular challenge.

However, my problem went further than this. Many plays are devised or developed collaboratively, and this suggests that dramatic writing is not a blueprint for a physical act which will take place later, but part of a more flexible, interactive process of working. In this kind of work, the physical predates the written and the notion of authorship itself is problematic.[3] Lizbeth Goodman, describing the creation of *Lear's Daughters*, points out that 'devised playtexts are rarely written in finished form. As a result the accessibility of definitive versions of written texts is greatly limited'.[4] She also notes that this form of 'collective authorship' creates a sense of 'solidarity', an aspect of drama practice which Andy Kempe explores in more detail in Chapter 5. In encouraging my students to write plays, it was important that they understood the connections between the written discourses of dramatic text and physical discourses of theatrical practice.

An understanding of, and involvement in, the relationship between the physical and the written seemed to me to be a crucial part of what students need to experience in order to be successful readers and writers of plays. My aim was to help them to see that the process of writing plays, unlike other forms of writing, is intricately associated with, and negotiated, by physical enactment and experimentation. It was clear that I was asking for a very different set of practices in reading and writing than those which my students had encountered and acquired in their work with other kinds of texts. Clearly, as Aston and Savona point out, 'The habits of reading cannot be unproblematically transposed across differential forms. The dramatic text must be read on its own terms'.[5]

I was concerned to explore how students might gain a real sense of the ways in which dramatic writing draws upon a very different set of narrative codes and practices. As a teacher, this meant that I reconsidered the status, purpose and method of scaffolding which would help students construct this kind of text; I was interested in creating a classroom environment which encouraged students to experiment with using the visual and physical 'languages' of drama, as well as the written and spoken word. I found that an electronic classroom offered a range of starting points for this project, where working with computers, digital cameras and video created opportunities for students to engage in a process of working which enabled them to read and create images and written text simultaneously. They were also able to see their texts as dynamic, provisional entities.

PROVISIONALITY AND PHYSICALITY

The notion that the written dramatic script is provisional, unfinished and open to physical interpretation presented me, as a teacher of English, with an important opportunity both to challenge the status of writing and to reconsider its value.

A play script is incomplete in itself, an outline of prospective action. It is the tip of the iceberg, a synopsis merely, a sketch of the real thing. It is also, by its nature, an unfinished product, necessarily still in process. As an English teacher I would be asking my students to think again about the hierarchy of the written and the physical. I would be proposing a new relationship between these modes of communication where the linguistic was the least important, existing purely to facilitate or record the physical. I would be asking them also to consider the context in which writing is produced, its purpose and its audience. There are few other text types which carry such immediate and practical application.

I began by considering the function of a play script. In which form should students first encounter this text? Should I introduce them to the text in performance or on the page? Is a play a text which notates performance, which should be considered to some extent to exist *after* the event? Or is it a first version of a physical experience to follow?

We began with a discussion of this problem. I asked my students how they thought a play was written. We had considered some of the conventions of play making earlier in the year when we studied Shakespeare; their research projects explored the relationship between the playwright and the company for whom he wrote, the question of authorship and the idea that 'corrupt' texts were circulating at the time. Some students had been involved in devising their own pieces of theatre in drama lessons, and described a collaborative process where little dialogue was recorded. We considered some of the stages of hypothetical writing processes and wrote these on cards, which the students sequenced to create what they felt to be the ideal process for the creation of a play (see Figure 3.1).

This led to an interesting debate about the role of performance in writing and whether later revisions to scripts constituted revisions or new versions. The idea of who should be allowed to make changes to work was interesting, with many students hotly defending the right of playwrights to protect the versions they had created. Indeed they noted that in the *New Connections* anthology, Nick Drake had written that the plays 'were not to be adapted or altered in any way without consultation with the playwrights [who] proved more than happy to discuss their work, and to be consulted about possible

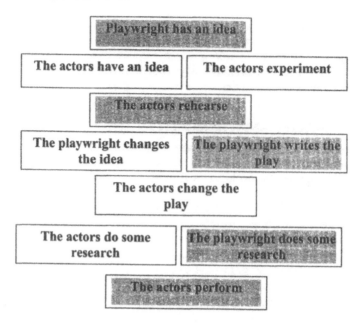

Figure 3.1 The cards offered to the students for sequencing. The shaded cards are those that are most selected. Interestingly, all of those referring to the actors' role in the writing process were discarded at this point

small changes'.[6] We also looked at other descriptions of the writing process, such as the one outlining the problematic authorship of *Lear's Daughters*, and related this process to the improvised drama they had experienced in other contexts.

I wanted the students to conceive of play scripts as part of the process of creating dramatic/theatrical texts, rather than a separate entity from performance. This way of thinking influenced how we read and interpreted the play *Cuba*, where I introduced the idea that we would read the script as potential performers or directors. I hoped that this would help the students recognize, when they began to write their own scripts, that scripts as written documents are only part of the process, and are similarly 'unfinished'. As Susan Melrose points out, this sense of provisionality is part of the magic of reading a script: 'Reprinting the play as script, explicitly toward a staging, in a form which leaves adequate space for users' notation seems magically to transform our relationship to it as thing.'[7]

In order to capture some of this magic, I created an electronic version of extracts from the text with space for digital photographs of performance to be entered using a scanner. The text extracts were typed into Page Maker with frames created for the photographs in advance and spaces created for the discourses of technical design and actors'/director's notes. In this way we were able to view the text being read as a working document, one which was

Work in Progress

The narrator, B., is 'sorting through' in her parents' house after the death of her (long-widowed) mother. 'sadness acting' of any sort is strictly to be avoided though. She is flooded with memory and this is likely to be exhilarating beyond all grief.	*Drop photo in here* *Drop photo in here*	**Director's notes**

Figure 3.2   An extract from the electronic script. Picture frames and text frames were set up in advance to accommodate photographs and notes. The division of the stage directions into manageable sections helped with differentiation

essentially unfinished and appearing in the context of use. We continued to use this writing frame throughout the work; it was integral to the process (see Figure 3.2).

The students' ability to manipulate visual image and written text on computer not only suggested the provisionality of the drama script, but also pointed to, and anticipated, its physical realization. Throughout my preparation I was interested in the fact that script and performance are often regarded as two distinct spheres. In the classroom I wanted the reading and writing of plays to involve the discourses of both of these fields, the written script and performance practice. In a discussion of playwriting, Melrose seeks to reinstate the physical over the linguistic in dramatic writing. She argues that in the past, dramatic writing has rather ignored the body, which was considered to 'intrude' into the written text, or merely to 'illustrate' the playwrights' words.[8]

This idea of the body as intrusion or illustration seemed to me to usefully characterize some of my previous approaches to the physical experience of dramatic text in the context of the English curriculum. I reflected that if I had used dramatic staging of scenes at all it had been to exemplify discoveries made in the classroom. Interestingly, earlier in their school career there is a sense of the implied physicality of language when they are taught to 'Use punctuation to replace intonation, pauses, gestures' as part of the National Literacy Strategy.[9] Here children are encouraged to see kinaesthetic grammar as analogous with the grammar of written text, working from the non-verbal to understand the function of the verbal.

The status of the physical in students' progress towards literacy was not something I had considered before. In order to redress this balance in my own teaching, I wanted to explore the place of the body in the dramatic text, and to encourage students to employ their understanding of silence, of the relationship between the non-verbal and the verbal in their scripts. Among the students, there was a consensus of opinion that scripts contained 'characters', 'dialogue' and 'stage-directions', and I felt that stage directions might be the obvious place to begin work which looked at the relationship between the physical, the provisional and the written text.

STAGE DIRECTIONS AND PERFORMATIVITY

In order to encourage students to visualize the physicality implied in written scripts, I wanted to begin by reading Lochhead's play with a close study of the function of stage directions. A significant number of the students had already encountered play scripts, and asserted that stage directions were there 'to tell the actors what to do'. When I asked them which elements of playscripts were most important, there was a strong feeling that stage directions were least important because 'the actors could decide what to do themselves' and because 'what they *say* tells the story'. Aston and Savona refer to the fact that 'Stage directions frame the dialogue in two senses: literally, in the layout of the page, and theatrically, in that they impart to the printed text the status of a blueprint for theatrical production'.[10] I was interested in the notion that, far from fulfilling an ancillary purpose in the reading and writing of plays, stage directions might be seen as a guiding framework in both processes.

We began by looking at the voice operating in stage directions in the opening scene of Lochhead's *Cuba*, when a grown-up Barbara is in the attic looking at old photographs. The students investigated the discourse of 'telling', of command, which they felt in our early discussion was the primary function of the stage directions. However, they soon found that Lochhead's use of metaphor ('she is flooded with memory', 'two or three years before hemlines even thought of climbing toward the idea of the mini-skirt') establishes a mode of 'telling' that is more than utilitarian. I was interested in how the students would respond to this as actors, and how this would modify their preconceptions about the function of stage directions. I gave the students the scene with the dialogue blanked out and, in groups, they created a silent version following the stage directions alone.

As a result of improvising a silent version of the scene, several groups identified the difficulty of precisely conveying complex emotion through the language of stage directions. Lochhead's directive that '"sadness acting" of any sort is strictly to be avoided ... She is flooded with memory and this is likely to be exhilarating beyond all grief' caused some hilarity in performance.[11] The language was felt to be melodramatic, creating Victorian swooning to represent floods of exhilarating emotion. There was, therefore, an early engagement with Lochhead's voice in these directions, an acknowledgement that metaphor and idiom are part of the discourse of this kind of text. Our discussion focused on two apparently contradictory things: the desire for absolute precision in the description of acting styles, and the sense that such precision is difficult to achieve in practice.

In order to look more closely at the craft of writing, and in particular at how the dramatic purpose of the scene is constructed, the students began to uncover the complexity of the sentence structure in Lochhead's stage directions. In the first sentence, 'The narrator, B., is "sorting through" in her parents' house after the death of her (long-widowed) mother', the choice of the idiomatic expression 'sorting through' suggests the kind of colloquial voice we are about to hear through the characters in this play. Lochhead is therefore laying before us the dramatic world in which this character operates. The complex structure of the third sentence allows Lochhead to weave together instructions relating to movement, action and reaction, lighting and staging.

> B. drags a big dusty old cardboard box across centre stage, stops, wipes her dusty hands on the seat of her trousers, picks out a dusty old book, blows, registers that it is a copy of Palgrave's golden treasury, sees that tucked into it, though much bigger, is a real large-size school photograph – we only see the back of it – which she holds in front of her, perusing, as behind her, central, lights come up on a still tableau.

The voice is one we associate with narrative storytelling, a voice which narrates events which have happened rather than one which instructs in what is required to happen. The students identified this voice as one which creates a sense of action and feeling as it appears before us on an imaginary stage. They also experimented with hearing different inflections within that voice, and this illustrated its multiple functions. A choral reading of this part of the play, while the actress playing B. acted out these 'instructions', provided an opportunity for the students to find these different voices and attribute them to a speaker. They created a script for these stage directions, dividing the text between five different speakers, that is those who, respectively, described movement, thought, feeling, lighting and the setting of the story. By dramatizing the text in this way we were able to consider the different tones of voice used by the different speakers and therefore to discuss what purpose each voice was fulfilling. We were also able to consider how the stage directions were integral to the dramatic action itself; the group recognized that one of the primary functions of this particular part of the text is to enable the reader, the prospective actor/director, to 'watch' a version of the play imaginatively.

Watching the scene staged in this way also created a sense of the text not as a blueprint for production but as a description, a notation, of a production that has gone before. The playwright's voice, manifested in stage directions, was seen as merely one voice among others in the play. Each group then selected a moment in their mimed version of the scene and we used the digital camera to record these frozen moments. We inserted the stills into the spaces I had already set up beside each of the stage directions.

We had begun to consider the function of stage directions in detail by
teasing out the multilayered voice in Lochhead's initial directions. In order to
begin to establish a vocabulary for describing function in this context, we
created a list of performative verbs, which describe the active effect of the
stage directions. Their performative vocabulary included describes, establishes, states, suggests, creates, introduces, sets up, destroys, undermines, tells,
insists, allows, points to, mentions, quotes, echoes. We collected these words
on a transparency for an overhead projector (OHT). By creating a colour
code for each function and by changing the colour of the text on the computer
screen we were able to see clearly which parts of the early stage directions
carried particular functions; those parts which carried more than one purpose
were able to be coloured only once and so the pairs negotiated until they
could agree on its principal function. They then allocated the most appropriate performative phrase to their stills in order that we could reflect on
which function seemed most important when we had enacted the scene
physically.

DIALOGUE, ACTION AND INTERACTION

The students' original idea that the stage directions told the actors what to do
had been replaced by a more flexible notion, one that recognized the voice of
the playwright in creating the dramatic universe of the play. As part of the
process of preparing the students to write their own plays, I now wanted to
look more closely at the relationship between stage directions and dialogue,
the part of the text which the students believed told the actors what to say.

Speech, in drama, is an event, an act; Keir Elam, drawing on speech-act
theory, suggests that dramatic dialogue is a 'linguistic interaction'. He blurs
the boundaries between saying and doing.[12] For my students, the idea that
dramatic dialogue can be seen in terms of its particular impact or effect was a
helpful analytical tool. In this context, I was interested in exploring with the
students how Lochhead's play exploits different kinds of utterances, including
the public voices of magazines, the trite proverbial language of the adult world
and Tennyson's poetry.

The students began to question how stage directions are used to frame
dialogue and what relationship these parts of the text had with each other.
They worked together to write their own versions of the lines in the play before
they read Lochhead's script. Using the electronic scripts we had created from
the stage directions, the groups were asked to create one line of dialogue
between each of their stills. This meant that they had to make a number of
decisions; they needed to decide who was speaking between the stage
directions and who was listening to the speaker. They drew on their list of
performative verbs to decide what function the line needed to fulfil. I wanted
them to work three-dimensionally, constructing their lines through physical
experimentation and discussion. Running through this work was an interesting debate about whether stage directions pre-empt the voices heard by the
audience or confirm them.

To help them get started, we brainstormed some of the different ways in which we talk to one another and decided whether each line should be a statement, a reflection, a command, a question or an exclamation. As the students worked, it became clear that some of the stage directions were conjunctive, supporting and exemplifying the dialogue. For example, the stage direction '*Stops and pep talks herself*' was seen by the students as a clear indication that the following line was intended to 'create confidence' or 'establish that B. is trying to cheer herself up' and should therefore be an exclamation or statement. One group followed a narrative thread in the stage directions noticing that B. is 'beyond tears' and in the next direction 'hugs her arms around her stomach and rocks a beat or two back and forward'. They decided that she needed to move from calm to panic in her line.

Other stage directions were disjunctive, providing a commentary on, or tension with, the dialogue. Several groups picked up on the question in the stage directions describing the families ('*Different families?*') and were alerted to the need for the dialogue to create something this text could argue with, a statement about how different the families are. Having made their decisions about the function of the lines in the text they improvised their ideas, performing and reworking the lines, which were finally noted on their scripts.

As they compared their own work with Lochhead's version of the scene, they were able to explore the particular dramatic purposes that dialogue performs. I allocated a small section of Lochhead's play to each group to rehearse a reading using any information from the stage directions that seemed important. It became obvious, however, that there was another layer in the process; some stage directions seemed to be contained in the dialogue, as 'intra-dialogic' instructions. To explore this aspect of playwriting, the students created stills implied in the dialogue with digital cameras, and pasted them alongside the appropriate line in the script. This enabled them to see how the dialogue carries within it its own stage directions. There was a clear identification that intra-dialogic stage directions are contained within the voices in the text. Through physical enactment and an experience of 'reading' this electronically we had challenged the group's original notion that instructions for physical action belong in one kind of text alone.

There were further challenges. As well as creating a sense of what is happening on the stage, the dialogue also seemed to suggest an absent world. In order to look closely at this, groups created pictures of the kind of past implied by their own versions of lines in the play and then they repeated this process for Lochhead's lines. One group's line following the stage direction 'she is well beyond tears in this' read:

B. I was only 14. How could I have known?

Lochhead writes at this point:

B . . . she was so proud of you, Sairy, when you were born that was the first thing I did she ever really approved of.

The still memories of Lochhead's line suggested an unhappy past, with the mother turned away and disapproving. The group's own line led them to an image of a young B. alone in the space. There was not as much information in this line, they reflected, making the task more difficult. A comparison of digital photographs of these 'memories' led to a discussion of how lines of dialogue help to create impressions that point to a life beyond the stage.

In the students' versions of the scene, they also used both dialogue and stage directions to make decisions about who they felt was listening to each line. One group picked up on the fact that the narrator, B., was either Barbara or Bernadette, central characters in the play (though importantly at this point in the play we do not know which) and played their line to two summoned ghosts. When B. said, 'I was only 14. How could I have known?' the two ghosts reacted with disgust. Interestingly, this line followed recognizable conventions of an opening; the group had not decided on a narrative for their play but wanted to *suggest* an event that would be explained later. I asked why their narrator was looking back, and they explained that the line had to be memory because the stage directions described someone looking at a photograph summoning 'ghosts'. I had also asked this group to consider how powerful speaking was in the play, what the narrator's speech seemed to achieve, and they reported back that 'speaking only makes people unhappy or remember', that 'everyone speaks but no one listens'. In this way, the stage directions not only framed their thinking about the dialogue very clearly, but also enabled them to engage with the play emotionally.

CREATING SCRIPTS: ENACTMENT, PHYSICALITY AND ELECTRONIC TEXTS

Throughout the work on Lochhead's *Cuba*, the students had worked on a range of activities which looked closely at how to read a dramatic text visually and physically. Reading and writing had been closely linked during the project, with writing used often as an essential part of the reading process; drafted versions or rewritings enabling the students to imaginatively play the role of the playwright in the creative process as well as the roles of the characters. I was now concerned for the students to use the knowledge and understanding they had acquired about dramatic conventions to create their own scripts. In particular, I hoped that the work we had already undertaken would enable them to create a sense of the kinaesthetic and the visual within their own playwriting.

In my own preparation, I began with the question of how to frame their first encounter with the text they would be creating. I decided to begin with a visualization of the space in which the performance would take place. In this way I hoped to focus the writers from the outset on how their written text comes to signify performance. I laid down some clear frameworks. Like Lochhead's text, their play would begin with a narrator and a flashback. They would write in pairs, and create only the first scene. We took the idea of an attic and considered why this had been chosen in Lochhead's play by brainstorming words which described the atmosphere and associations of this space. We created a list of other places that might stimulate memories of all kinds and we used this as a bank of ideas. I had set up stored electronic images of these spaces on computer, and the students manipulated these to experiment with different dramatic atmospheres and effects. It had been clear during the reading of *Cuba* that the stage directions had effectively framed the group's thinking, both about the dialogue as it was written and about the 'gaps' in the dialogue which were open to interpretation. I wanted to use stage directions as a writing frame, but also to construct this frame three-dimensionally.

In the drama studio, I asked them to create a memory and to show the rest of the class a series of 'photographs' of the memory. One of the pair then mimed finding an object that evoked this memory and I videoed the performance of this. We used the video to 'transcribe' the action together on an OHT. To support some students with their contributions to the shared writing we worked with a list of sentences that described action in the present tense and they selected from these. We then used a copy of Lochhead's opening scene on the OHT and looked for the references to emotion in the opening stage directions. We looked again in particular at the metaphor used to describe emotion ('flooded') and the voice of the dramatist issuing directions about the actor's presentation of the emotion ('sadness acting' of any sort strictly to be avoided). Using these and a fuller bank of examples of metaphors for describing feeling which were left on the OHT we looked at how to describe the emotion that our videoed actor was showing. Students collectively directed a reworking of the scene and we redrafted our description accordingly, looking more closely at sentence structure in our shared writing. We imagined the worst possible interpretation of our directions and had them hilariously played out before us by volunteers. To avoid such we built in some direct instructions on style by replacing some of the words in Lochhead's sentence. This three-dimensional frame was interactive, with the writing informing the rehearsal and vice versa.

A reflection upon the recursive nature of this process was an important part of scaffolding the draft of their own opening stage directions in pairs. I set out clearly delineated writing times and rehearsal times to ensure that there was an even balance of enactment and notation but, as the process developed, these distinctions became more fluid, with several students demanding clipboards! I experimented with different kinds of framing devices for different individuals during this process. Some wrote their stage directions on cards and placed them in appropriate places on the floor to use as prompts for improvisation of dialogue, moving in the physical spaces between them, just as our reading of Lochhead's dialogue had operated in the spaces between stage directions on the page. Another group projected the stage directions on the wall and elected a scribe to note key words and lines as the action took place, so that the written text took shape in the background of the physical action. One group continued to use photographs to frame their work with some students drafting speech in bubbles and choosing stage directions from a list. This text was turned into conventional script form with help from a learning support assistant. Some groups moved outside the constraints of my original frame altogether and began to work on the devising process much more independently.

Swapping their notation of this part of the scene for performance allowed the students to examine how clearly their physical scene could be reproduced in its scripted form. Videos of subsequent pairs' performances gave rise to some useful work on comparative interpretations. We considered exactly how scripting could usefully close down decisions and tie actors to particular effects and to what extent groups wanted to work outside these instructions.

APPRECIATION, ANALYSIS AND ASSESSMENT

Our experiments with creating scenes had involved students in a discussion in what we began to refer to as the 'tingle factor'. What language should we use to discuss successful dramatic writing? Melrose suggests that the effect of theatrical practice is often difficult to describe in words. At its most powerful, it is, she suggests, 'unspeakable'. She argues that: 'Only certain kinds of knowledge about theatre are transmitted through language.'[13] There are important implications here about the discourse we use as teachers when describing the reading and writing of scripts. I hoped that students would acquire the language of analysis and also recognize the power of the unspeakable. The challenge seemed to lie in rendering private feelings, thoughts and emotions public. I needed to find a way to structure an evaluation which included both personal experience and analysis, a language for describing something that, at its best, we recognized as indescribable.

The discourse of the physical also had a powerful role to play in this work. It had been a feature of this particular writing process that students demonstrated their recognition and creative exploration of dramatic conventions in physical and written form. The project therefore required an assessment process that reflected this.

The process of reading and writing plays described above had resulted in a range of outcomes. Each student had a script with electronic images and text based on their interpretation of Lochhead's play. They also had an electronic image of the set of their own play and at least a short opening scene which, in some cases, was taken to performance and videoed.

I had been concerned during the year to find ways of sharing the criteria relating to assessment with the students themselves, creating student versions of National Curriculum assessment criteria given to the class at the outset of a scheme of work and describing what achievement at different levels would involve. This helped me to set very specific targets for students in each unit of work. In England and Wales, the National Curriculum in English places the practice of drama within the context of speaking and listening, which means that there is not a specific dramatic vocabulary available for its assessment. In order to highlight the status of the physical process in the construction of this particular text I adapted level descriptors to include a specific reference to the way in which skills would be demonstrated in this case.

Importantly, it is a feature of the real use of play scripts that understanding is demonstrated through rehearsal and performance. The electronic images of groups enacting their interpretations of the play that Lochhead's stage directions describe were evidence of their understanding of the function of stage directions. Those achieving at the highest levels demonstrated a subtle understanding of spatial relationships and worked as actors to present a physical interpretation of Lochhead's instructions. The students' own scripted scenes, both in visual (on video) and written text enabled me to assess to what extent they had explored and understood the conventions of script, script-writing and performance. The visual redrafting we had carried out when experimenting in the drama studio was a valuable store of information about the understanding that had underpinned their decision-making.

I also wanted to find a way of including the students' own evaluation of their work. I also felt that their critical engagement with the final product would tell me a great deal about their awareness of the conventions we had explored and the 'tingle factor' these conventions had produced. To capture their critical analysis of the results they were given the opportunity to provide a detailed oral commentary on the final performances. By choosing from questions on cards prepared by me in advance or constructing their own, the members of the audience talked to the actors about their decisions. This ensured that the questioning was very focused, gave me the opportunity to scaffold the vocabulary of evaluation and enabled the performers and audience to evaluate their work as part of the physical experience, rather than as a process separate from it.

The questions themselves became a form of three-dimensional writing frame afterwards. We created a display of the questions, categorizing them to show what aspects of the writing and performing process they uncovered. I was able to refer to them during later work on other texts where an analytical response was required. I wanted to use the strategies described here in many kinds of writing within the English curriculum. I was able to include this very physical asking in what, I reflected, had previously felt like a rather two-dimensional, voiceless, desk-bound analysis.

The variation in framing devices to support the reading and writing of plays certainly raised the assessment levels of many students. The exploration of the essential physicality of writing had been enhanced through using an electronic medium to reproduce the physical space. This helped to store some of the imaginative depth produced by the process so that it could be tapped when we were writing in the computer room. This coherence seemed to be reflected in the physical memory evident within the writing with many students success-fully representing in writing the complex conventions that had experienced at first hand.

In his self-assessment one member of the class reflected on his group's playwriting in the drama studio: 'We wrote our play while we were going along and then we changed it and did it again.' Exploring the physical dimensions of their writing had led them to make a substantial connection between form and function and to see written text as a dynamic, changing entity. The processes, however, did not meet with universal approval. 'It was really hard', said another student, 'to write and walk'.

NOTES

1 Lochhead, L. (1997) *Cuba*, in *New Connections: New Plays for Young People* (London: Faber & Faber), pp. 115–62.
2 Wray, D. and Lewis, M. (1997) *Extending Literacy* (London: Routledge), p. 27.
3 This idea is developed in more detail by Andy Kempe in Chapter 5.
4 Goodman, L. (1993) *Contemporary Feminist Theatres* (London: Routledge), p. 97.
5 Aston, E. and Savona, G. (1991) *Theatre as Sign-System* (London: Routledge), p. 72.
6 Drake, N. (1997) 'Introduction' to *New Connections: New Plays for Young People* (London: Faber & Faber), p. ix.
7 Melrose, S. (1994) *A Semiotics of the Dramatic Text* (London: Macmillan), p. 246.
8 Melrose, S. (1994) *ibid.*, p. 252.
9 The National Literacy Strategy was a new initiative in 1997, in which primary school aged pupils are given specific programmes of study in literacy. I am here referring to DfEE (1997) *The National Literacy Strategy* (London: HMSO), pp. 46–7, Year 5, Term 2.
10 Aston, E. and Savona, G. (1991) *op. cit.*, p. 73.
11 Lochhead, L. (1997) *op. cit.*, p. 117.
12 Elam, K. (1980) *The Semiotics of Theatre and Drama* (London: Methuen), p. 159.
13 Melrose, S. (1994) *op. cit.*, p. 49.

Chapter 4

'You Mean I Have to Learn All This?':
Performing Scripted Plays

Bryony Williamson

Drama is a performing art. Drama is not a branch of literature. The essence of drama is live performance in front of an audience.[1]

CHALLENGING ASSUMPTIONS: 'WHAT ABOUT MY PAPER ROUND?'

In the first three years of secondary education, drama tends to include two different approaches to learning. First, the drama curriculum usually encourages students to develop improvisations and to act out polished scenes they have devised. Second, in my school students most frequently study scripted plays in the English classroom, where literature is a key consideration. Both can be valuable learning experiences. Arguably, however, this chapter deals with neither; rather it is concerned, as Don Shiach's statement above suggests, with the realization of a script in performance. The performance of a play articulates both with the English and drama curricula, although the project that I am going to discuss was extra-curricular which, interestingly, raises new issues and also explores old ones.

In this chapter I focus on performance of a particular play, with a particular group of students, at a particular school. The aim was to motivate challenging students, and for them to demonstrate to the rest of the school that performance requires skills and understanding that are to be valued. I wanted the students to have the experience of the concentration and effort required to bring a script to public performance. They would also learn specifically about creating a character, interpreting a text, and communicating meaning to an audience. Before that could happen, we had a long way to go. This is not every experience, but it is mine.

Act I, Scene 1, first rehearsal
    Candice: You mean I have to learn all this?

Dwayne: Can't do Mondays or Wednesdays – that's basketball. And
   Fridays – I have to pick my brother up from school.
Graham: What about my paper round?
Tsige: Where's upstage?
Paul: I can't even read this.
Dwayne: And I can only stay till 4.15 tonight.
Alice: I've never been in a theatre.
All: Nor me!

This was the first play that I had ever directed, and it was at this moment that I realized what an enormous amount of teaching I was going to have to do to overcome the assumptions I had made. For example, I had to begin by teaching some of them about the physical space they would perform in: where stage left and right were; where the wings were; what I meant by front of house. They did not know what to expect from a rehearsal; how to warm up; that they needed to be in character all the time even if they were not speaking. The role of the audience was a mystery; after the first performance Tsige said: 'They were so noisy. I could hear them laughing, but when I did my monologue they were so quiet because it was sad. It was weird knowing what they thought.'

I had assumed a level of knowledge they had yet to acquire: luckily they learnt quickly. I had also assumed there would be more than forty pounds in the productions budget, but that is another story! Because this extra-curricular project would provide a sustained creative and intellectual challenge to students, its value both to them and the wider school community was never an issue. But it was also a challenge for me, and realizing it was one of the hardest things that I had ever done.

DIFFERENTIATION: 'IT'S NOT MY FAULT I'M THICK'

Our aim was to perform at Cambridge Arts Theatre, a newly refurbished professional theatre, as part of a national initiative to promote new plays with youth groups. British Telecom, a private sponsor, had commissioned new scripts from twelve playwrights and linked with the Royal National Theatre to enable schools and drama groups to perform the premieres. Our play was *Shelter* by Simon Bent, specifically selected by me because the age group, characters and issues (friendship, loyalties, personal survival and homelessness) fitted the group who had expressed an interest in performing.[2] The characters in the play were aged between 11 and 17 and their mix of personalities produced both dramatic conflict and provided the cast with a wide range of roles. Differentiation began in the choice of students for certain roles. I had to ensure that students were cast in roles which set them appropriate challenges, and the target of performing to a paying audience was attainable. The challenges varied, but the main problem centred around physically getting the students to rehearsals. They forgot, had other commitments, were late, left early. I found rounding them up at the end of school was essential, and went to their homes to collect them for Sunday rehearsals. I decided it helped to make them feel wanted.

Before anyone could miss a rehearsal, however, the first question was the selection of the cast. One of the purposes of this project was to motivate all the students in the school, including all academic abilities, and therefore differentiation was vital. The cast included students in the 'top' sets for English, and those who struggled with reading. Some had taken part in amateur theatre productions and some had never even spoken out in class at all. In terms of personality, they might be described as a mix of sporty, withdrawn, extrovert, bullied, dedicated, insecure and wild. The thing that tied them all together was that they had got to the auditions and demonstrated a huge amount of enthusiasm and curiosity about the play.

It was agreed from the outset, by myself and the cast, that differentiation by outcome was not on the agenda; everyone had to perform equally to the highest standard. 'I'm not being on stage with someone who can't act – it'll make me look bad 'cos I'm in the same play as them', as Candice put it. Thus the expectation of achievement was built in from the start, and there is no doubt that peer pressure contributed considerably to the performance.

We discussed the concept of differentiation by support: I felt that it was important that we did not try to gloss over the fact that some students were going to find the first few rehearsals, when we were reading the play, very difficult, whereas some were going to take to it like ducks to water. There was a lot of insecurity to get over. 'I'm not doing this if people are going to laugh. It's not my fault I'm thick' (Paul). 'You're not thick, just not very good at reading. Who cares? You're going to be acting, not reading to the audience,' said Simon, neatly identifying a new experience for the group. As a consequence of discussing the kind of support that cast members might need, students found that they supported each other honestly, and their determination that problems could be resolved, was inspiring.

From this initial meeting, the students set up their own line-learning sessions, asking other members of staff to help. I would often arrive at a rehearsal to find them already started, working on details: 'That's good, but I think it would be better if you didn't look at her – it's like a confession, you're ashamed of saying this' (Peter).

This collaborative work could not have been forced; I did very little formal organization of these initiatives. It was also the first time I had seen differentiation really working as an open partnership, with everyone (including myself) learning together and accepting new challenges. The group was able to share knowledge in this way as they shared a common script; no character or role was their sole preserve or invention, and thus all could contribute.

I have examined so far only the students' mutual support: my support was differentiated too. The extra assistance, explanations and the feedback given was accepted easily due to the ethos the cast had created. I found that students asked for my help frequently, and appropriately, and positive criticism was welcomed. The same students, interestingly, responded in an entirely different way to me in class time – usually more aggressively and less openly. This challenged the way I taught, and I am now more generous with praise and inclined to wait for a student to ask for help: ownership of the task and learning is vital for progression.

There are particular educational issues associated with working with students outside the constraints of the curriculum. In some ways, this offers particular opportunities, as Guy Claxton implies:

> The problem that [teachers] face, with a greater or lesser degree of conscious awareness, is that much of what they are required to do, as conventional school-teachers, pulls them in conflicting directions. The structure of syllabuses, timetables and examinations demands a form of education that, whatever the rhetoric says, actually works against the goal of good learning.[3]

Working on this play outside school time taught me that although this may be true, these difficulties can also be overcome. The students learnt about self-discipline, negotiation, pride, achievement, self-reliance, teamwork, and a whole host of other things that Claxton is addressing. I learnt that if differentiation is alive and well, and living in extra-curricular land, then it can be brought into the classroom. The only difference (arguably huge) is that students elected to work on *Shelter*. However, through such strategies as offering a choice of texts in the classroom, a real audience for the work, creating an atmosphere of support rather than competition, I have found that the same spirit can be encouraged within the timetable.

But before I am accused of being unrealistic and seeing all with rose-tinted glasses, I will close this section with an extract from my diary at the time. 'Why am I doing this play? I can't stand it. They can't get to rehearsals, can't get on the stage, can't remember anything I say. This is such a nightmare. I'm sick of it.'

LEARNING: 'I'M ONLY DOING THIS FOR A LAUGH'

So far I have described some of the issues that needed to be addressed when working on *Shelter* but many of these difficulties are not confined to performing a play. I want now to turn to look specifically at what happens in terms of the opportunities for learning that occur when working with scripts. Both texts and improvisations require teamwork and imagination to bring them to performance, but realizing a script requires students to develop and interpret a role which makes it a different experience altogether.

When working on a script, someone other than the teacher or student has set the agenda – the playwright. Most students are comfortable with improvising; they often create characters more or less like themselves, and are in control of how this person moves and speaks. They work together to create a plot. Here, however, their ideas have to fit in with someone else's restrictions, and they have to look beyond their own horizons. Graham, when working on his role in the play, wanted to change the script to match how he hoped he would behave in the character's place: 'Can't I just not say this? It makes me look really bad if that's how I talk to her when she's sad.' When the answer is, inevitably, no, there is a conflict of interest which leads students to realize that they are playing a character that someone else has imagined, and the parameters are already set. In other words, the skill of interpretation, rather than creation, is required. This discipline leaves the students free to concentrate on the subtle development of role, and focus on the particular skills and understanding required for performance. For example, one of the characters in *Shelter* was very excitable and full of energy. The student playing her decided this was because she ate lots of sweets, and so was constantly on a sugar high. This led to the development of several moments of business when chocolate was passed from one character to another, offered, declined or stolen, depending on their relationship. Thus a layer of richness and understanding was inserted into someone else's words. When this student had the responsibility for making up everything, including her own words and plot, this level of detail was absent: she simply had enough to think about already. The repeated rehearsals also enhanced this effect; the cast had enough time to assimilate directions and build on them. Each became expert on their own character and was able to develop the nuances and subtleties that brought them alive.

> I'm saying this, but I don't really mean it. Look at where I've come from, what I say earlier. I've got to remind them [the audience] of that, so I've got to turn the same way. Then they'll remember.

Here Alice was realizing that characters change and develop, and that process helps a playwright to communicate meaning. The fact that the play was one and a half hours long gave the students the opportunity to learn how to sustain interest and pace over an extended period.

Learning about the use of space, movement and the relationship between audience and actors occurred during the struggle to find meaning. Candice, during rehearsals, said of her character:

> Nikki wouldn't stand with everyone else. She thinks she's in control, but she's not. She's really just as lonely, being manipulated. We could use light to make her alone, or a different level, lower. We can show it to them [the audience] without saying it out loud.

Her objectivity was possible due to the nature of the work she was discussing – someone else's.

Working with a script, and developing a role in this way, should mean that students get the chance to work with high-quality writing on a wide variety of themes. Increasingly, their experience of drama revolves around naturalism; after all, no one in the popular British television soap opera *EastEnders* has ever woken up to find they have turned into a beetle, much less tried to pour a pint with six legs. Students build on the experience they have: drama lessons with this age group would consist of improvisations on divorce, dating and bullying if allowed. However, drama needs to be seen as distinct from exploring issues for personal and social education. Here, as new genres and styles are introduced as models of good practice, the quality of students' writing and performing increases. They are able to explore dialect, accent and register and therefore their confidence in experimenting is supported as they see so many different 'right' ways to treat an idea and they can learn how specific styles can be manipulated – for example the irony or comfort of a chorus, the loneliness or humour of a soliloquy. *Shelter* combined naturalism with the stylized use of monologues to explore the backgrounds of the characters, thus increasing the dramatic experience of the students. In one moment in the play, Tsige's character spoke directly to the audience about her devastation at being told by a teacher that she would only ever clean toilets. This vulnerability was usually masked; in the 'public' moments she was buoyant and aggressive. The play was performed in a studio space, with the audience very close to the actors. 'It was like I was touching them when I was doing my monologue – the rest of the time they were a million miles away', said Tsige, articulating how a playwright reveals different facets of a character to the audience and to other characters in the play.

While concentrating on one script develops a particular depth of under-standing, the performance of scripts can create an ethos that spills over into other areas of the curriculum. Active performance promotes imagination and problem-solving, and illuminates the concept of taking something from a page and making it happen. There are particular issues which link with the English curriculum, such as the history of theatre, the use of dramatic language, the way dialogue suggests an accent or dialect, and how spoken English is written in script form. I was able to use a section of the script of *Shelter* to study the use of slang words and students rewrote part of it. 'You look like a tart' became 'You look like a lady about to earn money by selling sex,' and I was able to link this to Hamlet's speech, 'Get thee to a nunnery'. My purpose was to stimulate the dramatic imagination of the students, and to provide an insight into the way language can be used to create and communicate meaning on stage. The skills required to do this are similar to those necessary for any project requiring a transition from the abstract to the practical, but the experience of performance is unique.

ASSESSMENT: 'NOBODY MADE HER TELL ME I WAS GOOD'

It is generally acknowledged that assessment is useful as a process by which pupils and teachers gain insight into learning. In this section, I shall begin with the experience of assessing *Shelter*, and go on to explore how this extra-curricular experience can enrich teaching and learning in the classroom. In the UK, there are general guidelines for assessment, outlined in the *Ofsted Inspection Manual*:

Assessment practice should have a positive impact on pupils' motivation, attitudes and self-esteem. This is more likely where pupils see assessment primarily as a means of improving their standards of work and promoting their general development.[4]

As learning was undoubtedly occurring, the assessment of a performance as an extra-curricular activity is just as vital as assessment in the classroom, but it has a variety of different aspects. First the question of who actually does the assessing must be addressed: 'You mean people are going to pay to see us? What if they don't like it? What if they ask for their money back?' (Graham).

Obviously the ultimate goal of rehearsing the *Shelter* script was the performance in front of a paying audience. The playwright and representatives of the Cambridge Arts theatre were also going to be present: 'But he knows what he wrote, he thought it. What if we're not the same?' (Candice). The tensions created by these issues sharpened our minds. Other schools were going to be watched by the theatre officials, and thus the students were subjected to a curious mix of norm and ipsative-referenced evaluation,[5] depending on who would be in the audience. Either way, summative judgement would be swiftly delivered – in the form of laughter, applause and even autograph-seeking on occasion.

The purpose of assessing in the classroom, as opposed to the extra-curricular performance, is also different. The extra-curricular script works to a moment in time: the class activity takes place in an ongoing scheme of work, and the assessment of both must reflect that. Here the assessors were family, friends, staff, governors – a wealth of experience, status and feedback that is rare in the classroom. The cast were surprisingly adept at filtering it.

> Well, she's my mum, so she has to like it, but that woman, [the governor] nobody made her tell me I was good, she just did. And she remembered some of my lines, so she must have been listening. (Paul)

Reporting by peers followed, and was evident in the demand for tickets for the second night. I often obtain audiences for regular drama lessons, either to watch polished or devised pieces, or scripted work. Here, however, finance is not a consideration, nor the inconvenience of coming back to school after hours. The delight at missing double maths is usually enough to prompt an uncritically positive response, and while the experience of having any audience is useful, the performers find their opinions of less importance. Thus the role of a large paying audience is the clearest distinction in assessment of extra-curricular as opposed to classroom performance but there are others too.

Self-assessment played a key role and, as always, could be accurate or very misleading. In rehearsal, two members of the class assessed their performance as below the standard of the others (although this was true at the time, they undoubtedly had potential) and removed themselves from the play. In the classroom, I would have used assessment to diagnose difficulties and decide what the students needed to do next, but this was not possible in an extra-curricular situation: the students knew they held the trump card as they did not have to be there: 'Look Miss, I know what you think, but I'm just not doing it, OK!' (Daniel). Neither did they allow me to challenge their negative self-assessment. However, this was not always the case. Others recognized that they needed to talk about the process they were going through and became involved in celebrating their strengths and taking responsibility for their weaknesses. They became adept at formative assessment and would tell me what they were going to do next: 'This scene doesn't work, so we're going to try standing the other way round. Then the audience sees my face more. It'll be easier to understand. Watch – you'll see what I mean' (Candice).

The confidence and enjoyment in problem-solving was evident, particularly when it was focused on themselves. Once the cast had realized that, having got the words right, it was up to us as a team to negotiate the best way of interpreting the script, experimentation flourished: 'I don't think that's going to work, but it's made me think we could do it this way' (Tsige). Thus monitoring was continual, personal and individual. This enabled self-assessment to be challenged or supported by the rest of the cast, who evaluated each session at the end. They began to push each other and applaud effort, always directing the learning forward. The suggestion is not that this does not happen in classrooms, but the fact that those students faced the assessment of their audience was a great motivator.

Finally, I come to the role of the teacher, my role, and direct you back to the quotation from the *Inspection Manual* at the beginning of this section regarding motivation, attitudes and self-esteem. As the cast began to appreciate the task ahead of us, their enthusiasm and confidence failed. They were excellent at spotting weaknesses and moments of inconsistency, which left me able to focus only on the positive, identifying good practice and providing evidence and insight into why such moments were successful. Claxton sums up the process, experiences and vulnerabilities of learning:

> You have to be prepared to tolerate not-knowing and not-being-able-to-predict. You may have to flounder, thrash about, seek help, and admit you can't do it on your own, clutch at straws of advice or intuition, before the learning begins to come good.[6]

More than ever, as the students were risking more, it was my role to steer them through this.

Throughout the whole project, two things were being assessed: first, the play as a new script and second, our ability to realize it in performance. The audience had to assess both, and here the students had a head start as they had already enjoyed the play and felt confident in its quality. My assessment of their work was part of the process of directing the play, and necessary to give an overall coherence to the rehearsals and performance. However accurate the student-centred assessment was, my comments needed to evaluate and develop them. In this case, my summative assessment was perceived as valid by the students because it was based on our discussions in rehearsal, part of the process of continuous formative assessments.

During the process of working with the students on the play, I found that there were opportunities for assessment which were informed by classroom practice. Writing about the place of drama in the National Curriculum in England and Wales, David Hornbrook has commented:

> For all its lack of foundation status, the National Curriculum inevitably puts pressure on drama to bring its assessment procedures in line with those of other subjects. If drama is to retain its integrity outside English, then we must establish more precisely what we mean when we speak of 'being good at drama'.[7]

In preparing the play, the cast had spent much considering what being 'good' at drama meant in this context. The rehearsal period had taught them that the realization of a script in performance was a complex intellectual and creative process.

Despite the fact that this particular project was undertaken outside curriculum time, it met many of the National Curriculum criteria. In practical terms, for the classroom, the following areas might be used when assessing the performance of scripted plays:

- individual interpretations of characters; use of speech, movement, gesture and intonation
- individual performances in relation to the whole play; consistency of interpretation and dramatic development of role and ideas
- individual and group understanding of the ideas and themes within the play
- group communication of the play's meaning.

All of these must be weighed, arguably, against the playwright's intentions – not the students' desires. It is not the play's structure or writing or message that is to be assessed (although, as I have previously mentioned, an audience could not ignore this) but the student's ability to interpret and realize it, both as an individual and as a group. Here it is understanding which is demonstrated, not through discussion but, importantly, through practical performance. Analysis has often happened in practice, without the need to articulate it, and this style of learning enabled many students who had been previously regarded as low ability to reveal their potential in other areas of the curriculum. They achieved confidence as learners, particularly in speaking and listening, reading and writing; performing a script provided a real context for learning, and evidence of a wide range of different skills.

The key difference between assessing scripted and devised pieces is what is being assessed; with scripts, only the acting matters. This 'narrow' focus creates huge complications of subjectivity, and it is perhaps this that keeps drama dynamic and challenging. I know a student has interpreted a script well when the hairs on the back of my neck stand up!

THE FUTURE: 'WHAT CAN WE DO NEXT, MISS?'

As to the future, the role of drama is changing in the UK. There are local initiatives which aim to develop the arts in education, and nationally there is evidence that drama will have an increased role in the National Curriculum. As a subject and a way of working, it is understood to foster linguistic development in a number of registers. Its relevance to the promotion of social skills and citizenship is being explored. However, the enthusiasm which was generated by the production and performance of *Shelter* was obvious. It was a learning experience the students will not forget. I shall leave the final words to Candice:

> He [Simon Bent] wrote her, but he couldn't do her like I do. He couldn't give her a body and bring her to life. He thought it, but I'm doing it. When they watch, it's me they watch, me they listen to, me they believe. Will it be someone like me performing my play when I write it?

NOTES

1 Shiach, D. (1987) *From Page to Performance* (Cambridge: Cambridge University Press), p. 1.
2 Bent, S. (1997) *Shelter* in *New Connections: New Plays for Young People* (London: Faber & Faber), pp. 459–526.
3 Claxton, G. (1990) *Teaching to Learn* (London: Cassell), p. 162.
4 DfEE (1993) *The Ofsted Inspection Manual* (London: HMSO), p. 73.
5 In ipsative assessment the criteria are set and defined by the students in relation to the demands of the task itself, and are not norm-referenced.
6 Claxton, G. (1988) 'Teaching and learning', in R. Dale, R. Fergusson and A. Robinson (eds) *Frameworks for Teaching* (London: Hodder & Stoughton), p. 22.
7 Hornbrook, D. (1991) *Education in Drama* (London: Falmer Press), p. 127.

Part Two

Teaching Drama 14–16

PROGRESSION AND LEARNING

By the time students reach the age of 14, if they are lucky enough to experience continuity, they will have undertaken nearly ten years of drama education. Wherever it has taken place, and however haphazardly, students at the age of 14 are likely to have had experience of working in various forms of drama. They may have engaged in role-play, simulations or enactments; they may have read, written and/or performed scripted plays; they may have created improvisations and crafted devised drama. Some drama may have been perceived primarily as a cross-curricular learning medium, some may have been part of an English curriculum, and elsewhere drama may have been regarded as a separate subject. If this is something like the case, what new experiences might they expect if they follow courses in drama in between the ages of 14 and 16? What areas of learning might they consolidate and revisit?

In this part of the book, there are a range of suggestions about how students might progress in drama. Andy Kempe, whose chapter begins this part, focuses explicitly on progression. He suggests that as students progress they are able to make increasingly informed choices about how the drama will develop, drawing on both their knowledge of dramatic form and on their practical experiences of working creatively in the medium.[1] Both Andy Kempe and Bruce Wooding describe how students' devised and scripted drama might be informed by the work of other practitioners, and Jane M. Gangi and Robert D. Taylor discuss creative ways of interpreting a range of dramatic texts. This develops the work described in the first part of the book, where the drama was either crafted by teachers or focused on the conventions of particular genres, styles or dramatic forms which had been very carefully selected. In this part, 14–16-year-old students are given increased opportunities to structure their own dramas using their personal experiences and their knowledge of dramatic form. Indeed, throughout this part, there is an awareness of how students' assumptions might be challenged and affirmed, and how they might extend their dramatic repertoires in their practical and analytical work.

COLLABORATION, DIFFERENCE AND IDENTITY

Unlike many other areas of the curriculum, as students progress in drama they are not expected to abandon the exploration of issues and ideas which affect them as individuals in favour of more depersonalized forms of learning. Indeed, as many of the contributors in this part point out, all critical responses, as well as creative work, are informed by individual experiences and the local cultural context in which the work takes place. However, drama is also a collaborative art form, which relies on students reaching shared interpretations. One of the questions which all these contributors address, in different ways, is how to sustain a balance between individual thoughts, ideas and feelings and collaborative working practices.

Andy Kempe explores how making devised drama might foster the kind of working environment which enables young people to explore and communicate shared ideas and feelings. His aim, however, is not primarily concerned with the social benefits of the work, nor in achieving ideological or group consensus about the content. Rather, he is interested in encouraging students to work towards *artistic* coherence in their work. Bruce Wooding, who is similarly interested in the dramatic representation of ideas, takes another approach to the relationship between individual experience and group collaboration. Working with two very different groups of students, he invites them to represent their own identities and to acknowledge cultural difference in their scripted drama.

Working collaboratively does not mean that all students have to work in similar ways, nor that does it assume that they have similar cultural reference points. Indeed, this leads to particular questions about the role of the interpreter and the choice of dramatic texts to which students are introduced. Merrilyn Evans, whose discussion of teaching Shakespeare takes account of the different ways in which individual students learn, acknowledges the difficulty of teaching 'canonical' dramatic texts as part of an English curriculum. Her work is designed to encourage students to explore the plays creatively and critically; she hopes that this process will enable students to be less 'reverent' and engage in dialogue with the plays. Jane M. Gangi and Robert D. Taylor, whose work also interrogates classical Western texts, explore contemporary plays which represent the pluralist society in which they live and work.

In this part of the book, contributors explore the balance between individual learning and group collaboration, representations of identity and cultural difference, and critical and creative interpretations of dramatic texts. Taken as a whole, this part raises some important practical suggestions about how we might continue to balance student-centred and subject-centred approaches to drama education as they progress.

NOTE

1 Andy Kempe's discussion of progression draws on Jonothan Neelands' work in this area in Neelands, J. (1998) *Beginning Drama, 11–14* (London: David Fulton).

Chapter 5

'So Whose Idea was That, Then?': Devising Drama

Andy Kempe

AN ORGANIC OUTCOME

> *devise*: to imagine: to compose: to suppose: to contrive: to describe: to depict: to meditate: to bequeath.[1]

Etymologically, the word *devise* is linked to both *device* and *divide*. It is a good word to apply to a drama that has grown out of a group's combined imagination, skill and effort. Drama is, after all, a device for exploring our ideas about, and felt responses to, whatever stimulates us. In the process of making drama we imagine, compose, suppose. We question 'what if ...?' In dramatic writing and performance we contrive to communicate thoughts and feelings to an audience by finding ways of describing and depicting them. The whole process involves reflection and meditation on what is being discovered and why this is worth communicating to others. And that last synonym, *bequeath* – what a splendid word to link to drama with its resonance of gift. Drama, though temporal and transient, should leave both participants and audience with something of value to be taken away.

In the collaborative process of devising drama, the work is *divided* between the participants depending on their individual interests, knowledge and skills. It is what David Hargreaves calls 'An exemplar of differentiated team work'.[2] Such a description indicates the socializing potential of an ensemble approach and acknowledges that while roles and responsibilities may be differentiated, the status of individuals involved in the project is not. Mike Shepherd of Kneehigh Theatre Company recognizes the contribution that such an approach makes to the sense of worth enjoyed by each individual member of the devising company when he says that 'everybody doesn't have to do everything – far from it – but there's a common ownership within the company'.[3] When the different contributions of each individual are combined and allowed to feed off each other, the final whole is clearly greater than the sum of the individual parts. It is a symbiotic process in that while it demands creativity, imagination and critical thinking, such enterprise stimulates the very same things. The relationship between input and outcome is organic: what is created begins to take on a life of its own. Whether in the rehearsal of a scripted play or in the germination of a wholly new work, the evolution of ideas into workable forms can seem quite magical. For Peter Brook, however, there is no great secret to it: 'a constantly changing process is not a process of confusion but one of growth. This is the key. This is the secret'.[4]

The aim of this chapter is not to dwell on the social outcomes of a collaborative approach in making and performing drama, important as they are. Nor is it my intention to try and dissect the organic nature of the devising process, fascinating as that might be. Rather, it is to consider how pupils, under the tutelage of the teacher, can progress in their knowledge of and skills in drama by seeing a play through from inception to reception. For a group to come up with an idea for a play of their own; to be able to structure the piece; to develop and rehearse it; to tailor the work for an identified audience; to complement the acting performances with appropriate use of design and technical elements, and to critically evaluate the production and the audience's response, evidence the extent to which students have progressed towards taking 'responsibility for making *informed* choices about the form and direction or their work'.[5] While no one student need necessarily be expected to acquire an expertise in every facet of the art form of drama, it seems to me reasonable to suggest that an outcome of drama education is that each student develops an understanding of what is involved in the process of making, performing and appraising it. If students are to take control of choosing what they wish to communicate, how to do that, and to whom, then it is presumably the teacher's role to ensure that they acquire the wherewithal to achieve this.

ROOTS AND PARADOXES

Given that devised drama almost certainly predates the production of scripted plays and has continued to re-emerge periodically alongside them over the centuries, it seems curious that the work of companies such as Thèâtre de Complicité, Forced Entertainment and Forkbeard Fantasy is largely regarded as being on the avant-garde fringe of the professional theatre world. Hodgson and Richards have noted how, in Great Britain at least, the reluctance of theatre companies to develop their own material was due in part to the censorious power of the Lord Chamberlain's Office.[6] It was not until the removal of these powers by the 1968 Theatre Act that innovative teachers and directors such as Albert Hunt were enabled to explore the educative and artistic potential of devising new drama and performing this to live audiences.[7]

In the 1950s and early 1960s the prevailing culture of British theatre revolved mainly around the presentation of 'well-made plays' by classically trained actors separated from a predominantly middle-class audience by a proscenium arch. The Lord Chancellor's insistence on seeing every word intended to be spoken in performance contributed to the continuing predominance of the scripted play. Peter Slade's 1958 book *An Introduction to Child Drama* may be seen as something of a reaction to this moribund situation.

Slade presented a rationale for seeing the purpose and product of drama in schools as being essentially different from that of the professional theatre. For him, improvisation was conceptually linked with children's 'natural' play and the linchpin of drama in education. However, a conceptual chasm began to develop between celebrating children's abilities to create and explore through improvisation, and extending and developing this capacity in order to devise and show complete dramas. In the absence of professional models of devised work, Slade considered 'polished improvisation' as being no more than a stepping stone towards dealing with a scripted play rather than being a viable and worthwhile artistic project in its own right. He asserted that: 'True improvisation comes first, then a polished improvisation, which is getting nearer to a play.'[8]

By the second half of the 1960s, however, developments in the types of plays being staged and new ways of staging them were being recognized by drama educationalists.[9] Nevertheless, the notion that making and performing plays was towards the summit of the hierarchy of forms of drama may lie behind Gavin Bolton's 1982 statement that 'it is possible that pupils even at the secondary level may not acquire the necessary skills to create a group artistic product and yet still have a worthwhile course'.[10]

Notwithstanding this orthodoxy, in the UK secondary school drama teachers became increasingly adept at taking their students on to the newly introduced Advanced (A) Level during the 1980s. One of the requirements of this examination (taken by students at 18 years of age) was that the group devised their own piece of theatre. In 1986 the General Certificate of Secondary Education (GCSE) was introduced as the terminal examination for 16-year-olds and here again syllabuses offered considerable scope for students to demonstrate their ability to devise, show and comment on their own work rather than perform and answer questions on 'set texts'.

Whether by default or as a result of a ground swell of appreciation regarding students' abilities to devise their own work, teaching pupils how to take responsibility for the form and content of their work in drama by improvising around situations and structuring ideas became an imperative. The Arts Council's 1990 document *Drama in Schools* reflected this in its proposal of a framework for drama education resting on pupils' abilities to make, perform and respond to drama.[11] The process of working collaboratively to *realize* (that is, to bring into being) a drama from a given stimulus is now an option in most drama examination syllabuses at aged 15 and above. As a result, many teachers are structuring the drama curriculum throughout the secondary school to ensure that students develop the ability to recognize the potential of different stimuli and posses a range of strategies for giving form to their ideas.

IMPROVISING AND DEVISING

In the context of drama education, it may be helpful not to be too precious about exactly what constitutes *devised* drama. Ultimately, we need to ensure that students are provided with plenty of opportunities to experiment with different ways of realizing a wide range of texts and making new dramatic narratives of their own. As Liles and Mackey point out,

> Collaborative devised theatre implies that the work is original and created by the company. It may contain extracts of previously published work such as music, play texts, novels, short stories, poems or journal articles.[12]

How, one might ask, can a work be original if it contains previously published work? This apparent paradox is resolved by Alison Oddey's notion that 'devised theatre is concerned with the collective creation of art, and it is here that the emphasis has shifted from the writer to the creative artist'.[13] In other words, students learning how to devise drama are liberated from attempting to realize the intentions (dramatic or otherwise) of the authors whose work they use as a stimulus, but simply employ the work as a resource which serves their own specifically dramatic intentions. For example, some 15–16-year-old students were presented with a book about political assassinations. The group were told about some of the more celebrated cases. The result of further research was that the group collected extracts from T.S. Eliot's *Murder in the Cathedral*, Shakespeare's *Richard II*, Marlowe's *Edward II*, Weiss's *Marat/ Sade*, Jarry's *Ubu*, Robert Patrick's *Kennedy's Children* and Paul Ableman's *She's Dead*. Excited by the dramatic possibilities emerging from this theme, the group researched wider and uncovered other source material. This included the statement by the Irish Republican Army (IRA) about the assassination of Lord Mountbatten and the original Teletype manuscript of President Kennedy's assassination.

A chase through Roget revealed an array of synonyms which was developed into an unsettling piece of choral speech entitled *Homo Thesaurus* by one group. Meanwhile, another student discovered that using a blackboard, pointer and chalked stick men to illustrate a description of how traitors were hanged, drawn and quartered created a similarly startling juxtaposition of comedy and horror. The dramatic collage was enriched further as the group began to experiment with songs and dance. The story of the Bulgarian diplomat murdered in London by a poisoned umbrella in 1978 appealed to three boys who depicted the incident by sardonically re-choreographing Gene Kelly's routine and calling their sequence *Assassinging in the Rain*.

The culmination of this term-long project was a two-hour piece called simply *Assassin*. It involved some 40 students, specially written music and songs (performed by a group billing themselves as Lee Harvey O. and the Sharpshooters) and an extensive slide show reminiscent of *Oh! What a Lovely War*.

Work such as *Assassin* can represent much more than simply a montage of extracts or showcase for students. Within this one project the students were exposed to a wide variety of genres and the work of a range of major playwrights which demanded different acting styles. They also learnt that by juxtaposing different forms with elements of the content, new, often ironic, dramatic narratives emerged making the final production a moving and disturbing essay.

STARTING POINTS

Oddey schematizes her project to make and communicate through drama by identifying four preoccupations which underlie such work. She asks:

- What is it I want to devise and why?
- What is it I want to say and share with others?
- Who will be my audience for the work?

She finally demands of herself that she must 'understand the kind of theatre I wish to create'.[14] Such questions may well be apposite for students at the advanced end of their school drama career. However, in the context of teaching students *how* to devise drama, these questions may be more appropriate:

- How do I achieve a balance between providing a working structure and allowing the students to exercise their own creativity?
- How do I ensure that the devising process extends the students' knowledge and understanding of and skill in the art of drama?
- How do I assess the progress each individual student has made while recognizing that the final product may appear to be more than a collation of individual contributions?

The first of these questions is to some extent addressed by accepting that a good deal can be gained by just starting and seeing what emerges rather than pre-planning the outcomes of the devising process and working towards those aims. Far from being an abdication of responsibility, this is likely to be more demanding for the teacher who must be sure to watch and listen to what is being generated and match that with other pedagogical aims.

Improvisation is a fundamental element of devised work. Hodgson and Richards articulate this by stating that 'every improvisation is to some extent a play'.[15] Trusting in the students' ability to generate something from nothing, and perhaps more importantly, encouraging them to trust in this ability, is pivotal to the devising process. For me, Keith Johnstone's 1981 book *Impro* remains an inspirational work by revealing just what can be achieved from simple starting points. While his proposal that 'an improviser shouldn't be concerned with content, because the content arrives automatically' appears to be unhelpfully vague,[16] it is supported by Brook's (biologically spurious yet nevertheless appealing!) recognition that 'the less one gives the imagination, the happier it is, because it is a muscle that enjoys playing games'.[17] Even when pre-published texts are used, it is through playing around with how to juxtapose and present ideas that new narratives are created. Brook's assertion, that 'A play is play',[18] is reflected in educationalist Malcolm Ross's view that inspiration is primarily derived 'from the act of making, from working directly in the medium'.[19]

Although these references are now quite dated they may still resonate with contemporary teachers. Certainly, Hodgson and Richards' analysis (written in 1974) of what could constitute a starting point for a devised play seems little different from ideas forwarded by Oddey or Liles and Mackey. I do not think that we should be perturbed by this as the process of devising drama inevitably relates to some of the basic ingredients of the art form. Drama involves *characters*, in a given *space*, at a certain *time*, being involved in some kind of *action*. Any one of these ingredients may serve as a starting point. There is however a key difference between simply improvising in order to release creativity and setting about the earnest project of devising drama. This difference is summed up by Brook's adage that 'in the theatre, "any-old-how" is the great and subtle enemy'.[20] Agreeing with this would seem to indicate the need for teachers to adopt an interventionist approach when teaching the devising process in order to introduce different activities which will show the students ways of selecting, structuring, editing and shaping the material generated through improvisation and research.

STARTING WITH CHARACTER

One effective launch-pad for devising drama is the close observation of real life characters. It is certainly the method favoured by Mike Leigh whose *Nuts in May* (1975), *Abigail's Party* (1977) and *Secrets and Lies* (1996) have become classic examples of devised dramas.[21] However, Leigh's focus on the rhythms of everyday speech presents a tremendous challenge for younger students who, left to their own devices, all too often rely on what they perceive to be naturalistic dialogue rather than experimenting with more diverse forms of communicating characters' thoughts and feelings.

A way of introducing students to such forms involves giving groups a photograph or painting of a number of real or fictitious people. Without discussing or speculating who the characters might be, or what the context is, the students are asked to re-create the poses as accurately as they can and become consciously aware of how holding their bodies in such a pose makes them feel. They are asked to imagine that this 'frame' is the middle point of a 'three-frame story'. The next task is to create a still image which would precede this central frame and one that shows the final outcome. When shown in sequence, the three frames must depict a coherent narrative. From this platform, students go on to develop the narrative by, for example:

- animating each frame through spontaneous improvisation
- having characters step out of the frames and addressing the audience directly about how they are feeling, what they are thinking or perhaps what they remember of the moment in retrospect
- improvising duologues between some of the characters depicted or others who are implicit in the embryonic narrative

- considering how popular songs might add irony to the narrative; giving the story a title and using this as an acrostic to create either a prologue or epilogue to the piece in much the same way as Ben Jonson does in *The Alchemist*.[22]

Each step of a process such as this may usefully be recorded and restructured to ensure coherence and maximum dramatic effect. I discuss some ways of doing this in the section on notation and structure (pp. 72–3).

STARTING WITH SPACE

A different way into the devising process may be taken by focusing on the working space itself. A particularly productive exercise involves inviting students to use an assortment of everyday objects (brooms, poles, rope, boxes, pieces of fabric) to define a performance space within their normal workroom. They are asked to create a ritual which would give an audience a clear signal that some sort of performance is about to take place.[23] From this beginning, the students are asked to discuss what resonances the process of defining the space in this way has for them. They move on to identifying what specific place has been inferred by their ritual and finding a way of signalling that place to an audience by creating and using some sort of simple set or prop. This process in turn leads them to consider which characters would be found in such a place and how they might be introduced to an audience. The ball is now rolling and potential narratives start to emerge.

Kneehigh Theatre's Mike Shepherd endorses this way of working when he says that, for his company, devised work comes principally from 'being willing to take the space without pre-conception, and this notion that anything can happen. And things always do, of course'.[24] In a similar vein, innovative company Forkbeard Fantasy often take a similar starting point in their multimedia work and note that many of their shows start with an idea for a set or a prop. One example is *Work Ethic*, which came about as a result of having an idea for a set built entirely out of cardboard boxes.[25] Costumes may be used in a similar way. Inviting students to dress up in items of clothing selected from a broad range of fashions can generate ideas about intriguing characters whose 'backstories' can then be investigated through strategies such as hot-seating. Emerging narratives can then be developed, ordered, edited and reshaped. A great benefit of working with both space and costume in this way is that it illustrates to students how dramatic characters are constructs and that reading them as 'real' people can lead an audience away from the discourse of the drama.

ACTION, GENRE AND AUDIENCE

The implicit action of historical incidents, pre-published stories or factual accounts, contemporary news items or local legends may all be used as starting points for devising new dramatic narratives. The example of *Assassin* which I outlined above illustrates one approach. One group of 14–15-year-olds built a semi-fictional, semi-documentary play about the experiences of local people in the Second World War by interviewing neighbours (and, memorably, one of the school's cleaners), and improvising around the stories they heard. While researching this project it was discovered that the pilot who had flown Prime Minister Chamberlain back from the famous meeting in Munich with Hitler had mysteriously crashed in the area and was buried in the local cemetery. In turn, this snippet of information led to further research with a different group who developed a 'spy' drama from their findings, illustrating that young people tend to know a lot more about genre than they are often given credit for. Another example of this would be the group of 15–16-year-old students in a special school who were set the task of working within the perimeters of a given genre. These students had no problem identifying the archetypal characters of a horror film and using improvisation to physicalize them. They went on to suggest locations in which they would be found and from there developed background stories for a number of the emerging characters. Work such as this can of course be valid in its own right but by recording and plotting the different scenes into a sequence it can equally serve as the base on which a performance project may be built.[26]

In my own work with students throughout the secondary age range I have come to see that focusing on story is a more potent force in drama than selecting an explicit issue for exploration. Stories arise because of characters: the fact that characters have a story to tell indicates that there are, inevitably, issues at work. In his discussion on devising drama specifically for young audiences, David Pammenter notes:

> the focus on content or on reality-based content is not intended to denigrate or preclude the telling of a traditional story ... Rather, I am saying that theatre is a social art and therefore the practitioner has a social responsibility for the conception of the material.[27]

While sharing Pammenter's concern that Theatre in Education (TIE) companies set about their projects with clear intentions, it seems to me that when teaching students how to devise theatre, the identification of an appropriate audience for the work may justifiably come towards the end of the process rather than being the bedrock of the whole thing. For example, a group of 14-year-old students were shown a heap of rubbish and apparently inconsequential objects and invited to play with combining some of the objects. It was not long before one of them found a way of strapping an old teddy bear to a worn-out broom and proclaiming that he was Bert Dirt whose increasingly impossible mission was to tackle the world's litter problem with only his friend Gerry the bear for company. It was suggested that the group drew on the genre of popular TV cartoon hero series in order to develop this idea. They quickly created an evil adversary for Bert, who was stitching up both ends of the consumer market by creating products which came with an excessive amount of packaging then selling a range of automated sweeping machines to dispose of it all. Identifying the genre suggested a host of other arch characters such as the villain's 'moll' and 'assorted heavies' along with a plethora of brainwashed consumers. Over a period of around eight working hours the group devised *Rubbish*, a 30-minute show which, they decided, should be taken to the local primary school – and it duly was.

In the examples given above I have illustrated how a devised drama may come from existing stories, a prescribed genre, the working space or the students' own immediate responses to what may appear to be the most inconsequential piece of stimulus. Whatever the starting point, it is the teacher's role to provide the students with a variety of identifiable structures and range of dramatic forms. In addition to releasing creativity students need to be shown how to martial it and so tackle the great and subtle enemy that 'any-old-how' will do. This in itself implies that students need somehow to identify what they need to do to make their work better and be able to reflect critically on how they have addressed the problems. From the teacher's point of view, monitoring the students' conscious engagement with the task allows for an assessment to be made regarding the contribution of each individual and the degree of progress they are making through collaborating in the process of devising drama. Clearly, listening to and observing the students at work can provide some insights here, but establishing procedures by which individuals document their thinking can not only better inform the teacher about what development is occurring but also, as I argue below, accelerate that development and enrich the work further.

NOTATION AND STRUCTURE

Liles and Mackey claim that because devised theatre 'is transient and ephemeral' documenting it is problematic.[28] However, published examples of devised pieces are not difficult to find, and endowing students with strategies to record the different stages of the devising process can help students acquire the particularly difficult skill of editing and shaping their work and then reflecting upon their journey.[29] Keith Johnstone likens this element of improvisation to a man walking backwards:

> He sees where he has been, but pays no attention to the future. His story can take him anywhere, but he must still 'balance' it, and give it shape, by remembering incidents that have been shelved and re-incorporating them.[30]

There are a number of accessible and imaginative ways of recording developing work. One such is the 'washing line' technique which simply involves giving each part of the structured process a title, writing these on a sheet of A4 paper, and then pegging them in sequence on a washing line stretched across the working space.[31] In this simple way, students can instantly recall what they have done so far and, by physically swopping around the order of the captions, they are ultimately able to consider how the whole dramatic narrative may be reordered to create different effects. Alternatively, key scenes and moments of the devising process may be recorded in photographs. Giving the developed pictures to groups in the following session helps students to get back into the work very quickly. Rearranging the sequence of these stills offers the possibility of speculating on alternative narrative structures and has the added advantage of drawing the students' attention to aspects of semiotics such as the use of space, gesture and expression.

Recording key moments on film has another extremely useful function. By pasting on paper 'thinks balloons', 'speech bubbles' and narrative captions on to the stills, students are able to record key lines of dialogue and/or direct address. The stills can be used as stepping stones on which to build the developing piece of drama. Drawing on this popular comic book format is in no way demeaning for students; on the contrary, it is using exactly the same device that experienced and sophisticated film directors use in order to ensure that each image carries the maximum meaning in the most economic way. Employing as many practical strategies as possible to explore the relationship between the images in such sequences can add further dimensions of irony and subtext to the drama.

One of the principles of progression in drama, as articulated by Jonothan Neelands, is that 'Students should become increasingly selective and complex in their use of "sign" and gesture to make and represent meanings'.[32] Encouraging students to employ visual images to record their work alongside, or as a complement to, their written journals, will allow for a wider range of learning styles to be catered for. Adopting a creative and eclectic approach to notation might further extend students' appreciation of drama as a visual and well as a literary art form. For example, recording the devising process through the use of storyboards, sketches and diagrams can prove to be a far more effective way of explaining the genesis of a drama project and capturing its essence than lengthy verbal descriptions. Encouraging students to use different forms of notation in their journals, including script-writing, helps them progress further and faster towards taking responsibility for their own work. By establishing that practical work is productively complemented by such documentation, we are more able to assess the extent to which students' progress towards their individual potential is being achieved.

ASSESSING DEVISED WORK

Terry O'Connor of Forced Entertainment observes that when working collaboratively 'it is difficult to pinpoint exactly where the move for a particular feel for a show or idea really comes from'.[33] In the context of drama education, working in such an organic way has considerable benefits in instilling mutual respect within the group while enhancing an individual student's self-esteem as he or she recognizes both what has been taken from and given to the project.

In this chapter, I have argued that for students to devise drama successfully they need to learn how to recognize the potential of different types of stimuli.

By calling on a variety of forms and locating their work within a cultural context, students can give a greater sense of structure to their imaginative responses. Through this process, devising drama becomes a sound measure of what students know, understand and can do. The examples of projects undertaken in schools cited above provide evidence that secondary-aged pupils are capable of devising drama in much the same way that professional companies do, and they illustrate what some of the actual learning outcomes of working in this way are.

It seems to me that teachers now recognize more clearly both the need to, and the benefit of, assessing the extent to which each individual student has progressed towards the point where they can devise their own sophisticated dramas unaided. The fact that the devising process can obscure exactly how ideas arose or who contributed which particular idea need not be a problem in assessment if we are clear what it is we wish to assess. Requiring individual students to employ a range of devices for recording, visually, aurally and through notation, what is being created, allows the teacher to monitor and report on elements of each individual's contribution to and understanding of

- the value of background research
- the different ways of communicating through drama (e.g. use of dialogue, monologue, direct address, physical theatre, design and technical effects) and how these forms are generated and manipulated
- the structuring and sequencing of the drama
- the evaluation and appraisal of their own and other people's contribution to both process and performances
- the value of considering the audience's response.

In addition to this evidence of progress, the teacher will also have the opportunity to assess each individual's performance and skills in working collaboratively through observation of the process, and critical appraisal of the final piece. And if that final piece appears in some way greater than the sum of all of the individual contributions, then each individual should be rewarded – even if they personally cannot remember who had which idea!

NOTES

1 Extracted from the *Oxford English Dictionary*.
2 Hargreaves, D. (1982) *The Challenge of the Comprehensive School* (London: Routledge & Kegan Paul), p. 152.
3 Quoted in Liles, S. and Mackey, S. (1997) 'Collaboration: devising group work', in S. Mackey (ed.) *Practical Theatre* (Cheltenham: Stanley Thornes), pp. 113–62.
4 Brook, P. (1993) *There Are No Secrets* (London: Methuen), p. 119.
5 Jonothan Neelands identifies this as the first of three 'key principles of progression in drama'. See Neelands, J. (1998) *Beginning Drama, 11–14* (London: David Fulton), p. 18
6 Hodgson, J. and Richards, E. (1974) *Improvisation* (London: Eyre Methuen), p. ix.
7 See, for example, Hunt, A. (1976) *Hopes for Great Happenings* (London: Methuen) and Hunt, A. (1972) *John Ford's Cuban Missile Crisis* (London: Methuen).

8 Slade, P. (1958) *An Introduction to Child Drama* (London: Hodder & Stoughton), p. 90. The conception that the constraints of this form of theatre could be damaging to young people is voiced in Brian Way's (1966) *Development through Drama* (London: Longman). On p. 269 Way proclaims that 'there is only one entirely and totally *wrong* environment for drama in education: that is the conventional picture-frame stage, raised up at one end of a large room or hall' (my italics).

9 For example, Way, B. (1966) *op. cit.*, pp. 282–3, advises teachers of the time not to dismiss the improvisational method he espouses on the grounds that it is 'not proper theatre' but to consider 'the extraordinarily exciting developments in professional theatre over the last few years'. He goes on to say that while it is not his intention to explore the production of scripted plays, the use of improvisation as a part of the rehearsal process is educationally and artistically valid.

10 Bolton, G. (1982) 'Drama as learning, as art and as aesthetic experience', in M. Ross (ed.) *The Development of Aesthetic Experience* (Oxford: Pergamon), p. 145.

11 Arts Council of Great Britain (1990) *Drama in Schools* (London: Arts Council), p. 10.

12 Liles, S. and Mackey, S. (1997) *op. cit.*, p. 113.

13 Oddey, A. (1994) *Devising Theatre* (London: Routledge), p. 4.

14 Oddey, A. (1994) *ibid.*, pp. 27–9.

15 Hodgson, J. and Richards, E. (1974) *op. cit.*, p. 103.

16 Johnstone, K. (1981) *Impro* (London: Methuen), p. 142.

17 Brook, P. (1993) *op. cit.*, p. 27.

18 Brook, P. (1968) *The Empty Space* (London: Methuen), p. 157.

19 Ross, M. (1984) *The Aesthetic Impulse* (Oxford: Pergamon), p. 111.

20 Brook, P. (1993) *op. cit.*, p. 16.

21 See, for example, Clements, P. (1983) *The Improvised Play: The Work of Mike Leigh* (London: Methuen).

22 There are a number of techniques for generating dramatic writing that genuinely excite students and can create quite startling work. In a devised drama which retold the story of Perseus, the students were challenged to use the names of the major characters as acrostics and develop this into pieces of choral speech to introduce the character. Dialogue was then generated by mixing the names of the speakers. For example, the scene in which the invisible Perseus discovers the naked Andromeda chained to a rock inspired this:

*P*lease Zeus and the Gods on Olympus! What is this I see?
   *A*aaaah! Who speaks?
*E*nd your cries sweet maiden. It is I, Perseus.
   *N*o – sorry, I've never heard of you! Nor can I see you. Show yourself to me.
*R*eveal myself I will. (*He does*)
   *D*on't look – I've got nothing on!
*S*o I see!

23 I am indebted to Lib Taylor for pointing out that pupils' attention could be drawn here to the way classical Greek or Noh theatre traditionally starts. Further comparisons may be made to the way certain 'rituals' are still associated with attending the theatre in the Western world, for example, the way it is established that we are about to witness a theatrical performance.

24 Quoted in Liles, S. and Mackey, S. (1997) *op. cit.*, p. 119.

25 Forkbeard Fantasy (1995) *Work Ethic* (Walton on Thames: Thomas Nelson & Sons), p. vi.

26 A fuller description of this project can be found in Kempe, A. (1998) 'Scunny stuff: exploring genre and irony in special needs education'. *Drama*, 5(2), 53–6.

27 Pammenter, D. (1993) 'Devising for TIE', in T. Jackson (ed.) *Learning through Theatre* (London: Routledge), p. 60.

28 Liles, S. and Mackey, S. (1997) *op. cit.*, p. 114.
29 The Theatre in Education movement has, in fact, provided a particularly rich source of examples of work arising from collaborative devising processes. See, for one such example, Redington, C. (ed.) (1987) *Six T.I.E. Programmes* (London: Methuen).
30 Johnstone, K. (1981) *op. cit.*, p. 116.
31 My recognition of the potential of this technique came about through the creative approach taken by drama teacher Noreen Boylan.
32 Neelands, J. (1998) *op. cit.*, p. 18.
33 Cited in Oddey, A. (1994) *op. cit.*, p. 36.

Chapter 6

'I See a Voice': Visual Approaches to Teaching Shakespeare

Merrilyn Evans

> I see a voice ...
> To spy and I can hear my Thisbe's face.[1]

Is this nonsense or wisdom? Is there any real meaning to be found in these apparently ridiculous words of Nick Bottom? Perhaps, seen in the context of the play, there is some sense in his nonsense. The arrogant, foolish, muddled thespian who speaks these lines in *A Midsummer Night's Dream* is reflecting the fact that this is a play in which most of the characters are unperceiving, in fact 'blinded' to what is closest to them. Paradoxically it is when their sight is altered in sleep that they begin to see and feel differently. If, as teachers, one of our aims is to encourage students, too, to gain new insights, Bottom's apparently contradictory words can serve as a useful model for a teaching approach to Shakespeare.

If we begin by looking, rather than by speaking or listening, we may actually 'hear' more than might be expected. 'Seeing' language through pictures, physical images and action is a means of recognizing and working with the variety of experiences and learning styles that our students bring into the classroom. The performance text is so multilayered as to appeal to all the senses and on many levels. One outcome may well be that we 'see' a voice, and the text emerges in new and varied ways. J.L. Styan has made a similar point:

> Whether we are scholars or students, actors or playgoers, Shakespeare, like beauty lies in the eye of the beholder ... it is an endless pursuit ... an inexhaustible process because Shakespeare himself draws constantly on our own power to perceive and experience.[2]

Styan's terminology implies that the ability to 'see' is concerned with inner perception as well as with vision in an optical sense; the word 'experience' is used to convey the sense of physical participation as well as intellectual understanding. He clearly conveys the notion that a play text is not fixed and immutable but is always available as an object for rediscovery. It is in this sense that I would hope that students would begin to 'see' the voices in Shakespeare's plays.

Practical involvement with the plays, discovering and reinventing the text through performance, must help to demystify the study of Shakespeare. Engagement with the text in an individual and personal way will dispel the notion that Shakespeare is 'the most examined, the most hated and terrifying author we have'.[3]

Sadly, the idea that Shakespeare is sacred territory is so often conveyed to children before they tackle the text that they commence their study convinced that they will not be able to understand. Joseph Fiennes – star of the film *Shakespeare in Love* – captured this sense of veneration in an interview: 'Shakespeare's sacred ground isn't he? An academic's hero. Everyone's hero. So there was this feeling of trepidation in taking him on, yes.'[4]

For some time teachers have been engaging students in the multiple possibilities of text in practical and sensory ways, which eliminate such feelings of reverence and exclusivity. Most often, however, such work has primarily focused on the way meaning is conveyed through language and it is only relatively recently that there has been a renewed interest in the sense of the plays as scripts, complete ultimately in performance. In this chapter, I shall explore how recognizably visual approaches might be used in teaching Shakespeare, where teachers encourage students to work in a range of learning styles to explore multiple interpretations, different responses and new visions of the plays.

VISUAL TEXTS AND MULTI-MODAL LEARNING

Current thinking on developing children's learning is increasingly focused on the concept of multi-modal learning. Michael Fielding, a social psychologist, has suggested that we learn through different senses: 'The most important sensory channels as far as the teacher is concerned are the auditory, the visual and the kinaesthetic.'[5] In terms of planning for differentiated learning, Fielding's research is useful as it enables us, as teachers, to identify teaching strategies suited to the different ways in which young people learn.

- Auditory learners remember what is heard and said while also needing to talk through new material; they enjoy listening to others reading aloud.
- Visual learners find writing or drawing helpful, preferring to watch and remember what is seen, and find assistance in graphs or pictures.
- Kinaesthetic learners work through problems physically; they like moving around, collaborative work and role-play; they remember what is done and experienced physically.

I have suggested that offering physically active and recognizably visual approaches are helpful ways of planning for the strengths, strategies and preferences in learning styles of young people. Indeed, these methods are particularly appropriate for the kinaesthetic or visual learner who can be most fully stimulated by the teacher who has recognized such differences and planned accordingly.

Shakespeare's plays have been reinterpreted in so many different ways, and in a such a variety of media, that they appear to present an endless range of possibilities; in this respect they are truly multi-modal. A focus on multi-modality in education is to be welcomed, argues Gunter Kress, who concentrates less on preferred learning styles than on the fact that learning today is increasingly about transferring knowledge gained from one mode of communication and understanding to another. Kress argues that new forms of communication have implications for teaching: 'The curriculum [is] coming into crisis with the move in public communication from language to the visual and from 'mind' to the body.'[6] Yet, rather than something fearsome, this could be seen as a strength on which teachers might build. Children are especially capable of multi-modal learning: that is, using both traditional textual and verbal language and physical and visual signs. They are constantly making shifts from one to another within their daily existence; many are increasingly competent in the uses of information and communications technology (ICT), including the manipulation of electronic texts. Thus, teachers could capitalize on their pupils' expertise, experience and abilities. Arguably, the combination of students' expertise with multi-modal texts and the reinterpretation of Shakespeare's plays in a variety of electronic forms is a further reason for offering an increasingly varied approach to teaching Shakespeare.

In the work described in this chapter, I have tried to bring together these three interrelated aspects of education. First, I intended to focus particularly on Shakespeare's plays as visual texts, where students might develop their own interpretations of the plays in performance. Second, I was interested in how active approaches to Shakespeare's plays might appeal to those with visual and kinaesthetic learning styles who may be ignored in more traditional approaches to education which focus primarily on the perceived difficulties of Shakespeare's written language. Third, I was interested in acknowledging in my teaching that students live in a multimedia age, and are often adept at reading physical and visual images, and creating multi-modal texts. This account of a package for 'reading' Shakespeare's plays follows these intentions, and I have found it useful to subdivide the process of working into four key areas:

- diagrammatic: using charts and drawings
- physical: creating and reading body pictures, tableaux or still images
- televisual: using video, film, television, Internet, multimedia
- pictorial: interpreting production material, posters, programmes, photographs.

These four areas of learning allow pupils to explore the imagery of the text by creating images themselves in drawn or physical form or using multimedia; to register their discoveries in pictorial or note form; to discuss and examine performance through visual resources from theatre production and from video adaptations and to investigate interpretation and design.

In the following sections, I shall describe work exploring *Macbeth* which builds on this way of thinking and which I have undertaken with mixed-ability classes. Some have specific literacy difficulties and find reading aloud or at sight particularly taxing. The activities were planned to operate through differentiated learning styles, responding particularly to the needs of the visual and kinaesthetic learners in the group. I wanted the students to learn to represent their ideas physically and visually, and to collaborate in reaching a range of interpretations of the play. My main objectives were as follows:

- By encouraging students to visualize the settings of the play, to consider how the setting creates dramatic atmosphere and mood in a theatrical interpretation before the visit of a touring production.
- By representing physically, to interpret the role of Macbeth and his journey in the play, particularly focusing on key issues such as the hero and kingship.
- By using archive photographic material, film and video, to consider how visual imagery in different performances creates meaning.
- By visualizing abstract concepts, to explore how poetic imagery contributes to the dramatic development of the plot and themes of the play.

Throughout the work, my aim was to encourage students both to consider interpretation of performance texts and to experiment creatively with their own ideas through multi-modal approaches to learning. By bringing these two elements together, I hoped that students would experience, perceive and 'see' the plays as multi-modal texts in themselves, which, as Styan suggested, await reinterpretation and rediscovery.

VISUAL LANGUAGES AND ABSTRACT CONCEPTS

I aimed first to introduce the play to the students by focusing on visualizing and physicalizing abstract concepts articulated in the play, and to use this as a basis for developing their understanding of role and plot. The work began by exploring the concept of the 'hero' – a concept indicative of the play's journey. The students' previous notions, judicially interspersed with my comments to them about Renaissance attitudes, were used to develop a focus on Macbeth's decline from honour to savagery and ultimately catastrophe, through the decisions and choices he makes.

Drawing on their experiences from reading, television, films or theatre, the students undertook a quick brainstorming activity where they covered a large flip chart sheet with their ideas on heroic literary, filmic or theatrical figures. The chart remained in the classroom throughout the work, as a visual reminder of the students' ideas; it could be reintroduced in other lessons to be reviewed, challenged or added to. Building on this initial exercise, and alternating between solo work, pairs and small groups, the students created 'frozen' images which they formed simultaneously around the room to suggest some of the key abstract concepts they had associated with a hero, such as strong, brave, noble. The images were viewed in the style of a living picture gallery and the tableaux were discussed.

Next the class developed their understanding of the dramatic significance of the setting which located the story in space and time. By visualizing the settings in the play and his part within each scene, they also built up their understanding of the role of Macbeth. In theatrical terms, the different locations for the dramatic action provide an atmospheric backcloth which signify Macbeth's status and state of mind, and thus provide the designers with particular challenges. I identified the following settings from crucial scenes in the play: A Camp, A Heath, Inverness – Macbeth's Castle, A Park, Macduff's Castle and England. I withheld the final setting of the play, Dunsinane, to allow speculation about the play's outcome and, by refusing to reveal the content of the last scene, to introduce the concept of suspense. One of the play's significant settings, written on a piece of paper, was handed to a group of four or five students who were asked to draw what the setting suggested to them on a large sheet of paper and then to enact significant words associated their scene in three still images. For example, the group with 'A Park' (Act III scene 3) were given the words 'travellers', 'light' and 'assault' to portray.

Every group spoke the title of their scene; showed their drawing, and then re-enacted their series of physical pictures. The speedier groups were encouraged to create accompanying sound effects and in the following lesson, a '20-minute performance' was presented. By adding five named characters, five lines of dialogue and two properties to every scene, each sequence was built up and cemented into a performance with a short running commentary from the teacher to fill in the missing narrative strands. The presentations provoked discussions about the relationships between role, setting and plot; the students were able to understand loosely the narrative structure of the play and began to speculate about possible outcomes. They were already prepared to suggest alternative interpretations relating to the motivation of the main characters. As the work on role and setting developed, the students began to understand the theatrical unity within a dramatic text, with real emphasis on how dramatically significant visual images, motifs and abstract concepts act in conjunction to bind the play together.

The third area of study was to introduce the students more specifically to the poetic imagery in the play, which contributes both to its theatrical unity and to the dramatic development of ideas. I was again keen to use approaches to teaching which would encourage them to visualize and physicalize the language. Apart from selecting the words from the text which had a particular resonance in the play, as a teacher I had no control over exactly which physical pictures might emerge. This is the challenge and opportunity offered by working in this way: the students' real creativity can be shared and enjoyed. Their freshness and innovation allow the teacher to revisit a text. Despite such unpredictability presenting the teacher with an element of risk, the rewards can be great. For example, several students observed how frequently blood or violent actions had been present either by use of gesture in the tableaux or in the spoken words; the frequency of 'light' and 'dark' language or concepts like deception and secrecy were also readily noted.

Completing the play in the 20-minute format, offers a grasp of it *as a whole*, including some impression of the dramatic craft involved (narrative structure, suspense, dramatic irony). Alternatively, protracted study often eliminates the feel of a performance and prevents the sense that in real production the play would only be two to three hours long.

Through the process of visualizing abstract concepts and narrative devices, a complex debate began to emerge: was Macbeth to be considered a hero? Or indeed, what now (in their thinking) was a hero? From relatively simple starting points, contradictory concepts were formed and discussion began: earlier pictures of 'noble' or 'brave' – found in the text (Act I scene 1 particularly) as well as their brainstorm – were juxtaposed with a striking image of a friend performing the 'cleaving' action of a 'butcher' (Act V scene 8) – an image not to be forgotten in a hurry!

The concretizing of imagery also proved crucial for their written work; the group recognized that by creating physical pictures from Shakespeare's words, they had a framework by which to discuss issues, the central characters and some of the networks of imagery in the play. The students had demonstrated to themselves that here was a strong story which they could 'own' by performance and about which they could express a personal view in both their written work and in their visual and kinaesthetic representations of the play.

Through a mixture of teaching methods which encouraged the students to articulate their ideas in visual form, and focus on the visual dynamics of the play itself, by drawing settings and physicalizing dramatically significant themes, words or actions, each member of the group had:

- grasped the story-line in sequence and knew the main settings of the play
- memorized and spoken a line of dialogue and heard at least another 30 important lines from the play spoken by their classmates in the other sequences
- knew the names of the central characters and some features of each
- begun to engage with the imagery of the play.

In speeches where the density of imagery and tightly packed poetic language can present a truly bewildering montage of ideas for students to grasp, isolating and concretizing some of those images in a form that is recognizable and holds visual associations for *each* pupil, has, I have found, real benefit in developing individual understanding and personal engagement. I wanted the rest of our work to track further the changes and development in Macbeth's character so these techniques were therefore applied to three of the major soliloquies:

- 'If it were done when 'tis done' – Act I scene 7
- Is this a dagger?' – Act II scene 1
- 'To be thus is nothing' – Act III scene 1

W.H. Clemen has argued that the first of these speeches marks a development in Shakespeare's imagery to become 'bolder, mightier and more dynamic'.[7] Allowing students the freedom to make physical images, for example 'vaulting ambition' which included a leap-frogging motif, or 'angels trumpet tongued' which involved sound effects and a tableau of angels with extended arms over Macbeth curled below, began to demonstrate palpably the energy and power of the language. Ultimately this work provided visual prompts which were available to the students to explore in written discussion of the interpretations of the play which they had explored in practice.

INTERPRETATIONS, PRODUCTION VALUES AND VISUAL IMAGES

In his work on the teaching of Shakespeare, Rex Gibson has proposed that active approaches to learning are those 'involving a wide range of resources: video, film, programmes, photographs, posters, reviews, some traditional criticism'.[8] The use of archive material would also enable students to investigate different dramatic and critical interpretations of the plays. Gibson's comment is a reminder of the rich potential of Shakespearian text which has been translated through so many media but he is also highlighting the particular importance of recognizing visual elements in learning. Increasingly, this list needs amending to include the possibilities of multimedia work and the use of the Internet.[9] In this context, Gibson recognizes that the ability to read the visual, aural and kinaesthetic qualities of Shakespeare's plays in performance is an important factor in learning to interpret, and create, their theatrical potency. The implication here is that both the plays themselves, and the ways in which past productions have been recorded, rely on multimodal forms of communication. Furthermore, both the film industry and educational publishers have recognized the cultural significance of Shakespeare; there are now multimedia websites and CD-ROMs particularly designed for use in schools which support students learning, and which rely on their capacity, as Kress suggested, to move easily and fluently between one mode of communication and another.

One benefit of using video is that it opens up opportunities for all children to express opinions about what they have 'read' and interpreted visually rather than as response to the printed word. Although video may well be a 'prop' if not used critically and if it is seen *simply* as a visual stimulus, planned viewing can be an excellent way into deeper discussion about the range of decisions that are involved in making or staging a version of the play on stage or screen. From his classroom experience, Bob Allen commends the use of Roman Polanski's *Macbeth*,[10] and endorses the view that 'reading' a filmed version of a text actually requires a considerable degree of media experience and sophistication.[11]

Using a filmed version of Shakespearian text prompts the class in the following ways:

- To 'read' the text: who is it for? What sort of market might it reach? What appear to be the producer/director's intentions?
- To examine manipulation of text and therefore audience, by camera work.
- To observe the ways cuts have been made and for what purpose.
- To notice visual imagery and forge links with previous work or textual study.
- To formulate ideas about the effects viewing has on their thoughts and feelings.

To encourage students to engage in critical and creative readings of film the Roman Polanski film of *Macbeth* (mentioned earlier) and a Grampian TV film of *Macbeth*, starring Jason Connery,[12] were incorporated into lessons. The opening sequences, based on Act I scene 1 and concerned largely with the 'weird sisters', were watched twice in each version. The first time was to allow the students to watch and absorb without comment while on the second occasion they were asked to sketch the groupings and positioning of the women on screen. By noting details of their appearance and observing their interaction together or with Macbeth, they were preparing for a class discussion in which emphasis was placed on each director's treatment of the witches. Using Bernice Kliman's helpful and detailed commentary, the students contrasted Polanski's wide shots of the vast expanses of beach and the tiny dispersing figures of the women who are 'practising witches not supernatural beings',[13] with the tightly clustered 'sisters' in the Grampian film, standing high over the opening battle sequences, laughing gleefully.

After performing for themselves the tableaux they had drawn from the films, the students also debated the textual justification for the images which the director had chosen to emphasize. Subsequently the class devised their own versions of the opening scene. By using a range of levels and heights, one group conveyed a sense of brooding power and gave reality to the impression that the witches are overseeing Macbeth's activities. Further possibilities within a range of performance spaces were drawn and discussed and this exercise was then linked with an examination of six sets of photographs of the witches from Royal Shakespeare Company (RSC) productions.[14] Design styles ranged from the hallucinogenic hippy to bag lady/battle scavenger. The students were encouraged to explain their responses to the archival material; they were asked to consider the likely visual impact on an audience; to make observations about particular design styles, and to see if they could forge the link between this material and a range of theatre critics' comments on the same productions.

A consideration of the wide-ranging interpretations of the play through past productions enabled the students to extend their own ideas and re-examine the interpretations which they had explored in earlier sessions. They now understood the play as something organic and unfixed that can be worked on in a variety of ways. Extension work involved designing their own style for the witches; producing a scene with a small group and examining the use of the supernatural in the overall design of the play. I was particularly keen to introduce Edward Gordon Craig's ideas on design realization in

Macbeth. Although he considered the play was, in many ways, unstageable he nevertheless offered an interesting insight into possible staging of the play when he declared: 'Behind it all I seem to perceive the unseen forces.'[15] He indicates that ideally a director might allow the witches or 'spirits' to materialize at other significant crisis points for Macbeth and Lady Macbeth. Turning this concept into a performance reality is a challenging task for more advanced students.

I think there are several important points to be drawn from all of this. These techniques can be applied to a moment in the text where filming offers a particularly stimulating or controversial version, assisted further if there are contrasting production photographs or classroom portrayals to include in the discussion. A favourite example would be looking at the relationship of Macbeth and Lady Macbeth hinted at by their spatial relationship with each other at the end of the banquet sequence. The distance between the couple is accentuated by the camera work in the Grampian TV version, with Lady Macbeth (Helen Baxendale) obviously tearful and shown gnawing thoughtfully at her finger. Macbeth (Jason Connery) extends a hand to her and waits. One student astutely said: 'She doesn't want to take it, miss, she's scared because of what that hand's done'. Her observation was *so* accurate: this Lady Macbeth watches her husband slowly and then, very reluctantly, ultimately allows him to take her by the hand. Comparable photos of a 1982 RSC production show Sara Kestelman as Lady Macbeth,[16] head buried on her arms at the table, equally distanced from her husband (Bob Peck) yet a slightly different slant is offered here, for he is turned away from her, deep in thought (see Figure 6.1).

Increased access to video and filming equipment means that students might learn to develop their expertise and knowledge as film-makers. Through working in this way, one student began to talk about the camera angles in the filming and then observed that the repeated focus was on 'hands' – Baxendale's, Connery's, the two together – so that this formed a visual motif, which climaxed in the sleepwalking scene. Using experience of working practically with video, it became possible to incorporate work she had done on preparing a script for camera into her coursework.

An additional strategy, and a useful visual introduction to classwork on dramatic text, lies in making deductions and predictions from the visual presentation of the textbook. Unfortunately, the edition I have to work with includes antique and ugly line drawings and it was this lack of visual stimulation that led to alternative ways in but another issue arises from this: keeping my class from the printed text for two sessions meant that they had proved to themselves they could 'handle' Shakespeare. By the time we moved to the printed text they had acted small excerpts from memory and formed their own opinions. The key speeches we used were enlarged on to A3 sheets without the clutter of marginal notes, diversions or page divisions. For students with literacy difficulties, this method has real advantages. Such sheets can also become working documents that can be used for performance scripts; lines can be highlighted for learning; colour coding can be applied to

Figure 6.1   Sara Kestelman (Lady Macbeth) and Bob Peck (Macbeth) in the RSC production (1982)
Source: Donald Cooper/Photo*stage*

track images and the pages can ultimately be included in folders of written coursework.

SHAKESPEARE, VISUAL INTERPRETATIONS AND ASSESSMENT

In the light of the expressed aims of this work, assessment focused strongly on observing the students' creative engagement in the production process and their demonstration of their understanding of that process. The tasks set embraced all the elements expected of drama work within the curriculum: making, performing and responding, but additionally this work was designed to fulfil many of the criteria expected of a course in English. The focus of my students' assessment lay in their demonstration of

- an understanding of the design and realization process as a means whereby the designer and director are able to explore the themes of the play through visual symbolism
- an understanding of the development of the main characters within the dramatic structure of the play as performance text and how this too could be expressed through visual and physical processes in performance
- an understanding through their own physical and visual exploration the imaginative world of the play expressed through imagery and how this transfers to stage or screen.

Visual and oral presentations provided the opportunity for the students to demonstrate this understanding and to justify and explain particular design or production styles to a small group or to the whole class. Complemented by acting performances, such tasks allowed them to demonstrate their developing knowledge of the theatrical process.

Differentiation for a range of learning styles was built into the practical work from the outset but this was also evidenced in the range of recording procedures available to the students. In other chapters in this text, the authors have written of assessing a final performance where such an assessment is supported by the individual performer's written comments. This work was no exception. The student's log of the activities included diagrams, sketches, charts and notation of script which formed a partner to assessment through more traditional written tasks: standard argumentative essays; more sophisticated media comparisons of portrayal of character or reviews of performances on stage or screen. Alternatively, students might be assessed on their multimedia presentations, now possible through the use of the manipulation of digital images and text, or through creating or re-creating a script for performance or filming.

SEEING VOICES

The work described in this chapter is intended to explore one particular approach to teaching Shakespeare's plays. There are many others. In part, this approach was motivated by an interest in the performative qualities of the scripts, an interest in their interpretations and production values and, as a teacher, in working with multi-modal teaching and learning styles and multimedia texts.

In all these areas, of both dramatic practice and written work, there were real opportunities for differentiation. All students, including those who prefer kinaesthetic learning styles, have been able to engage in movement, work collaboratively and change from one activity to another. The emphasis on the visual has enabled students to draw, note and watch although there is still work to be done which will appeal to those preferring the auditory modes. More importantly, I would contend, all the students have had to use other modes than their preference. As well as teachers recognizing that work needs to match the learning styles of their children, equally important is the need to help children recognize their own strengths, and work in ways which match personal preference. However, the pupils also have a responsibility to foster the development of the techniques they least like, building on the knowledge that after completing the sort of work described here, they can comfortably function in other modes.

Writing with reference to his own early experience with film, Peter Reynolds recalls: 'I was fortunate enough to see Shakespeare before I read him.'[17] There is much to be said for offering all kinds of visual experiences as we teach Shakespeare, ultimately engaging a wide range of learners and accommodating their diversity of learning styles so they too may be able to 'see' the voices in the play and join with Bottom in saying, 'I have had a most rare vision'.

NOTES

1 Shakespeare, *A Midsummer Night's Dream*, Act V, sc. 1, line 190.
2 Styan, J.L. (1984) *The State of Drama Study* (Sydney: Sydney University Press), p. 43.
3 Styan, J.L. (1984) *ibid.*, p. 24.
4 O'Farrell, M. (1999) 'Interview with Joseph Fiennes'. *Independent on Sunday* 17 January.
5 Fielding, M. (1996) 'Why and how learning styles matter: valuing difference in teachers and learners', in S. Hart (ed.) *Differentiation and the Secondary Curriculum* (London: Routledge), p. 88.
6 Kress, G. (1995) *Writing the Future* (York: NATE), p. 57.
7 Clemen, W.H. (1951) *The Development of Shakespeare's Imagery* (London: Methuen).
8 Gibson, R. (1994) 'Teaching Shakespeare in schools', in S. Brindley (ed.) *Teaching English* (Buckingham: Open University Press), p. 147.
9 For example, an excellent website exists on Baz Luhrmann's film of *Romeo and Juliet* at www.romeoandjuliet.com. Pictures and brief biographies can be used for extensive discussion and activity.
10 Polanski, R. (dir.) (1972) *Macbeth*, with Jon Finch as Macbeth and Francesca Annis as Lady Macbeth.
11 Allen, B. (1991) 'A school perspective on teaching Shakespeare', in L. Aers and N. Wheale (eds) *Shakespeare and the Changing Curriculum* (London: Routledge), p. 51.
12 This low-budget film, made in Scotland, uses shareholders as extras and offers background to the production in a useful postscript. The certificate 12 suggests that it is aimed at the school market. Such issues are all relevant to media discussion.
13 Kliman, B. (1992) *Shakespeare in Performance – Macbeth* (Manchester: Manchester University Press), p. 129.
14 The RSC Archive at the Shakespeare Centre, Henley Street, Stratford-upon-Avon, CV37 6QW allows teachers to have access to any photographic material from all the past productions, early 1900s to present. Prior application means that material can be sorted and it is then photocopiable. Video viewings by individuals or small groups can be arranged with prior notification. Productions used: 1996, 1994, 1986, 1982, 1976, 1952.
15 Walton, J.M. (ed.) (1999) *Craig on Theatre* (London: Methuen), pp. 168–78.
16 Photographs of the 1982 production starring Sara Kestelman and Bob Peck, available from the RSC.
17 Reynolds, P. (1985) 'An active reading of Shakespeare's stagecraft', in R. Adams (ed.) *Teaching Shakespeare* (London: Robert Royce), p. 118.

Chapter 7

Authoring our Identities: Dramatic Narratives that Write the Self

Bruce Wooding

When are we going to get a decent mirror to see ourselves in?[1]

When I planned the work discussed in this chapter, I was particularly interested in how students might use drama to question and represent their own experiences and identities. I wondered if it was possible to enable students to explore and promote their identities as an explicit agenda, while also considering *how* their sense of selfhood may be represented, realized and projected in the drama form. In so doing, I also recognized that this way of working articulates with the work of many performers, particularly created by those from groups labelled as 'minority', who have used theatre and performance spaces for similar dramatic purposes.

I wondered how I could develop a mode of drama education that takes account of multiple social, personal and cultural perspectives and identities. I hoped to develop an approach to drama teaching which has more than one 'centre in the curriculum', providing, for example, Afrocentric, Anglocentric, Asiacentric, Eurocentric lenses.[2] Each perspective would be made explicit to students, both by asking them to realize their own self-identities through drama, and also by exploring diverse dramatic texts and considering the representations contained in them.

In this project I wanted to encourage the students to reflect explicitly upon their experiences and then consider how these could be crafted through scripting and rehearsal into a formalized piece of drama. Previously I had researched the use of play scripts as a way of widening the voices heard in the drama classroom.[3] Also I had worked on a devised play in a primary school in the East End of London, where a group of female Bengali students told me that in their stories and plays they pretended to be white characters as they believed this would get them better results in the government's national tests. This seemed to me to be a worrying state of affairs and I wondered why students felt the need to self-censor. Somewhere a gap must be occurring in the curriculum. These two experiences made me wonder if, as many performance artists do, we could explicitly draw from real experience, and frame the outcome in a performance that grew from the personal voice of the actors. Indeed the 'real voice' is as important as the imagined one, and both are important areas for the drama learning experience.

Perhaps by reflecting on their own identities, students could begin to reflect and explore the identities of others. This seems useful for all schools who are developing approaches to education which aim to be inclusive and multi-cultural. Writing about intercultural dialogue in relation to drama, Richard Schechner states:

> The best way to ... understand, enliven, investigate, get in touch with, outwit, contend with, defend oneself against, love ... others, other cultures ... the other in oneself, the other opposed to oneself, the feared, hated, envied, different other ... is to perform and to study performative behaviours in their various genres, contexts and historical processes.[4]

As drama education practitioners, we have a key role to play in the develop-ment of an education that begins to meet the needs of our culturally diverse society and goes some way to developing the 'understanding' Schechner outlined. He continues:

> The task for cultural workers is to express as clearly as we can both the emotional and the logical sense of the changes taking place. We need to find ways to celebrate individual and cultural differences, even as people work towards economic and political parity. Is such a different egalitarian-ism possible?[5]

Obviously this is not an easy task. Identity and culture are sites of struggle, and it is important to consider how, in a complex and pluralist society, it might be possible to widen discourses of both multiculturalism and identity. Stuart Hall argues that identity is continually renegotiated according to context:

> [S]ince our racial differences do not constitute all of us, we are always different, negotiating different kinds of differences – of gender, of sexuality, of class. It is also that these antagonisms refuse to be neatly aligned; they are simply not reducible to one another; they refuse to coalesce around a single axis of differentiation.[6]

So according to Hall, the lens becomes wider than the traditional sociological broad categories of class, gender and race; identities are fragmented and draw from many experiences. Something pretty key to drama! Cultural theory indicates that multiculturalism is not just an issue for groups defined as 'other' or outside the dominant culture. In a pluralist society, our identities are complex and arguably each of us contains multiple cultures or identities. If we, as drama practitioners, take account of such cultural, performance or identity theories in our work, we might find new depth and meaning in our practice. It is one way to take account of the different forms of identity and the range of cultural experiences that students bring to the classroom.

We may also want to consider how the political issues can be conjoined to pedagogic issues pertinent to drama education – imagination, students' identities, ideas and experiences, production, reception, representation, performance, various types of text, and so forth – those themes that have been recurrent throughout the history of drama in education, all be it in various wrappers. Drama is informed by two things: knowledge about dramatic forms and personal experience. This leads to aesthetic involvement with the work – a balance between self (personal experience) and other-understanding (about dramatic forms, experiences of others). This is one of the most valuable things drama has to offer; it is about *both* self-understanding *and* the representation of social, cultural and artistic values. They are not mutually exclusive.

When I began the project I am about to describe there were three key questions in my mind. These arose from my reading, theatre-going and school-based experiences.

- How can we value cultural diversity by introducing dramatic forms or texts which reflect a variety of cultural perspectives and recognize different 'lenses'?
- How can we acknowledge individual identities in drama in ways which challenge the perception that the dominant culture is 'better', and recognize that students in schools move between multiple identities?
- How can we address this imbalance by using real – or lived – experiences within the process of making drama?

In this chapter I hope to share my exploration of these questions. I addressed the questions in two very different contexts – a state secondary school and private classes for young people at The Central School of Speech and Drama in London. I chose two settings as I wanted to begin to see if *all* students might get something from considering notions of culture and identity. This was important for me as I wanted to challenge the view that cultural diversity should be explored only in schools with an obviously diverse population.

I'M ALSO BLACK AREN'T I?

The school is a large comprehensive school situated in the inner city of London. Once you enter through the security doors you are greeted with some super artwork. Indeed, the school is currently transforming itelf: new rooms are being built and a redecoration programme is brightening up the old, tatty buildings. The school is lively and full of energy. Male and female students are taught in single-sex groups. There is a large Bengali population and I worked with a group of 15-year-old girls over a period of five weeks.

The intentions and aims were to encourage students to

- consider how genres frame realities
- consider how identities are represented
- use this knowledge and understanding to write their own scripts
- begin to realize these scripts in performance.

In the first session I needed to establish a working relationship with the group as well as outline the project. I needed to see what the students were willing to give to me, as an outsider to their school, while also setting the perimeters for the five sessions I had to work with them. We began with a small group improvisation. Each group was given an instruction card that read as follows:

> Make up a quick improvisation that tells me something about this area and the community. You could do it in the style of a holiday programme or a docu-soap like 'Paddington Green'. The end product should be two minutes in length and you will have about five minutes to prepare.

By framing the initial stages of the work in this way each group was being asked to consider how certain genres shape realities in certain ways. They were beginning on a journey in which we could explore the notion that performance is not free of ideology; as writers, performers and producers they would need to consider the intention and purpose of their work as well as the audience's reactions to it. This was reinforced in the second exercise.

I used a simulation exercise that employed both teacher-in-role and mantle of the expert.[7] The scenario was that the students had been television researchers who had been researching the East End of London looking for ideas to include in a new docu-soap. It was their task to report back to me as the producer of the series. This exercise threw up issues about representation and stereotype. For instance, in role as 'posh' TV researchers the girls were happy to focus on sleaze. Once out of role, they admonished such behaviour as they thought television created a fake representation, even though they felt it made good TV. I showed a range of videos that helped to raise further debate about production and reception. I showed short extracts from Paul Rotha Production's film *West Indies Calling* (1943), Peter Brook's *The Mahabharata* (1989), Chopra's *Mahabharat* (1995) and Ayub Khan-Din's *East is East* (1996). We were able to consider how people are 'othered' or how people can choose to represent themselves. I used this as a way into framing the students both as critics and dramatists.

The students were then given a sheet with blank jigsaw pieces on it. They were asked to consider the fragments that made up their identities. I was asking them to move beyond a simplistic impression and to consider a notion of identity which takes account of the different ways in which they see themselves. They identified the following key ideas:

- personality, described as brainy, smart, mature
- psychology, including the way we behave, attitude, what makes us 'tick'

- reactions to others, such as friends, parents, carers
- emotions
- geographical area where raised
- physical/personal appearance
- home or community culture, including religion, food, customs, music, history, language.

Groups were encouraged to explore, through improvisation, some of the ideas that they might include in their work. This work was developed by writing scripts and through rehearsal and improvisation. I made a large display of colourful speech bubbles to help signpost and scaffold their writing. The questions on the display were as follows:

- Who is your character?
- Where is your character?
- What action takes place?
- What story are you telling?
- What message are you trying to give?
- How does the piece use/include your identity?
- What are you saying about the community?
- Have you avoided stereotypes?

By session four, the girls had selected two scripts to develop; focused, multiple authorship had begun to occur in both groups. They were able to get their ideas down on paper and were open to the drafting process, thus developing improvised pieces into script. We explained what had or had not been produced by each member of the group. The girls chose to develop complex social issues in their drama, and I was given a sharp reminder of the difficulties they face when one Friday preceding a nail bomb exploded in the local community where some of the students live. They chose to represent the following ideas in their scripts:

- an abused girlfriend's story
- a suicidal wife in an arranged marriage
- a girl being treated differently from her brother
- the relationship between an Asian family, their 'Coolie' daughter (i.e. mixed race – part Black and part Asian) and the daughter's Black boyfriend[8]
- living in a youth area.

The girls' ideas were rooted in their experience and generally based in London youth culture. They began to explore some interesting ideas about identity, particularly when we critically watched short extracts from each developing piece to enable reflection on the work in progress. This helped keep the students on task during a period of extended rehearsal, in which there were many changes before a finished product emerged. While script can look flat in comparison to the active world of the drama classroom, the following extracts provide useful evidence that exemplify the way the students had begun to explore and express a complex notion of identity. The performative qualities of the drama are indicated but, obviously, in live performance their use of space, movement and body deepened the drama.

Karana wrote a play exploring the different treatment of boys and girls. She created a character, Yasmin, who strives to achieve but whose father does not treat her with respect. She runs away to attend a rave and ends up involved in a road accident. The play closes with a catharsis for the family in which they recognize how their actions had affected her. The script blends melodrama and naturalism, and the personal experience/playwright's position is integrated into the fiction of the play. In the following extract the father represents traditional values; he comments on Yasmin's modesty of dress and her examination results.

> Hussain: I want you to come straight home with your results.
> Yasmin: OK.
> Hussain: Now Yasmin, don't go [*vexed voice*]. How many times have I
>   told you to wear your hijab properly? Why can I see hair at the back?
> Yasmin: Sorry daddy.

While the role of the father is a popular and populist version of the Bengali father that I have often seen used in my classes, Karana's piece showed some complex reflections about race, identity and group belonging as the play developed. Here we can see a complex debate contained in the 'fiction' of the drama as Karana hints towards the ways in which identities are fragmented and change.

> Thamina [mother]: Why do you have to be so hard on Yasmin?
> Hussain: Because Yasmin is spoilt from the beginning so I'm going to
>   straighten her up a bit.
> Thamina: What do you mean by spoilt?
> Hussain: Can't you see she stays with English and black people. They are
>   bad influence.
> Thamina: And what about Ali, our son, he is also my child. How come he
>   is not treated like Yasmin?
> Hussain: [*stumbles over his words*] Be, be, because he is a boy. Yes Ali is a
>   boy.
> Thamina: [*amused*] Ali is a boy that why let he be different than Yasmin?
>   If Yasmin heard this, do you know how she will be feeling [*raises her
>   voice*]? It wasn't her choice to be a girl, which does not mean treating
>   her different.
> [*Hussain walks out of the room. Not even caring what Thamina was saying*].

The character of Yasmin is created by her gender and ethnicity along with the contexts of home and school. External factors are influencing the 'I' of the role. This drama raised useful areas for reflection on identity and freedom: is identity a social construct?

Building on the jigsaws we had made to explore fragments of identity and the docu-soaps we had created to discuss the issues involved in the production and reception of dramatic representation, Rujia also recognized that identities are complex sites of struggle. Her group wrote a narrative that explored a 'Coolie' girl's experience with her ragamuffin boyfriend, Jazz, who assumes that she is black. The play explored the tensions that the girl experiences as Yasmin tries to hide her Asian roots and admit to her Black roots only when she is with the boys. Also the question of blackness is raised – who *defines* identity is a theme of the play. This group were able to author a piece that examined the troubled relationship between identity and loyalty within the bounds of contemporary 'street' culture. In this particular scene the scarf takes on a symbolic role: it carries the identity and the cultural 'tie'. Here we see a representation where racial loyalty is valued above personal ties and where wearing a metaphorical mask is essential to existence.

Yasmin: Tanzina please don't tell Jazz you're my cousin, or he'll dump me . . .

Tanzina: . . . but why Yas you know what sort of a guy he is. What if he finds out you are half Asian? What are you going to do then?

Yasmin: Let's not worry about that right now. All you need to do is play along . . . and here [*gives her scarf*] this is yours, OK.

[*They walk over to the guys*]

Jazz: Hey babe. Guys, this is my girl Yasmin. [*to Yasmin*] Who is this?

Yasmin: Er, my mate Tanzina.

Tanzina: Hi [*the guys ignore her*].

Jazz: What are you doing with that Asian bitch Yasmin? I told you not to hang about with them . . .

Yasmin: Yeah . . . but . . .

Jazz: No buts, from now on I don't want you to go anywhere near her. Understand?

Tanzina: Yasmin we better go now. Come on.

Yasmin: No I can't go now. You go and I'll come later.

[*Tanzina gives the scarf to Yasmin and goes*]

Jazz: What is this?

Yasmin: [*hesitating*] This is my scarf.

[*The guys laugh*]

Jazz: Scarf [*shouting*]. What is this scarf for? [*Throws it on the floor and pulls Yasmin*] What are you doing with a scarf?

Mother: Yasmin?

[*Yasmin turns around shocked. Tries to hide behind Jazz*]

Jazz: Who is this bitch?

Mother: Yasmin you should be home by now. Are these your friends? How come you never introduced them to me?

Jazz: Is this your mother? Yasmin answer me!

Yasmin: [*hesitant*] Yeah.

Jazz: You're Asian . . .

Yasmin: No . . . no I'm mixed race.

Jazz: Shut the fuck up. You're still fucking Asian bitch. What do you
think you were playing at? Huh? [*Pushes Yas out of the way.*]

Yasmin: No don't do this Jazz. Please I was going to tell you . . .

Mother: [*interrupting*] Leave it Yasmin. He is not worth it [*as Jazz and his
friends leave*] Here, wear your scarf.

Yasmin: How could this happen mum? I'm also Black aren't I? Dad
married you didn't he?

Here we see a violence in the male character's dialogue. The violence and abuse
is inscribing the girl's identity within her love relationship. The mother in this
play was a particularly strong character who protected her daughter and was
able to argue with all those characters who did not allow her daughter a free
path. The reality of the girls existing in a macho school where boys dominate is
reflected in Jazz's sexist machismo but the experience is then moved to the
imaginary, where the women are powerful and able to stop the abuse.

I REALIZED THERE WERE HUGE GAPS IN MY ENGLISHNESS

The second group who worked on this project represented a real contrast to
the girls in the city school. One would not imagine nail bombs and the gang
dynamics of street culture disrupting their lives. The girls generally arrive in a
small fleet of cars to private classes at The Central School of Speech and
Drama, a major drama school in an affluent part of London. In this context, I
wanted to develop the original aims for the drama while also considering not
only that drama is about self-identity, but also how identity is constructed in
relation to others. I was interested in how drama can expand the students'
cultural and personal horizons by implementing a multicultural approach in a
situation which appears mono-cultural. The work in this context may have a
different political agenda, but maintains similar pedagogical and dramatic
aims.

We had been devising a play about a street community and a group of office
workers. The topic was that of 'breaking out', and was initially conceived in
the style of *Stomp* where the physicality of the body was to be a key form of
expression. I felt that the initial responses were naive and stereotypical, so I
hoped to deepen their work by asking the students to explore their own
identities and consider how these were formed. From this, we could draw from
our experiences and use it as writers to develop the imaginary roles and the
devised text as a whole.

The groups began by reflecting on the two key groups in the piece, the office
workers and the homeless community. Using the familiar drama in education
technique of role on the wall, they recorded the contrast between these roles,
thereby raising issues of how they might feel as opposed to how they may be
perceived or viewed. For example the office workers were deemed to be seen on

the surface as being superficial, selfish, neurotic, prim, efficient and inconsiderate while the inner self was seen as being fed up, manufactured, intelligent, stressed, over-occupied, methodological and capable. This simple exercise allowed for useful reflection on the complexities of defining an identity. We discussed the internal and external influences on identity, and the students raised the issue of the conflict between group and individual identity. The next task was to use the 'identity jigsaw'. Responses were similar to the girls in the city school but they also showed an interest in fashion/body/looks, education, social life, the opposite sex, role models, society, nationality and how significant life events shape identities.

In order to demonstrate how other performers have used their identities I showed them the picture *Untitled 93* by Cindy Sherman. Also we looked at Fakirs Musafar's *14 Inch Waist Belt* (1952) and *Chest Daggers* (1980).[9] Then we discussed how these performers are using their identities. For example we discussed the 'i' of Cindy Sherman in conflict with the 'eye' of the audience/critic. For Sherman, the intended narrative is of a woman waking from a hangover, but most people read the image as of a woman who has just had sex, or is about to.[10] Also we discussed how the extreme corsetry altered Musafar's body, and how this might alter his identity. This exercise worked in the same way as the video extracts with the students in the school context, but it gave a complex and perhaps, for some, a more controversial way to place the students within the field of contemporary practice.

Individually the students wrote short monologues using their identity as the focus for the script. The monologue was to include a time when they had celebrated their culture and a time when they had wanted to escape it. A wide range of responses came out: there were several on religion, one on the oppressive nature of school, some on friends controlling or bullying them and even one on rugby! Lail wrote:

> Suddenly I realised that I had huge gaps in my Englishness, though I had lived in London all my life and been educated in English schools – my parents are from Israel. So I was standing with my choir, a group of about 60, in the final rehearsal before an important concert and the choir master said, 'there's only one thing we haven't run through – we'd better do it quickly to brush up on the words'. The pianist started playing the introduction. I didn't recognise it and when I asked my friend, 'what song?' I didn't know the title. I had never heard it before and didn't understand how they all knew the words. Somehow I had lived up to the age of 13, in England, without learning 'Land of Hope and Glory'. The feeling of being the only person in a vast group not knowing something that they were brought up with was very strange. As well as disturbing me and making me realise that I would never be totally English, I also understood that this was what made me and I would never change it.

Here issues associated with being second-generation Israeli are raised, and she frames her identity by invoking a situation where she was 'othered'. Lail is able to describe a fragmented identity which displays a clash of cultures within a clear expression of emotion. Sophie wrote a piece illustrating that even the supposed dominant group have questions about their identity. She explores the tensions created as identity alters or is brought into question:

> The fact that I'm sort of Christian but I only practise when I'm with my grandparents, mainly at festivals and stuff ... in Religious Studies we started talking about Holocaust Theology ... why God let all the horrid stuff happen like wars, and so I thought that, although I'm a Christian [perhaps] God could have 'gone on holiday' and this touched a really sore point for some people in my class and one girl began shouting at me.

Sophie's monologue raised issues about one's connectedness with a particular aspect of culture (her religion) and her identity (her personal belief system). She had been able to author a piece that reflected on the ideas of multiple identities by raising the notion of groups within groups and beliefs within beliefs. Her script illustrates that even cultures perceived to be dominant in our society are often complex and problematic.

Both of the girls' pieces illustrate how the group's assumptions were challenged as they began to understand how their own identities were made up. Students experimented with form. Physical theatre, sound-scapes, song, choral speaking, dance, painting faces and a rugby scrum (Brecht would be proud!) were combined. This was effectively juxtaposed with the devised section that explored homelessness and the rat race, as the representation of alternative realities. Presenting surface level, stereotypical roles was now difficult as they had a personal frame for exploring facets of identity, dramatic role and narratives. By fragmenting these narratives they made an exciting group performance from the original scripted pieces; the voices were interwoven but the distinct identities still remained.

CONNECTING WITH DIFFERENT WAYS OF THINKING

In conclusion I feel that the work was a useful way into making issues of culture, identity and representation explicit to the students. I found that the use of monologues as a starting point, rather than naturalistic dialogue, enabled a more inclusive and original approach. In the city school, where I began with naturalistic narrative, the students ended up with very episodic work that was akin to the dramatic form of soap opera. The students lacked a wide range of dramatic forms to draw on which meant that very interesting ideas were constructed as a linear narrative, where naturalistic dialogue was laced with a large shot of melodrama. This meant that they could represent their experiences only in a genre which suggested inevitability and predictability; soap operas are often 'themed', and the characters can react to situations only in ways which both fulfil the audience's expectations and confirm particular character 'types'. This was not what the girls had hoped to represent and, although in the process of working they explored interesting ideas, their dramatic representation of ideas seemed limited by the dramatic genre. By contrast, the group who began with monologues were able to experiment with ambiguity; they found an aesthetic/form/style appropriate to what they wanted to express. As Sita Brahmachari argues, using such naturalistic dramatic forms limits an exploration of identity as the form itself carries with it particular expectations and cultural values.[11]

The following comments help illustrate how the students in both settings were able to engage with the work both emotionally and intellectually.

> It gave me the chance to play a role I had never thought about playing before.

> We did this work to introduce a sense of reality into our drama, making it easier to act. We could translate this work into different forms, e.g. physical. It was hard to think about your cultural identity, as you don't usually think about these things, you don't challenge your thoughts.

> We did this work so that we could realise the differences between people even from the same culture, so we don't always have to resort to stereotypes. Also we can realise the complexities of a character. It made us look at ourselves more.

> Usually at my school we don't usually look at the ideas behind plays we just perform them on the one level.

> We did this work because it is such a vast subject majorly influencing our life – or even defining our life – that under normal situations is not analysed or discussed. Actually I've never seen a play that represents my cultural identity . . . but I'd like to.

From these comments we can see that students found ways to bring their realities to their drama – a useful skill for any writer or performer. The work had challenged them, both within and outside of the drama. Students had the opportunity to connect with a different way of thinking and this led them to new considerations about culture and identity as well as how to manipulate role and dramatic form. Students were able to find new depths in the texts they created and read.

> The hardest thing was to actually focus on ourselves and to write what we felt.

> To start with it was very difficult to talk about your feelings and what is important to you to someone you don't know very well.

These comments indicate potential problems and areas of sensitivity connected with such work. It was important not to push the students to talk about, explore or expose experiences which made them feel uncomfortable. However, students were given opportunities to explore their own identities in relation to others, both within the group and within the wider field of performance. From the work that the students undertook, I think we can begin to look at how cultures are represented in drama and begin to let our students enjoy projecting their own culture. Students might progress by moving on to a wider range of world texts (physical, electronic or written) in order to provide them with a range of 'centres' in the curriculum. Hopefully, through a more culturally open and diverse curriculum we can encourage all students to recognize that others' identity is not dangerous, but rather an essential and accessible part of any pluralist society.

I am not naive about the complexities facing us; asking students to explore and represent the contradictions in their lives and in their identities requires more than passive tolerance. Indeed the debate about representation, identity and culture is heated in the world of performance as well as the world of education. Bharucha, for example, notes that culture has a definite context and in theatre it is not enough merely to present a flavour of a country: '[Culture] is what differentiates a curry from a stew, and I'm not just referring to the taste, but to the entire history of a people that shapes taste in particular ways.'[12] However, the debate is well worth considering, and may well be a useful one to explore with our students. Considering, in the practice of drama, theories of identity and representation may go some way to help us meet the moral responsibilities that go with being a teacher in a pluralistic and culturally diverse society.

NOTES

1 Friel, B. (1990) *Dancing at Lughnasa* (London: Faber & Faber), p. 2.
2 For a fuller discussion, see Asante, K.M. (1991) 'The Afrocentric idea in education', in F.L. Hord and J.S. Lee (eds) *I Am because We Are: Readings in Black Philosophy* (Amherst, MA: University of Massachusetts Press), pp. 338–49.
3 See Wooding, B. (1997) *Multicultural Education: A Consideration of Approaches, Positive Mental Attitude Pack* (London: Theatre Centre).
4 Schechner, R. (1993) *The Future of Ritual: Writings on Culture and Performance* (London: Routledge), p. 1.
5 Schechner, R. (1993) *ibid.*, p. 5.
6 Hall, S. (1992) 'What is this "Black" in black popular culture?', in G. Dent (ed.) *Black Popular Culture* (Seattle, WA: Bay Press), pp. 30–1.
7 See Heathcote, D. and Bolton, G. (1997) *Drama for Learning* (Portsmouth, NH: Heinemann).
8 'Coolie' is arguably a racist term which signals the prejudice faced by mixed race Asian and Black young people.
9 See Parafrey, A. (1990) *Apocalypse Culture* (London: Feral House), pp. 106–17.
10 Phelan, P. (1993) *Unmarked: The Politics of Performance* (London: Routledge), p. 62.
11 Brahmachari, S. (1998) 'Stages of the world', in D. Hornbrook (ed.) *On the Subject of Drama* (London: Routledge), pp. 18–35.
12 Bharucha, R. (1993) *Theatre and the World* (London: Routledge), p. 71.

Chapter 8

Reading Dramatic Texts in the Electronic Age: Modes of Response

Jane M. Gangi and Robert D. Taylor

Today's adolescents inhabit a media world previously unknown to their teachers. The communications revolution of the last few decades has meant that young people are surrounded practically from birth by dramatizations encased in electronic forms – in film, television, videotapes, video games, and personal computers; perhaps they have encountered live theatre performances as well. Implications of this radical communications shift have been discussed in David Hornbrook's *On the Subject of Drama*, where it is argued that part of the role of the drama teacher in the electronic age is to help students criticize, in the most positive sense of the word, the many dramatizations they witness daily.[1] In accepting Hornbrook's model of making, performing and responding, our purpose in this chapter is to describe several modes of response to a variety of dramatic texts, whether live or electronically mediated. Dramatic texts selected for use in the curriculum should reflect diverse cultures, and these selections should frequently move beyond the standard fare of naturalism and realism that electronic forms most often encase.[2] Not to do so risks leaving drama at a level in which classroom dramatizations do little more than imitate television.

We also explore the connections between dramatic criticism and theatrical creativity. To work creatively, students must have some sense of what has transpired before, and be equipped with a critical vocabulary to both analyse and experience dramatic work. As Sharon Bailin points out:

> The way we value works of art is related, to some extent, to their place in the discipline. It is connected with the evaluation of how well they have solved the existing problems of the art, and whether they are thus good examples of their kind, or whether they have dealt with new problems and pushed the art beyond old limits ... our valuing of art is related to a knowledge of the tradition and of how a work fits into it or departs from it.[3]

Our aim is to encourage students to question performative texts, to challenge theatre's conventions, and to experiment with dramatic form and content.

In describing modes of response, we offer several models because any one model has its limits. Indeed, part of the drama teacher's role is to create multiple frameworks in which students can respond intelligently and meaningfully to dramatic art. For this purpose, we have structured into all the models a wide range of questions, which aim to elicit high levels of thinking and interpretation.[4] In the examples that follow, culled from Louise Rosenblatt's reception theory, Augusto Boal's *joker* techniques, Robert Findlay's *basic tools*, Bertolt Brecht's *gestus* exercises and Robert Taylor's *reverse writing* and *moments of dignity* techniques, we aim to provide students with creative challenges when critically exploring performative texts.

RESPONDING TO DRAMATIC ART: READER-RESPONSE THEORY

Beginning with reader-response (or reception) theory teachers can facilitate post-performance discussions in which interpretation promotes an active role for the viewer. Because meaning is constructed by the viewer, multiple interpretations are implied; each audience member brings different past experiences, memories and personalities to the dramatic event. The aesthetic experience resides both in how images, sounds and words are read, and in how viewers interpret the silences in the drama and respond to what is *not* enacted. Wolfgang Iser makes the point that creative readers interact with the 'gaps' in the texts.

> [W]hat *is* said only appears to take on significance as a reference to what is not said; it is the implications and not the statements that give shape and weight to the meaning ... whenever the reader bridges the gaps communication begins.[5]

Reception theory values the personal associations of the viewer, because the text and reader are seen in dialogic relationship.

In the drama classroom, this means that the teacher acts as a facilitator to draw out students' personal understandings of the dramatic text, inviting them to articulate their own experiences and insights in relation to the act of viewing, whether through oral discussion, journal writing or visual depiction. There are no right and wrong answers (though some answers are more supportable than others). The questions elicit students' aesthetic experiences. However, although drama teachers may hope that students have aesthetic experiences when viewing drama, this does not automatically happen. Students often need to be encouraged to respond aesthetically; interpretive strategies such as autobiographical writing may enable them to understand the assumptions they bring to a performance, and help to bring about active reading and creative viewing.[6] This is consistent with African-American Lisa

Delpit's view that, in a fully inclusive curriculum, teachers will make the cultural conventions explicit to students.[7]

For all its contributions, reader-response has its critics: critical theorists argue it does not go far enough and the results of a pedagogy of personal experience may lead to solipsism. In the next section, while we begin with a model of interpretation which encourages students to use their personal experiences in responding to drama, we also move on to models of response drawing on Aristotle's poetics. Following this, we explore how Boalian and Brechtian approaches to interrogating values might be combined with Aristotle's taxonomy of dramatic structure in order that students are able to move to increasingly complex analyses of performances. In the second half of the chapter, we describe workshop activities and exercises which demonstrate in practice how these ideas might work in the drama studio or classroom.

RESPONDING TO DRAMATIC ART: CHALLENGING THE CONVENTIONS OF *POETICS*

Aristotle's *Poetics* can be a surprisingly accessible place for the teacher of drama to introduce pupils to performance analysis and interpretation. What is needed is as simple a route into the *Poetics* as possible. Robert Findlay offers a *basic tools* approach that we have found useful.[8] Using his analytical frame, we begin with *Oedipus Rex* as the model, and proceed from this play to more contemporary dramas.

Findlay's basic tools provide an elegantly simple device for dramatic analysis. They follow a three-stage process, in which students are led to increasingly complex interpretations of the play they have seen. Findlay identifies three tools, as follows:

- Tool 1: central figure
  Students are asked to identify the central figure in the drama; this is easy in traditional works, more challenging in contemporary offerings where several protagonists might carry equal weight.[9]
- Tool 2: action statement
  Students are asked to write an infinitive clause identifying the motivating action for the drama. For *Oedipus Rex* the statement might read: 'to catch and expel the person responsible for causing the plague in Thebes'. Equipped with this tool, the teacher and students can begin to discuss the drama, comparing use of the poetic elements, plot, character, thought, language, music and spectacle in the development of the motivating action. Here the students begin to understand the dramatic irony that the person Oedipus seeks is himself – that this is the basis for the dramatic tale.
- Tool 3: basic human situation
  Findlay then encourages students to map out the actions of the central figure, based on personal characteristics, disposition, basis for reasoning and so on, in a single sentence. He begins, '*Oedipus Rex* is a play about a man who . . .' and students are required to complete the sentence. Once this

tool is acquired, students avoid the pages of description and exposition that we often read in analyses of dramatic texts.

Reflecting on these exercises helps students feel more familiar with the territory of dramatic analysis. The next step is to introduce them explicitly to a summary of the *Poetics* as a collection of elements, from which Sophocles and his contemporaries constructed their dramas: plot, character, thought, language, music and spectacle. Armed with these six key elements, students might now compare the structure of *Oedipus Rex* with a contemporary drama, perhaps George Lucas's latest film, Native American Sherman Alexie's *Smoke Signals*, or films created by contemporary women artists such as Penny Marshall or Elodie Keene.

Once the students have become familiar with basic structures, they might be encouraged to go on to Boalian criticism in order to recognize how dramatic conventions are used to create particular effects and to lead audiences to respond in specific ways. Augusto Boal, although perceiving Aristotle's work as a 'coercive system', integral to the oppressive government of ancient Athens, provides us with a detailed breakdown of the *Poetics*, including a valuable pattern that students can use as a template against which to test various contemporary works.[10] Methods of performance analysis are, perhaps, best exemplified via historical models, and Boal uses Aristotle's example of 'an almost perfect tragedy' in Sophocles' *Oedipus Rex*. His pedagogic method is twofold: first, to critique the political motivation for the creation of the Greek model, and second, to display the strength – Boal's coercive power – inherent in the structure. Both are useful lessons for students as they begin to analyse the complexities of more contemporary dramatic structures in the electronic age.

Perhaps of even greater importance, when considering the application of dramatic theory to classroom practice, is the point that Boal's focus on the ancient Greek model leads him to suggest the replacement of the passive spectator with an active *spect-actor*, arguing that the 'system' is coercive because the empathy we feel for the tragic hero as we live vicariously through his actions requires us to passively accept the rules or laws that he broke. Teachers and students can successfully use Boal's techniques to raise complex questions concerning the implicit values in drama, and to 'test' other works, including electronic dramas as well as their own improvisations and writing. Focusing a Boalian lens on soap operas and television advertisements can bring about lively discussion.

Aristotle and the Greeks are merely the starting point. At this stage it is helpful to ensure that readers, particularly those following the workshop exercises offered at the end of this chapter, recognize that non-Western aesthetics value different qualities. For example, the plot structures of Asian dramas are not linear and often do not have a definable beginning, middle and end. Similarly, a Native American story may begin in the present, leap back into the past, go forward again, now backwards, and finally, 'having made a complete circle, [end] at its own beginning'.[11] Contrasts can be made with

Western and non-Western values, as Elaine Aoki suggests: 'The Western narrative ... is about overcoming, changing, hope, and promise while the Japanese narrative is about conforming, renewing and continuing.'[12] Further, Caucasian consumers could learn a great deal from less materialistic cultures, such as Native American groups.

Unlike most reader-response or reception theorists, critical theorists focus on the cultural contexts of characters and actions and make explicit the hegemonies of power. Working in this context, the role of the leader in post-performance discussions is to awaken the consciousness of the respondents to the social condition in which the marginalized and oppressed find themselves, identifying the oppressors and the oppressed. Boal's magical realist, the joker, provides a useful practical model for this process. Following Brecht, Boal's joker stands between play and audience, comments, parodies, guides, breaks illusion, discourages overinvolvement, and encourages detachment. Whatever the dramatic text, the joker might ask the spect-actor:

Whose beliefs and values are assumed and/or promoted?
What cultures are being affirmed or ridiculed? Whose voices are not heard?
Whose truth is here? Whose interests are served?
To what extent are the poor and the marginalized the 'appendages of other people's dreams?'[13]
What activist tendencies may have been paralysed by catharsis? (see Exercise Four)

The process of being both engaged in and watchful of is not unlike the African American sociologist W.E.B. Du Bois's notion of double-consciousness, 'this sense of always looking at one's self through the eyes of others'. Through the joker's questions, students might be encouraged to consider how some dramatic texts and forms of readership privilege dominant cultures.[14]

MOMENTS OF CULTURAL DIGNITY: A PRACTICAL PURSUIT

Perhaps one of the most aesthetically fluid concepts in dramatic analysis is the idea of dignity. Dignity is a significant concept in both classical and contemporary drama, and its various interpretations provide students with insights into the ways in which performative texts are constructed and values are questioned and reproduced. It is important, therefore, that students are encouraged to experiment with the concept both academically and practically. Recognizing the points of loss of dignity in classical and contemporary dramas allows students to connect empathetically to a series of smaller tragic moments witnessed or experienced in daily life. Improvising possible directions a dramatic scenario might take helps to identify moments of mutual respect and trust in real life – the moment of dignity – when appropriate behavioural decisions are made.

In the grip of a terrible recognition of fatal error, caused in large part by character flaw, the tragic hero will attempt everything in his power to regain a sense of dignity. Arthur Miller's ordinary characters are excellent examples, imbued with the sprit of nobility, the *spoudaios* the Greeks insisted upon in their own regal heroes and heroines. Writing in *Tragedy and the Common Man*, Miller argues:

> As a general rule, ... I think the tragic feeling is evoked in us when we are in the presence of a character who is ready to lay down his life, if need be, to secure one thing – his sense of personal dignity ... the underlying struggle is that of the individual attempting to gain his 'rightful' place in society.[15]

Willy Loman in *Death of a Salesman* is an ideal model for student character analysis: 'a human being in search of dignity' might have been a suitable subtitle for Miller's play. In Exercise Six, students are encouraged to investigate this 'rightful place', which might be referred to as the *moment of dignity*, in their own creative practice.

This creative approach to critical analysis is supported by Aoki, who recommends interpreting and exploring Asian/Pacific American literature through role-play and point-of-view improvisations.

> The students should read aloud only part of the [text], from the beginning to where the problematic situation is introduced. Then the students should be guided in the role-playing activity by first defining the problem, delineating alternatives, exploring the alternatives through dramatisation, and finally making a decision as to what was the best alternative.[16]

Scenes can also come equally well from the students' daily lives, as from classical and contemporary drama, mediated in any form. Indeed, using improvisation to compare published text and contemporary experience is valuable.

Practical exploration of the concept of dignity can take many forms. However, in encouraging students to interpret the idea creatively, we have found that Brecht's approach to epic theatre acting techniques in *A Short Organum* provides a useful model.[17] In Exercise Five, we experiment with *epic replay* and *gestus* exercises, and an idea we call *reverse writing*. In this dramatic pedagogy, when students are dramatizing a story, they comment simultaneously on all its elements. Thus the student participants (Boal's spect-actors) maintain a critical distance from the dramatization, and this distance allows them the space to comprehend the play's politics. This was central to Brecht's 'epic' live theatre; it was a politically motivated reaction against dramatic forms such as realism, naturalism and German expressionism which maintained the status quo by encouraging emotional empathy with the bourgeoisie. Brecht's way of working has inspired many later film-makers,[18] whose films include plot interruptions, songs, poems, projections and other non-naturalistic elements, which invite audiences to 'possess' the moment, and critically interpret the dramatic form and content, rather than identifying with the roles presented.[19] As part of the process of engagement with drama, we encourage students to experiment with montage, the multidisciplinary re-mounting and re-presenting of moments of pre-existing work, again electronic or otherwise. For example, in Exercise Six, continuing our pursuit of dignity, we recognize the potential for such practical deconstruction and reconstruction in the Dustin Hoffman film version of Miller's *Death of a Salesman*, which is set against *Private Conversations*, a splendid examination of the filming process.[20]

But how might we select further, even more contemporary, work for practical dramatic experimentation? Any form is appropriate, from surrealism to epic, Grand Guignol to documentary and the electronic media, so long as there is a necessary recognition of the contradictory forces evident in the movement of history and how these forces affect the social roles of individual people. In drama education, exploration of the diverse representations of moment of dignity offers one way to effect social change. In finding and using multicultural dramatic texts in the classroom, students are posed challenging questions and asked to reconsider the assumptions implicit in different forms of dramatic representation. Teachers may wish to start by looking at Caleen Jennings's *A Lunch Line: Contemporary Scenes for Contemporary Teens*, Belinda Acosta's *3 Girls & Clorox* and Drew Hayden Taylor's *Toronto at Dreamer's Rock*. The latter play has elements of fantasy as three Native Canadian adolescent boys – including one from the past and one from the future – reflect on what it means to be a teenager torn between two cultures.[21] The purpose is twofold: to give voice to the silenced and marginalized and to explore dramatic styles beyond the naturalism and realism that characterizes much of our students' media environment. For example, while Jennings's work contains dramatic scenes in the style of realism, it also contains scenes deriving from musical theatre, rap, and dance. Acosta's *3 Girls & Clorox* is realistic in style, but its minimalist sets invite greater audience imagination. In this way, students are encouraged to develop their understanding of particular social contexts, and extend their knowledge of dramatic form.

WORKSHOPS: PUTTING THEORY INTO PRACTICE

The workshops we describe aim to develop analytic and interpretative skills with our students, and encourage the selection of valuable, stimulating material in order to move on to the stages of making, performing (sometimes re-making and re-performing), and responding to work. We include as much practical activity in the drama classroom as possible, with a basic grounding in history and theory as a foundation. The practical, six-stage, developmentally sequenced workshops follow the same progression as the theory we have already discussed. The work takes students through a variety of exercises involving writing, group discussion, improvisation, performance and critical analysis, leading to the higher level of thinking and interpretation referred to earlier. Beginning with a reader-response exercise that promotes active view-ing, the workshop moves on through Findlay's *Basic Tools* and Aristotle's key elements, to Boalian and Brechtian-inspired work around *reverse writing* and *moments of dignity* techniques. The final stages of the workshop focus on

Miller's *Death of a Salesman* and Brecht's *Caucasian Chalk Circle*, but the techniques described may be applied to a variety of texts, mediated and live. The workshops provide an outline of activities rather than lesson plans; teachers will wish to adapt them to suit their own context and ways of working. For each exercise, the specified aims provide suitable criteria for assessment.

<h3 style="text-align:center">Exercise One: active reading</h3>

The aim is

- to promote an active role for the viewer
- to encourage multiple interpretations of a play in performance.

Preparation

Multiple copies of Belinda Acosta's play, *3 Girls & Clorox*, are available. Students read and/or enact key scenes in the play. In this play, an African American teenager, Thayon, attends on scholarship a private girls' school where, unlike other girls, she must also work in the cafeteria to help with expenses. In an attempt to fit into the school, and to hide her black identity, Thayon dyes her hair with disastrous results, witnessed by her new Mexican American friend Lidia. It is Lidia who reminds Thayon that you come to belong to a place 'because of what you bring to it, not because of what you erase in yourself'. The play offers a rich discussion between Lidia, Thayon, and Thayon's one white friend at the school, Sherry (a poor little rich girl) about the meaning of belonging and creating a life for oneself and for each other.

Activity One: seeing the performance

The students see a performance or rehearsed reading of the play. It is a short play which could easily be staged in a drama class as well as being suitable for performance.

Activity Two: questioning the performance

After viewing the performance, students discuss a range of prompt questions, designed to encourage personal responses to the performance.

- While you were viewing *3 Girls & Clorox*, what kind of thoughts and feelings did you have?
- Have you ever been in a similar situation?
- Have you ever known characters like Thayon, Lidia, Sherry, Trudy or Becky?
- How do you think Lidia felt when she saw Thayon's damaged hair?
- What would it be like to be in a school where you were the only one of your ethnicity, as Thayon (black) and Lidia (Mexican America)?
- If you had been in the situation, would you have done something differently?

- How would you have handled Thayon's problem?
- Why do you think Thayon treated her hair herself, rather than asking her aunt?
- Why did Acosta, the playwright, have the three protagonists come from diverse backgrounds?
- What questions do you have after viewing the play?
- Has anything been learned by the characters at the end of the play?

Exercise Two: Findlay's three basic tools

The aim is

- to utilize three basic tools, central figure, action statement and basic human situation, to gain understanding of dramatic structure.

Preparation

Students are introduced to the story of *Oedipus Rex*. Various strategies for this may be used, including active-telling, role-playing the narrative, depiction of key events from cue-cards, watching the play on video, or reading the script. The class is divided into small groups for a brief discussion of their first impressions of the work. Questions based on Exercise One may help.

Activity One: central figure

Students are asked to identify the central figure in the drama. In *Oedipus Rex* this is straightforward, but discuss examples with the class where there might be more than one central figure, or protagonists of equal status.

Activity Two: action statement

Ask the students to write an infinitive clause identifying the basic action of *Oedipus Rex*. Help them to frame this by asking, 'What is it that the central figure has to do? What is his motivating action?' A possible infinitive clause might be 'to catch and expel the person responsible for causing the plague in Thebes'. This becomes the action statement. Equipped with this, students can begin to see how everything in the work is related to this simple phrase. Help the students to understand this by discussing how the characters and every-thing that they do relates to this one driving force, either promoting the action or attempting to prevent it. Try the infinitive clause approach to more contemporary dramas for comparison.

Activity Three: basic human situation

In small groups, the class discuss the actions of the central figure, why he follows such actions, what motivates him, what drives him, and what kind of man he is. Does anything about the central figure surprise the students? As a diagram of ideas, emotions, thoughts and deeds, the students map out these actions as they relate to the action statement. From this diagram, the students can now construct a single sentence beginning, '*Oedipus Rex* is a play about a man who …' Completing this single sentence produces the basic human situation of the play.

Exercise Three: Aristotle's Elements – the building blocks for a system of performance writing

The aim is

- to enable students to recognize the six Aristotelian elements as building blocks for performance writing.

Preparation

At home, have the students watch examples of television advertisements, especially ones that use a format that relies on a very short, but recognizable, story. Have them make lists of important ideas, moments, events, dialogue, images, scenery, costume and music, noticed in these electronic advertisements. Discuss the results of their homework assignment in class.

Activity One: action statements

In small groups, the students agree upon a specific product to promote via a television advertisement. Have them work out an action statement for the advertisement, such as 'to persuade working moms to buy *Aristotle's Frozen Pitta Bread*'. Discuss the 'thought' behind advertisements and other performance media.

Activity Two: the significance of plot

The students write out a basic plot summary for a two-minute 'story-based' advertisement, following ideas they have gleaned from watching the professional examples on television. The 'product' must be put to successful use in the advertisement and this should be reflected in the plot outline. Discuss the significance of 'plot' in these advertisements and other performance works.

Activity Three: the importance of character

The students decide on how many characters will appear in the advertisement and how they will interact. Discuss the importance of character in various performance media.

Activity Four: dramatic dialogue

The students write dialogue and/or narrative for the characters. How do they speak? Do they have an accent? Can we tell who they might be from what they say? What if we change what they say, and how they say it? Discuss how language is important in drama.

Activity Five: the effect of music

The students decide what music they might like to add to their advertisements. Discuss how music might add to the advertisement in both an entertaining and effective manner. What might music have to do with the way a potential consumer might respond to the advertisement?

Activity Six: the concept of spectacle

The students decide how their advertisement will be shot (film or video), what costumes the characters might wear, make-up, lights, scenery. Discuss the concept of spectacle with the students and how this might affect the way an audience might respond to an advertisement or other performance.

Summary

Discuss with the students the six Aristotelian elements they have introduced themselves to in the exercise – plot, thought, character, language, music and spectacle. Discuss the elements and their relative importance in various performance works. For example, how would television differ from radio? How is MTV different from Radio 1? How is film different from theatre? Which element or elements are most important in a West End or Broadway musical? Finally, discuss the origin of these building blocks from Aristotle's *Poetics* and how the philosopher regarded *Oedipus Rex* as the almost perfect drama because of its structure.

Exercise Four: drama versus life – Oedipus might always make the same mistakes, but do we have to?

The aim is

- to question the values implicit in Sophocles' play
- to re-create and re-perform a contemporary version of the Oedipus myth, or story, making it more relevant to our own lives.

Preparation

This work uses Augusto Boal's critique of Aristotle from the opening chapter of *Theatre of the Oppressed*, the role of the joker in the same work and in *Games for Actors and Non-Actors* also by Boal.[22] Aoki's role-play and point of view ideas may also be incorporated.

Activity One: changing the plot

Discuss Sophocles' play with the class, focusing on the fact that, given the fixed plot, things will always work out the same in whatever production of this play we see. In Sophocles' *Oedipus Rex*, Oedipus will always face the same catastrophic end, blinded and homeless – an end result worse than death, according to Aristotle. Oedipus will always make the same mistakes in Sophocles' version of the story, because that is the way the playwright constructed his ideas. However, Sophocles was doing just that. He was interpreting an old myth. He was free to change it where and how he desired. You might wish to share summaries of Steven Berkoff's *Greek*, Edward Bond's *The Woman* and other contemporary playwrights' versions of classical drama.[23] Now, we can do the same. If we wish to write a new play, a new version of the old story, once we know how to construct a dramatic script we can create our own version of this ancient myth. We can create our own play in which Oedipus might do some things differently.

Activity Two: introduction to Boal's analysis of Aristotle

Discuss how Boal charts Aristotle's system, exemplified in *Oedipus Rex*, in *Theatre of the Oppressed*: the spectacle of the citizens of Thebes suffering the plague as the play opens; the arrival of a dynamic and attractive hero whom the public appreciates, but who quickly shows a surprising negative side to his character, whose pride has brought him success and problems alike, and who is informed that he is, ironically, himself the murderer he now seeks. This creates a kind of fear in the public of Thebes (and, therefore in the audience) which leads to a concern for the central figure, but also the hope that this awful problem never comes to us; how through Oedipus' downfall, experienced vicariously and passively by the audience, we are made aware of our own flaws and persuaded to be more obedient to the rules that govern our lives – the resultant catharsis.

Compare Boal's summary with the students' basic human situations from Exercise Two. Explain how the playwright, Sophocles, might have meant this work as a warning to the citizens of Athens to obey their religious and civil laws – Aristotle's element of thought. Ask the class to alter the narrative of *Oedipus* by suggesting how they might construct a version in which he acts differently, at any stage of the story.

Activity Three: constructing our own play

Remember, we are now moving away from Sophocles' play. In small groups, have the students improvise sections of the plot incorporating changes they have considered above. With the teacher as Joker, ask questions as the improvisations unfold. The students should now work as spect-actors, active participants in the unfolding dramaturgy. Freeze the action and have other students replay the scenes to show how they would create their own versions of moments of the story. The aim here is to relate new versions of the ancient story to more contemporary life.

Exercise Five: reverse writing – Brecht's epic techniques in *Caucasian Chalk Circle*, scene i, The Noble Child

The aim is

- to show, through Brechtian acting exercises, how change can be fully demonstrated in performance only through total social *gestus*.

Preparation

Provide extracts from scene i of the play, from 'The city is still . . .' to 'Noon was the hour to die' (approximately two pages). It is the scene where the young soldier, Simon, falls in love with Grusha. Brecht's concept of social *gestus* is also used in this exercise.[24]

Activities

Suggested below are a range of activities which encourage students to experiment with the scene. It is suggested that they work in groups of four, with three actors (The Singer, Simon Sashava – a soldier, Grusha Vashnadze – a kitchen maid) and one person as director.

- Play the scene as you would normally choose to do it. Discuss the roles, including The Singer. What is she/he doing in the drama?
- Play the scene with opposite sex roles.
- Play the scene in the third person, where actors comment on the action, e.g. 'The soldier, Simon, said . . .'
- Play the scene as though it happened in the past. Improvise the scene as if it happened previously, where each character gives an account of his/her actions on that day.
- Now do it again adding stage directions, including movement (choreography), eye-contact, body language, etc. and all feelings, subtext thoughts and emotions, to build a total social *gestus*, along with the reported dialogue.
- Now have the actors mime the scene, with the director supplying the reported language as an entire narrative, including motivation and 'readings between lines'.
- Switch roles, including the director's job, so that everyone tries each part.
- Only when you are completely comfortable in doing the scene in all these various ways, return to playing the parts with the words as written by the playwright.

Exercise Six: *Death of a Salesman* – fluid moments of dignity

The aim is

- to recognize precise moments in drama when dignity is lost or found.

Preparation

This exercise is designed to form part of a unit of work on Arthur Miller's *Death of a Salesman*. By this stage, the students will have read the play and seen the film version directed by Victor Schlondorff with Dustin Hoffman in the lead role, and the teacher would introduce *Private Conversations*, a film examining the making of the Hoffman version at an appropriate moment.

Activities

Working in small groups, the students may be led through the following activities.

- Identify Findlay's three basic tools – central figure, action statement and basic human situation – with respect to Arthur Miller's *Death of a Salesman*. Discuss these with the class as a whole.
- Try to identify any specific moments when a character, or characters, lose or regain a sense of dignity in the play.
- Find a moment of dignity in the script and act out the moment with a partner, or partners.
- Discuss Aristotle's six elements of drama, as you recognize them in the text.
- Concentrating only on *spectacle*, how is the Loman house presented to the audience? Is it presented in a realistic fashion or is there an element of fantasy? If not, why do you think it was presented in this way? Look at the playscript. Is the presentation of the house different from what we see in the video version?
- Choose a short scene from the script and act it out. Use some of the epic theatre ideas in the *Caucasian Chalk Circle* exercise described above.
- Now watch *Private Conversations* video. Was your scene included? If not, repeat the process by acting out a scene that is included in the video. What additional information do you now have which might help you (a) understand the scene and (b) be able to perform the role better and/or (c) direct the scene more effectively?
- Watch *Private Conversations* again. What does Arthur Miller say about changing the lines for film? What does Hoffman say about 'artificiality'? The film set and the stage set are not 'real' houses. How do they differ from the 'real' and each other? What does this suggest that is different about video/film?
- How does the sequencing of film 'shoots' and 'takes' differ from stage performances? How might this affect the actors and directors?
- What do you make of the collaboration in the making of a dramatic performance, live or mediated? How do the artists in the video comment on this? 'An emotional symbiosis . . . a fabric'?
- How do the actors in the video respond to different ways of doing their scenes, in multiple takes? Can you relate this to your own Brechtian, epic theatre, exercises?
- What does the director mean by his phrase, '. . . must get inside' when he saw the need to, 'cut to close-up' in a very emotional scene? How would this be handled in a live performance?
- Is society to blame for Loman's situation?
- How do you relate, personally, to the suggestion that the work is about a 'conflict of family values and society's expectations of success'? Replay the *moments of dignity* scenes you identified earlier. Stop them at the precise 'moment' where dignity is lost or found. Freeze the image. Compare it to a freeze-frame from the movie, or pause the video at the same place.

CONCLUSION

In this chapter, we have provided a series of starting points for differentiation in models of response in the drama classroom. Whatever model for critique is used, when students are encouraged to explore multiple interpretations, the art of disagreeing agreeably must be taught. No technology can replace the vital role of drama teachers who provide for their pupils positive experiences in drama practice and discussion, experiences that can counterbalance their increasingly electronically mediated world.

Clearly, there is a need for a variety of modes; the complexity of today's exciting multicultural classroom renders any one mode of response too simplistic. It is essential that further work be conducted in creating, integrating and synthesizing non-Western modes of responding. We believe detachment and involvement can coexist; indeed, both stances enrich the other. The act of responding to drama guarantees not only that adolescents will leave our schools with a proficient critical vocabulary to interact with their media world, but also that they can become agents of change able to shape their own developing culture.

ACKNOWLEDGEMENTS

The authors wish to thank Pat Whitton, publisher of New Plays, Inc., in recommending various scripts and her contribution to this chapter.

NOTES

1 See Hornbrook, D. (ed.) (1998) *On the Subject of Drama* (London: Routledge), especially Jane M. Gangi's chapter, 'Making sense of drama in an electronic age', pp. 151–68.
2 See Brahmachari, S. (1998) 'Stages of the world', in D. Hornbrook (ed.) *op. cit.*, pp. 18–35.
3 Bailin, S. (1994) *Achieving Extraordinary Ends* (Norwood, NJ: Ablex), p. 38.
4 For further explanation of modes of questioning, see Aldrich, P.W. (1996) 'Evaluating language arts materials', in J. Van Tassel-Baska, D.T. Johnson and L.N. Boyce (eds) *Developing Verbal Talent* (Boston, MA: Allyn & Bacon), p. 222.
5 Iser, W. (1978) *The Act of Reading: A Theory of Aesthetic Response* (Baltimore, MD: Johns Hopkins University Press), pp. 168–9.
6 See Smith, M.W. (1992) 'Submission versus control in literary transactions', in J. Many and C. Cox (eds) *Reader Stance and Literary Understanding: Exploring the Theories, Research, and Practice* (Norwood, NJ: Ablex), p. 159.
7 Delpit, L. (1995) *Other People's Children: Cultural Conflict in the Classroom* (New York: New Press), pp. 25–6.
8 Professor Findlay typically uses this so far unpublished example in his theatre history classes at the University of Kansas.
9 Roger Howard's Material Theory provides several examples. See Howard, R. (1984) 'A material view of tragedy', in L. Bell (ed.) *Contradictory Theatres* (Colchester: Theatre Action Press).
10 Boal, A. (1985) *Theatre of the Oppressed* (trans. C.A. and M.-O. Leal McBride (New York: Theatre Communications Group). See, especially, 'How Aristotle's coercive system of tragedy functions', p. 36.

11 Bruchac, J. (1996) *Roots of Survival* (Golden, CO: Fulcrum), p. 205.

12 Aoki, E. (1993) 'Turning the page: Asian/Pacific American's children's literature', in V.J. Harris (ed.) *Teaching Multicultural Literature in Grades K–8* (Norwood, MA: Christopher-Gordon), p. 118.

13 McLaren, P. (1999) 'A pedagogy of possibility: reflecting upon Paolo Freire's politics of education'. *Educational Researcher*, 28(2), 50.

14 Du Bois, W.E.B. (1903/1995) *The Souls of Black Folk* (New York: Penguin), p. 45. See also Toni Morrison's *Playing in the Dark*, where she asks white readers to reflect on the extent to which white privileges still exist. Morrison, T. (1992) *Playing in the Dark: Whiteness and the Literary Imagination* (New York: Random House).

15 Miller, A. (1974) *Tragedy and the Common Man*, in B.F. Dukore (ed.) *Dramatic Theory and Criticism: From Greeks to Grotowski* (New York: Holt, Rinehart & Winston), p. 894.

16 Aoki, E. (1993) *op. cit.*, p. 128.

17 See Willett, J. (1964) *Brecht on Theatre: The Development of an Aesthetic* (New York: Hill & Wang).

18 We are thinking here of Julie Dash, Lina Wertmueller, Werner Herzog and Harold Pinter.

19 Boyum, J. (1985) *Double Exposure: From Fiction into Film* (New York: Penguin). See p. 32 for a discussion of Brechtian devices in films such as Jean-Luc Godard's *La Chinoise*. Teachers may want to check whether this film is appropriate for teenage classes.

20 See video tape 2 (vol. 2) *Private Conversations*, in A. Miller, *Death of a Salesman/ video recording/Roxbury & Punch Productions* (Troy, MI: Castle Hill Productions).

21 Jennings, C. (1989) *A Lunch Line: Contemporary Scenes for Contemporary Teens* (Charlottesville, VA: New Plays); Acosta, B. (1995) *3 Girls & Clorox* (Charlottesville, VA: New Plays); Taylor, D.H. (1990) *Toronto at Dreamer's Rock* (Calgary, AB: Fifth House). Taylor is an Ojibway whose plays are often toured in Canada.

22 See Boal, A. (1992) *Games for Actors and Non-Actors* (London: Routledge).

23 See, for example, Berkoff, S. (1994) *The Collected Plays* (London: Faber & Faber); Bond, E. (1979) *The Woman: Scenes of War and Freedom* (New York: Hill & Wang).

24 Anon. (no byline given) (1984) *Brecht for Beginners* (New York: Writers and Readers). 'Social gestus. The sum of movements, behaviour, facial expressions, language and intonation employed by an individual in relation to others and which reveal both his personality and his social position. "Words and gestures can be replaced by other words and gestures without in any way altering the social gestus."' (pp. 186–7).

Part Three

Teaching Drama 16–18

THEORY AND CONTEXT

Sharon Grady comments in her chapter that 'creators of performance employ many language systems to realize their artistic purposes'. Interpreting the different languages in which drama and theatre practitioners communicate with audiences, she suggests, requires students to actively combine theory with practice. At this level, when students have chosen to follow courses in drama and theatre, they often integrate practical work with an understanding of the social, historical and cultural contexts of different theatre practitioners and dramatic texts. As Steve Waters points out, this presents new challenges to students whose experiences of drama education up to the age of 16 have been dominated by spontaneous improvisation.

As the contributors to this part of the book make clear, students in the 16–18 age range develop their understanding of drama by recognizing, explicitly, the dual and reciprocal relationship between the contexts of production and reception. This approach to teaching drama marks the influence of critical and performance theories on educational practices where, as Janelle Reinelt and Joseph Roach have pointed out, an interest in context of performance has replaced the view that drama communicates ahistorical, universal and transcendental truths.[1] What this means in practice is that, rather than asking students to discover the universal themes or 'hidden meanings' implicit in dramatic texts, students are more likely to explore a range of possible interpretations. By engaging in alternative readings, by researching the ideas of practitioners, students might develop a wider range of cultural reference points from which to decode the languages of drama. As Sharon Grady points out, when students are introduced to diverse critical perspectives, they may accept, more openly, their own positions in relation to new or unfamiliar dramatic forms.

In her discussion of the integration of theory and practice, Melissa Jones describes how students extended their creative vocabularies by experimenting with the theories of Shaffer and Artaud. Steve Waters takes up this point, arguing that by locating drama and theatre practices in context, students gain a deeper understanding of the relationship between theoretical concepts and creative work. All the contributors to this part stress the importance of this combination of history, practice and theory, an interrelationship which encourages students to progress as both critics and as practitioners.

THE PROCESS OF DIFFERENTIATION

As students develop as practitioners, they almost invariably continue to work collaboratively, but their particular skills and interests may become increasingly differentiated at this stage. Some students become ever more proficient in design or directing, for example, while others may focus specifically on acting. This means that differentiation is intrinsically integrated into their work; many theatre forms rely not only on the participants' shared understanding of the languages of drama, but also on their different crafts and skills.

Elsewhere in this book there is discussion of possible processes of differentiation; Bryony Williamson described differentiation by support, Merrilyn Evans gave practical suggestions for differentiation by learning styles and Denise Margetts offered her class a range of differentiated tasks. In the 16–18 age range, as students become increasingly independent learners, they also develop a range of strategies which enable them to work together to develop and interpret drama which is artistically coherent, and which also gives them space to learn new crafts and skills. As Sharon Grady points out, this requires students to develop a practical and theoretical understanding of the sign-systems of drama and theatre form, and reach a working knowledge of how the languages of drama interact.

In this sector of education, there is an increasing attempt to avoid differentiation between an academic education and vocation training; in the UK, for example, it is now considered important that the 16 + curriculum as a whole extends students' key 'market-place' skills in communication, information computer technology, environmental awareness and so on. Indeed, the practice and study of drama, which relies on collaborative working practices as well as academic study, has a contribution to make to this area of work. However, as an art form which necessarily depends on social interaction, drama is always more than the sum of its individual parts. As all the contributors to this part make clear, when students are encouraged to make meanings for themselves, and apply their understanding of theoretical ideas to their practical work, they are better able to interrogate and represent a range of ideas in dramatic form, and to engage critically in a diversity of creative practices.

NOTE

1 See Reinelt, J.G. and Roach, J.R. (eds) (1992) *Critical Theory and Performance* (Ann Arbor, MI: University of Michigan Press), p. 415.

Chapter 9

Integrating Practice: The Practitioner and the Dramatic Text

Melissa Jones

CHALLENGING TRADITION

Drama has always reflected the spirit of the age, yet dramatic writing responds equally to the philosophies of theatrical practitioners and experiments eclectically with form. Simon Cooper and Sally Mackey describe the twentieth-century practitioners:

> [whose lives] were dominated by their desire for change: change to the prevailing theatre practice, which they saw as inhibiting experimentation. Above all, they were all people who took risks, since by challenging outmoded ideas they were forced to provide radical alternatives.[1]

Our theatre is imbued with elements of the work of many theorists; the writer, performer or director working today does not consciously set out to follow precisely the style of a given practitioner but draws, almost instinctively, upon knowledge gained from experiment and experience. Current theatre practice reflects a wide range of theories and the modern practitioner redefines the drama in relation to a variety of influences.

A brief survey of the impact of theatre practitioners on the modern theatre reveals a variety of influences. Peter Brook, who was probably the first to introduce the ideas of Artaud in England, wrote in *The Empty Space* of 'The Holy Theatre'.[2] His RSC experiment with Charles Marowitz in 1963 embraced Artaud's theories and seemed to reject the Stanislavski school of thought, which underpinned actor training at the time. Joan Littlewood's early work rejoiced in 'agit-prop' theatre; she developed her Theatre Workshop to challenge what she saw as 'bourgeois' English theatre in the early part of the twentieth century. At Stratford East her work reflected the impact of Brecht's visit to Britain and *Oh! What a Lovely War* employed many Brechtian staging techniques. More recently Max Stafford-Clark's Out of Joint production of Mark Ravenhill's play *Shopping and Fucking* shocked audiences, perhaps in the same way as Artaud had intended: 'Theatre also takes gestures and develops them to the limit. Just like the plague, it reforges the links between what does and does not exist in material nature.'[3]

Yet elements of the work of Brecht could be seen clearly in design and directorial decisions and in the play's structure. Timberlake Wertenbaker's *Our Country's Good*, directed by Max Stafford-Clark, has a Brechtian 'montage' structure but the depth of research and character detail undertaken during rehearsal could be ascribed to the influence of Stanislavski.[4] Essentially all practitioners are, themselves, influenced by the thinking of others who have redefined theatre form. The theatre is organic, constantly evolving. Theatre practitioners are practising professionals; theoretical writing has originated from practical experiment, from dissatisfaction and from a desire to challenge and to change.

As students progress in their study of drama, they should be encouraged to place their learning in context and to make connections between theory and practice. It is the experiment with form, born out of a desire to engage in the creative practice, that underpins the practical work in this chapter. The workshops detailed in this project originate from the desire to encourage recognition of the way practitioners challenged established theatre practice and to assess the impact of their thinking on modern theatre.

THEATRICAL INFLUENCE: ARTAUD AND SHAFFER

The aim of this project is to enable students to identify the connections between theory and practice and to understand that drama evolves as part of a gradual process and that engagement in creative practice draws on a wide range of influences. The work is structured to enable students, engaged in advanced study of drama, to understand the evolution of practice and to explore the work of the playwright and the ideas of a practitioner in relation to each other. The project stimulates creativity and experiments with style and form. The objectives include learning about the theory of a significant modern practitioner and his influence on the playwright in conjunction with their own practical explorations of theatrical style.

I am concerned with an approach that engages the imagination of the students and teaches through practical application rather then theoretical study. I want students to experience the freedom to experiment and to find an understanding of theory through practice. The practitioner Antonin Artaud has been regarded as extreme and many students find his work complex. Yet he left a legacy in his *Manifestos* that has had enormous impact on theatre, redefining its purpose, its relationship with the audience and its language of communication. Taking the work of a modern playwright, Peter Shaffer, who has embraced some of the theories of Artaud, as a basis for study I designed a series of workshop sessions which connected theory and practical work.

In devising the practical and written activities I sought to enable students to explore the theory in its dramatic context rather than in isolation. The focus was on the exploration of text using the theories of Antonin Artaud's *The Theatre and its Double* in relation to Peter Shaffer's plays *The Royal Hunt of the Sun* and *Equus*. The programme was devised to achieve the following aims:

- to understand Artaud's ideas about theatre
- to connect the work of Peter Shaffer with Artaud's theory
- to broaden the students' creative use of form
- to explore both practitioner and dramatic text in parallel.

The students undertook preparatory work on Artaud's ideas and on the texts before approaching the practical activities. As well as reading extracts from *The Theatre and its Double* by Artaud, the students found the chapter on Artaud in Cooper and Mackey's *Theatre Studies: An Approach for Advanced Level* very accessible. It was important for them to have a basic understanding of the theory and of the way Shaffer had redefined it before embarking on experimental exercises.

AN AFFECTIVE ATHLETICISM

Artaud's essay on the actor's training provided a starting point for practical activity. The first session engaged the students in Artaud's physical, vocal and ritual exercises. Breathing exercises were undertaken using a variety of rhythms to which were added sounds and then words. Suggested emotions were added to the breathing, experimenting with tempo. Artaud writes that 'an actor delves down into his personality by the whetted edge of his breathing'.[5] The work moved into exploration of Artaud's ideas of the 'primal scream' which he felt released the actor from inhibitions and enabled him to touch raw emotions. Initially students found, as Artaud suggested, that natural reserve and embarrassment prevented full engagement with this activity. Nevertheless as more physical movement was added, the lighting dimmed in the studio and confidence grew, the 'scream' was achieved and in discussion students articulated the release of energy that they experienced. Comparisons were made at this point with the work of Stanislavski and the importance he placed on physical relaxation and on tempo rhythm.

Artaud's fascination with Balinese dancers formed the basis for the next activities: 'In the Balinese Theatre one senses a state prior to language, able to select its own language; music, gesture, moves and words.'[6] Using a variety of masks, objects and percussion instruments the students created ritualistic pieces of theatre with the emphasis on movement, mime and sound – both vocal and instrumental. The work was undertaken in pairs and the task placed emphasis on communication both with a partner and with an audience. Through creating this 'wordless' theatre they explored the power of spatial language, sound and ritual in creating meaning. The finished pieces were presented and a discussion of communicated meaning enabled them to understand the power of non-verbal theatre.

The session finished with an introduction to Shaffer's ideas of 'total theatre' where 'not only words but rites, mimes, masks and magics' combine in the whole theatrical event.[7] In discussion it was recognized that the work they had just undertaken incorporated many of these elements.

At the end of this initial workshop the students had

- connected Artaud's ideas of physical and vocal training to actual experience
- experimented with the use of non-verbal theatre in communicating meaning
- evaluated their work and experience in relation to theory.

SOUNDS, NOISES AND CRIES

Artaud's use of sound provided the focus for the work in the next session. The aim was to engage the students in activities that opened up the ideas and enabled them to relate to Artaud's theory. By working on scenes from plays written by a Western playwright it was possible to see how Artaud had *influenced* Shaffer's work, yet Shaffer was not following slavishly the Artaudian theory. 'The sounds, noises and cries are first sought for their vibratory qualities, secondly for what they represent.'[8] Students were introduced to Artaud's rejection of Western 'dialogue theatre' and how he advocated an 'appeal to the senses' of the audience:

> How is it Western theatre cannot conceive of theatre under any other aspect than dialogue form? ... I maintain the stage is a tangible, physical place that needs to be filled and it ought to be allowed to speak in its own concrete language.[9]

In working on this section of the project, I was concerned with releasing the students from the very inhibitions that Artaud accuses Western theatre of possessing.

In *Equus* Act I scenes 20 and 21 Shaffer employs the 'Chorus' of the 'Equus noise' as a counterpoint to Alan's ritualistic enactment of the riding of Equus at night. After discussing the meaning of the scene the students worked as a group on creating this 'noise' vocally. They used a range of vocal styles from humming on a single note to creating a variety of distorted vocal sounds. The sound collage was recorded and replayed through a four-speaker sound system so that it reverberated around the studio. The students discussed the merits of live versus recorded sound.

The work continued with students playing the dialogue against a background of first the live vocal collage and then with the recorded sound. Finally they combined the two forms, playing the dialogue with live sound enhanced by recorded echoing sound. The effect re-created the assault on the aural senses that Artaud recommended. In preparation for the next session students looked at *The Royal Hunt of the Sun*, focusing especially on the stage directions, to identify potential uses of sound. They prepared extracts for a workshop in which percussion instruments, bells or any form of live sound was to be used. Thus the students were creating their own interpretation of the text while also experimenting with the concepts of Artaud.

Selected extracts included the opening of Act I scene 3 where 'Great cries of "Inca" are heard ... Exotic music mixes with the chanting'.[10] A student had prepared a selection of wind instruments, bells and pipes to recreate the 'exotic' music. She divided the group into two sections – one worked on a highly formalized 'Inca' chant while the other created the counterpoint with improvised percussive sound. The student director worked alternately with the groups to bring the sounds to a climax. The groups were then brought together to perform the scene. Through this work it was evident that the students had learned and understood Artaud's ideas and been able to apply them to Shaffer's play. The parallels with the *Equus* scene, the way live sound created by actors visible on stage adds to the dramatic tension, were also clear.

Another student prepared exciting vocal work on Act II scene 6 'The rape of the Sun'.

> Suddenly Diego gives a cry of triumph ... The Sun gives a deep groan, like the sound of a great animal being wounded. With greedy yelps, all the soldiers rush at the Sun and start to pull it to bits ... while terrible groans fill the air.[11]

This work included the physical movement, which illustrated their understanding of the first session's work. Members of the group took on the roles of soldiers while others became the sounds of the sun. The emphasis was on the use of sound to show violence and anguish, the studio filled with gesture and intense discord: the work of Artaud was being used with knowledge and understanding by the students.

The concluding session on sound involved the whole group in working on aural contrasts within the play *The Royal Hunt of the Sun*. Shaffer employs the use of choral song to emphasize the gentle communal society of the Incas; the 'toil song' in Act I scene 6 was the focus of the initial work. Students created their own vocal interpretation of the song and added percussive sound in keeping with the suggestions made by Marc Wilkinson, the composer. Wilkinson used maracas and a tabala drum to accompany the song. The students in this session added mimed gesture, although the focus was on the dramatic effect of vocal and percussive sound. Another student suggested the addition of a contrasting, threatening drumbeat to denote the Spanish military presence – a sharp contrast to the calm of the toil song.

Following this work the exercise continued by examining the use of sound at the end of the play, the death of Atahuallpa. The stage directions were examined before the practical interpretation.

> *A drum beats.* Slowly, in semi-darkness, the stage fills with all the Indians, robed in black and terracotta, wearing the golden funeral masks of ancient Peru. Grouped round the prone body, *they intone a strange Chant of Resurrection, punctuated by hollow beats on the drums and by long, long*

silences in which they turn their immense triangular eyes enquiringly up to the sky. Finally after *three great cries* appear to summon it, the sun rises.[12]

[my italics]

The students used voice and percussion to re-create the dramatic sound for this moment of the play. They improvised and worked collaboratively on the 'Chant of Resurrection' then added the drumbeats and silences to achieve dramatic impact.

In discussion, the students demonstrated understanding of how Shaffer used sound to create mood and atmosphere as well as to replace the need for dialogue. The toil song told of the harmony of the Inca culture while the use of anguished and discordant sound revealed the Inca's torment at the death of their God. This was related to Artaud's writing in his second Manifesto on the Theatre of cruelty.

The overlapping imagery and moves must culminate in a genuine physical language, no longer based on words but on signs formed through the combination of objects, silences, shouts and rhythms.[13]

To consolidate their learning from these sessions the students wrote detailed director's notes for their extracts and evaluations of the work in which they had been involved. In these notes they were asked to point out the way that Artaud's theories had influenced their decisions and to show awareness of the way Shaffer had employed Artaud's material. After this section the students had

- learned how Artaud challenged Western theatre's reliance on dialogue
- explored Shaffer's use of sound in *Equus*
- created their own work from *The Royal Hunt of the Sun*
- experienced working as an actor and director using vocal and percussive sound
- evaluated their experiments in relation to Artaud's theory.

RATIONALIZING THE IRRATIONAL

Artaud himself apologized for using the word 'metaphysical'.[14] The double, which Artaud called 'metaphysics', was the foundation for the ensuing workshops. This was a very difficult concept for students to understand and I was concerned that they would be anxious about the complexity of the language. I aimed to introduce the meaning and the idea through practical exploration rather than theoretical explanation. The workshops were designed to relate Artaud's ideas to Shaffer's plays.

Artaud's fascination with Oriental dance and its influence on his theory was the starting point for discussion.

In Oriental theatre with its metaphysical inclinations, as against Western theatre and its psychological inclinations, this whole complex of gestures, signs, postures and sound which make up a stage production language, this language which develops all its physical and poetic effects on all conscious levels and in all senses, must lead to thought adopting deep attitudes which might be called active metaphysics.[15]

The students explored the relationship between this statement and Shaffer's comments on 'total theatre'. The way Artaud wanted meaning to be attached to gesture, which would represent ideas and attitudes through signs rather than words, was considered in discussion.

Practical work related to two key scenes from the plays of Shaffer: 'The mime of the great massacre' (*The Royal Hunt of the Sun* Act I scene 12) and the blinding of the horses (*Equus* Act II scene 34). After reading the scenes, students identified Artaud's influences as non-verbal signs of communication, the use of mime and gesture and violent shock. The practical task was to use lighting in the studio, masks and sound to create meaning in the scenes. The students studied the stage directions describing the massacre and began by choreographing the movements of both Spaniards and Indians. They experimented with ways of interpreting 'wave upon wave of Indians are slaughtered and rise again' while considering how the Spanish soldiers 'relentlessly hew their way through the ranks'. As the work progressed the students gained an understanding of the importance attached to physical movement and gesture when dialogue is removed. They added vocal cries instead of 'savage music' and punctuated the movements with a relentless drumbeat. Eventually the drumbeat formed a rhythm for the choreographed slaughter. Interestingly, they had discovered how rhythm could be utilized in enhancing dramatic meaning through their practical exploration of the stage directions.

The problem of the 'vast bloodstained cloth', which is dragged out of the sun, proved more challenging. After experimenting with red lighting and with material, the students settled upon a visually stunning effect. Long strips of white muslin were dragged across the space, their light texture enabling a rippling effect to be achieved, simultaneously a red light flooded the area creating a bloodstained effect on the cloth. The 'howling' of the Indians and the 'screams' that 'fill the theatre' were created vocally. The result confirmed the students' knowledge of Artaud's theories.

The 'blinding' scene from *Equus* was approached with more confidence. The students worked initially on the movement of horses. They experimented with head movements and, although they did not have the raised boots, explored ways of creating the stamping effect of horses in a stable. The students had the use of one horse mask made from wire and they used this in turn to investigate how head movements by the actor affected the mask. The choreography of the blinding had similarities to the work on the *Royal Hunt* scene with the 'great screaming' accompanying the action. The violence of Alan's mime and the physical reaction of the horses were reworked to achieve the maximum shock effect. The students realized that the sound alone did not convey the message; it could be dramatically effective only when the gesture was invested with meaning. The dialogue immediately before and after the mime was added to complete the work.

In discussion the students identified the similarities in the two scenes and debated which was the more 'shocking'. It is interesting to note that they perceived the *Equus* blinding as more horrific. Perhaps, they thought, because they could identify with this more readily than with the deaths of hundreds of Indians from an ancient civilization. Shaffer's stated aim that his plays had a certain feature in common, 'a reliance upon gesture to enshrine idea – without which there is no theatre' formed the starting point for analysis of the work.[16] The wider meaning of the scenes and the way gesture, mime and sound were applied to highlight them were discussed. Students displayed an understanding of the way the central themes of worship, belief and the destruction of ideology were represented in the metaphysical interpretation of the scenes.

The concept of Artaud's 'doubles' for the theatre was revisited and the links between his ideas on metaphysics related to the comparisons he found between the plague and the theatre. In discussing Artaud's theory of the theatre as a double for the plague, comparisons with the themes of the two plays were made in relation to this statement.

> If fundamental theatre is like the plague, this is not because it is contagious, but because like the plague it is a revelation, urging forward the exterior-isation of a latent undercurrent of cruelty through which all the perversity of which the mind is capable, whether in person or a nation, becomes localised . . . It unravels conflicts, liberates powers, releases potential and if these and the powers are dark, this is not the fault of the plague or theatre, but life.[17]

Students were able to make connections between the cruelty of a *person* in *Equus* and that of a *nation* in *The Royal Hunt of the Sun* and see how Artaud's thinking had influenced Shaffer's work.

The students' understanding of the relationship between theory and practice was demonstrated in their own creative explorations. A written assignment was also set to consolidate and test their knowledge and understanding. They were asked to select one of the extracts and to show

- how the *issue* was examined in the practical work
- how *meanings* were created 'metaphysically' in the scene
- what Shaffer's intended *purpose* was
- how the scenes indicated the *influence* of Artaud.

From this section of the work the students had

- understood the theory of metaphysics explained by Artaud
- realized practically how meanings are created through non-verbal means
- combined several elements of Artaud's theatre techniques

- explored the ideas of 'shock' and 'extreme' in Shaffer's plays
- made connections between Artaud's written theories and Shaffer's living theatre.

MIMES, RITES AND RITUALS: PRACTITIONER, PRACTICE AND TEXT

Artaud's ideas of ritual, as interpreted by Shaffer, formed the basis for a series of lessons. Here I was interested in consolidating the students' learning by exploring *how* a playwright has taken elements of the work of a practitioner and used them creatively in his own writing. Shaffer was especially concerned with the elements of mime and ritual advocated by Artaud; therefore scenes from the texts which highlight this influence were selected for practical examination.

In *The Theatre and its Double* Artaud describes the quasi-religious elements of Balinese theatre:

> And the most constantly fused correlations constantly fuse sight with sound, intellect with sensibility, a character's gesture with the evocation of a plants' movement through the aid of an instrumental cry. The sighs of a wind instrument prolong the vibrations of vocal chords so identically we do not know whether the voice itself is held or the senses which first assimilated that voice ... our theatre has never grasped this gestured metaphysics.[18]

He sought a parallel in Western culture and made links with holy ritual and the danger of ritual in Dionysian theatre, which explored the violence of humanity. This background information was given to the students before the practical work began.

The key scenes from the plays were 'The robing of Atahuallpa' (Act II scene 4) from *The Royal Hunt of the Sun* and 'Alan's worship and riding of *Equus*' (Act I scenes 20 and 21). Clearly there are many other examples of ritual in both plays. The students worked in two groups to analyse the use of ritual in the scenes and to work on practical realization of them as pieces of drama.

The group who worked on the robing of Atahuallpa moved in slow motion with fine attention to detail as they mimed the removal of the bloodstained clothes and replacing them with clean ones. The stage directions indicate that 'tiny golden cymbals and small bells' hang from the wrists of the Indians. The students found some small bells and tiny percussion cymbals to add to the work. Synchronizing the percussion sound so that it enhanced moments of the robing ceremony heightened the sense of ritual. The description continues with the adorning of the Inca god with a necklace, cloak and rings, accompanied by humming from the Indians. A vocal sound collage was added to the ritual. The group discussed how their use of ritual and non-verbal communication created meaning. They decided that by performing the whole ceremony in slow motion the symbolic cleansing away of the memory of the massacre was portrayed.

This ritual marked the beginning of a new relationship between Atahuallpa and Pizarro; 'a clean sheet' as one student articulated it.

By contrast the group working on the *Equus* scene discovered that Shaffer had not slavishly followed Artaud's concept of non-verbal ritual. The words in the ritualized preparations for the riding of Equus are a vital part of the ceremony.

> Dysart: Go on! ... Then?
> [*Pause*]
> Alan: Give sugar.
> Dysart: A lump of sugar?
> [*Alan returns to Nugget*]
> Alan: His Last Supper.
> Dysart: Last before what?
> Alan: Ha Ha.
> [*He kneels before the horse, palms upward and joined together*]
> Dysart: Do you say anything when you give it to him?
> Alan: Take my sins. Eat them for my sake ... He always does.[19]

The students' investigation of ritual style realized that Shaffer had used verbal as well as gestural form. He uses Dysart as a mediator to demonstrate Alan's ritual. The language Alan uses has religious resonance, reflecting the play's theme of the conflicting understanding of worship. As they worked on the scene it became clear that the juxtaposition of the psychiatrist's questioning with the re-enactment of the riding of Equus was a powerful dramatic device. They were unable to create the turning of the circle, as suggested in the stage directions: 'The horses standing on the circle begin to turn the square ... The effect, immediately, is of a statue being slowly turned round on a plinth.'[20] The students used the wire mask and shone an intense spotlight on the actor playing Nugget. Instead of the circle turning they placed the actor on a raised block and he turned slowly on the spot as Alan recited his ritualized catalogue of enemies:

> Dysart: Who are your foes?
> Alan: The Hosts of Hoover. The Hosts of Philco. The hosts of Pifco. The House of Remington and all its tribe![21]

The groups performed their work and a comparison of style revealed the differences and similarities in Shaffer's use of ritual. Students understood how repeated gesture could replace words while appreciating that spoken rituals were at the heart of many Western ceremonies. Thus Shaffer had employed the most appropriate ritual for each piece. His treatment of the robing ceremony in *The Royal Hunt of the Sun* with visual and aural communication was entirely in keeping with the overall style of the play. In *Equus* Alan mimed the 'sandals of majesty made of sack' and the 'manbit' but spoke ritualized lists of enemies. There were obvious comparisons in content and style: the robing of a 'god' in both extracts, the use of sound to accompany the mime and the marking of a change in relationship between central characters. This session focused the students on

- Artaud's response to Oriental theatre and his concept of ritual
- the way Shaffer employs ritual form in different ways
- creative exploration of ritual as a dramatic device
- how dramatic meaning can be communicated using ritual form.

ASSESSMENT AND RECORDING

In reaching conclusions about the quality of students' work in this scheme I was concerned with establishing clear criteria, then gathering and documenting evidence. The aim of the project was to enable students to learn about the theoretical work of a practitioner and to understand how a playwright made creative use of his ideas. I was also eager that students worked inventively, engaging in exploration whilst applying their knowledge of style and form. Students were assessed according to the following criteria:

- their understanding of the *theories and influences* of Artaud
- their ability to use Artaud's ideas in *interpretation of texts*
- their *understanding* of the *meanings* created and *issues* raised by the plays
- their *skill* in *creative exploration* of Shaffer's plays
- their proficiency in written *analysis* of both text and practitioner.

The project was designed with these assessment objectives in mind, therefore opportunities for assessment were written into the original scheme. A range of devices for recording information was used, including notes taken during sessions, written assignments following the practical workshops and video of practical activity. As drama work is usually collaborative it was important to have an opportunity to judge the individual's ideas and understanding as well as his or her ability to be involved in the group creative process.

In the initial workshop students demonstrated their understanding of Artaud's key theories from their research and showed their ability to work creatively. When working on Artaud's use of sound students explored the text creatively; there was some fascinating, atmospheric use of vocal sound. The students' work on their own interpretations of *The Royal Hunt of the Sun* produced excellent creative responses that demonstrated their understanding of the influence of Artaud. Their directing notes and evaluations gave a clear indication of proficiency in analysis and ability to reflect creatively. A student's directing notes for *The Royal Hunt of the Sun* included:

Incas are heralded by the tinkle of tiny cymbals. A deep yellow spotlight fades slowly up to reveal Atahuallpa standing regally on a raised platform. He wears a golden mask which glints in the light. Gradually, as if coming from a distance, the Inca chant grows louder. Atahuallpa turns his head suddenly, the light flashes on the golden mask. With a sudden explosion of sound the Incas flood the stage. The yellow light also floods the area.

Following the work on metaphysics students revealed their knowledge of the key issues in the plays. A student commented on the destruction of worship:

Alan and Pizarro had faith in their 'god'; they were persuaded to trade that worship for belief in a different ideology. Both were betrayed.

In a written analysis of the work on theatre as a double of the plague a student reflected on theme, issue and meaning:

I wonder who was the more cruel – Alan for blinding the horses or society for its refusal to tolerate individuality.

In investigating Shaffer's use of ritual students approached the text with some detailed knowledge of Artaud's theory. They used this knowledge effectively in their creative work.

Clearly this project did not attempt to include every aspect of the work of Artaud, nor did it analyse the two texts in great detail. The work was intended to enable students to experiment, explore, create and collaborate while gaining knowledge of both Shaffer and Artaud. It was my intention to develop the students' knowledge and to extend their creative vocabulary, encouraging them to seek new dramatic form. The project was successful; the students are confident about their understanding of Artaud and many have been inspired to read further. The drama work devised by the group subsequently reflected the way they had been influenced and their willingness to adapt and to experiment, finding their own methods of utilizing the ideas of a practitioner. The next generation will challenge tradition: and so it goes on!

NOTES

1 Cooper, S. and Mackey, S. (1995) *Theatre Studies: An Approach for Advanced Level* (Cheltenham: Stanley Thornes), p. 183.
2 Brook, P. (1968) *The Empty Space* (London: Methuen).
3 Artaud, A. (1995) *The Theatre and its Double* (London: Calder), p. 18.
4 See Stafford-Clark, M. (1997) *Letters to George* (London: Nick Hern).
5 Artaud, A. (1995) *op. cit.*, p. 91.
6 Artaud, A. (1995) ibid., p. 44.
7 Shaffer, P. (1991) Author's note in *The Royal Hunt of the Sun* (London: Longman), p. xiii.
8 Artaud, A. (1995) *op. cit.*, p. 62.
9 Artaud, A. (1995) *ibid.*, p. 27.
10 Shaffer, P. (1991) *The Royal Hunt of the Sun* (London: Longman), p. 11.
11 Shaffer, P. (1991) *ibid.*, p. 55.
12 Shaffer, P. (1991) *ibid.*, p. 78.
13 Artaud, A. (1995) *op. cit.*, p. 83.
14 Artaud, A. (1995) *ibid.*, p. 26.

15 Artaud, A. (1995) *ibid.*, p. 33.
16 Shaffer, P. (1991) *op. cit.*, p. iv.
17 Artaud, A. (1995) *op. cit.*, p. 21.
18 Artaud, A. (1995) *ibid.*, p. 38.
19 Shaffer, P. (1973) *Equus* (London: Penguin), pp. 71–2.
20 Shaffer, P. (1973) *ibid.*, p. 73.
21 Shaffer, P. (1973) *ibid.*, p. 73.

Chapter 10

The Proof of the Pudding:
Teaching Theatre Practitioners

Steve Waters

This chapter concerns itself with teaching the ideas of Konstantin Stanislavski, Bertolt Brecht and Antonin Artaud at a post-16 level, and offers classroom strategies designed for students who have hitherto progressed through experiences of drama rooted in improvisation. Such issues arise from teaching the A-Level qualification in theatre studies which, in the UK, has offered a paradigm for addressing the theory of twentieth-century theatre through setting such practitioners for study. Behind this discussion lies a premise rooted in my own teaching experience, namely that students at this level can develop fruitfully through a pedagogy that embraces the intellectual and historical context of theatre practice, areas that many will not have encountered so far in their drama education.

The value of tackling such paragons needs to be considered before focusing on the small print of delivering their ideas in lessons. Their canonical status can and should be contested, and arguments may be offered in favour of more recent figures such as Peter Brook or Robert LePage; certainly the prescribed list on offer is Eurocentric and unmistakably male; the focus is chiefly on writers and directors, with only Stanislavski offering an insider's view of acting. Teaching Brecht necessitates a familiarity with Marxism and/or German history between the First World War and the German Democratic Republic, while Artaud's prose is infamous for its obscurantism and his practice is thin and ambivalent; even Stanislavski's career offers reversals and confusions.

Nevertheless these practitioners mark out the terrain for much of contemporary theatre and serve as exemplars of J.L. Styan's useful tripartite schema – Stanislavski, at the sources of naturalism and realism, offers insights into an aesthetic that now governs the mainstream of theatre and media practice; Brecht provides a toolkit for radical approaches to theatre form and function; Artaud supplies an entry point into Surrealism and the avant-garde of physical theatre and performance art.[1] With these figures as orientation points, students will gain a working map of contemporary theatre and invaluable templates for their own creativities.

For teachers, the philosopher's stone lies in achieving an equilibrium between theory and practice, given certain inherent problems that come with this terrain. First, with regard to practical work, few textbooks offer satisfactory solutions, with only Stanislavski providing a body of *études* and workshops that can be deployed as such – and even here the link between the exercise and the aesthetic can prove elusive. Second, it is my experience that students are often resistant to intellectual work; yet it must be acknowledged that practice alone will not unlock the import of these figures – in addition there must be lectures, research and reading. Nevertheless, such unwelcome elements of study may be linked with the creative tasks that students enjoy, thereby balancing the three critical elements of concepts, careers and creation which I outline below. Through such a symbiosis of academic and practical work, students will assuredly become better actors, devisers and producers of theatre.

The three elements are useful in that they offer a clear route through the often labyrinthine corpus of work each artist has left behind:

- Concepts: this involves workshopping the key practical and performance ideas that emerge from the practitioner as a springboard for devised work or staging a text.
- Careers: this complements the ideas, by examining how they are evident in the practitioners' texts, manifestos or performances, and examining their material context.
- Creation: tests the absorption of what has been learned through original practical work on the students' part.

The following discussion takes each of the three practitioners and attempts to examine how this tripartite approach might work. For the purposes of this chapter I have decided to take each of the three practitioners in turn as a vehicle for one of the three approaches: the concepts of Stanislavski delivered in workshop form; the intellectual context and career of Brecht; how creative work might lead to Artaudian presentations. Clearly in the classroom, it would be important to integrate the three strategies when working on the figure specified; indeed the schema might offer a useful approach to any given theatre practitioner.

CONCEPTS: STANISLAVSKI

The concepts of the practitioners are rarely systematic and call for a good deal of condensation and synthesis on the part of the teacher; equally they do not fit neatly into most teaching syllabi, and prioritization is necessary. As a consequence any teaching course will inevitably become an interpretation of the scattered agenda of the practitioner, even if remaining true to their spirit. What engages the students is work that yields visible practical dividends, turning elusive concepts into tangible theatrical effects. With Brecht and Artaud, this will mean working with improvisation rooted in their techniques or staging their dramatic output, while acknowledging the meagreness of Artaud's 'plays' and the protean nature of Brecht's praxis.

Unlike the other two practitioners, however, Stanislavski's concepts are geared to the staging of plays rather than offering a model for the making of theatre. As a consequence teaching Stanislavski leads to the rehearsal process becoming the object of study, and the students' work on his concepts can realistically occur only through the process of realizing a text. The choice of text is open: Chekhov's works seem well suited to this exercise, enabling students to compare their process with the closely documented productions[2] that made the reputation of the Moscow Art Theatre. However, using contemporary texts illustrates the enduring worth of his practice; one that has worked well for me has been Caryl Churchill's *Fen*, with its usefully detachable scenes, range of finely sketched characters and coherent milieu.[3]

The Stanislavskian rehearsal process obviously demands a longer period of time than most teachers have available so the System must be used selectively, leading to a process that is an interpretation of Stanislavski's sometimes obscure terminology and methodology. Some of the key concepts that yield clear results are discussed below.

The given circumstances

The given circumstances notion, outlined in *An Actor Prepares*, is taken in its broadest sense to refer to the research process necessitated by attempting to faithfully render the world of the play. For Stanislavski, it was notoriously exhaustive; for teachers, it is often a matter of valorizing knowledge and pre-textual work as such. *Fen*, which arose out of Joint Stock's research into rural conditions in East Anglia, is well suited to such an approach. Working with students from Cambridgeshire, some living on the peripheries of the play's world, enabled a drawing together of the class's given knowledge of the landscape and the nature of life therein through 'imaging' work, descriptions and anecdote. Students with experience of the agricultural labour in the text helped build up a class improvisation of back-breaking potato picking, dramatized in its opening scene, which gradually acquired nuance, as elements of class, climate and interrelationship were weaved in, moving ever closer to the action of the play.

Such work blends into the concept of the 'Magic If',[4] as the students' imagination is gradually populated with the landmarks of the text. With the assimilation of the play itself, group hot-seatings and off-text work become possible. Creative writing between lessons in genres familiar to drama specialists deepens the students' possession of the text and character before a scene is enacted.

This imaginative process is then reinforced by close textual work, using neo-Stanislavskian director Mike Alfred's rehearsal questions[5] as a tool of analysis. What are the stated facts about the character? What do they say about themselves? What do they say about others? What do others say about them? This leads usefully to the creation of sociograms, whereby the inter-relationships between characters can be enacted physically in tableaux, noting the complexities of status, yielding further improvisations off text. By now the class are some way from the specifics of Stanislavski but still faithful to his intent. Comparing this process with his own, for instance when at work on Gorki's *The Lower Depths*, as it is documented in *My Life in Art*, and Benedetti's biography of Stanislavksi, can be revealing.[6]

Units of action, objectives and super-objectives

Close scrutiny of the text is the next stage, stressing Stanislavski's notion of the necessity of 'a period of study'[7] before moving into staging. His analytical vocabulary is razor sharp in its capacity for breaking the action down into usable fragments and drawing out subtext. It is a good argument for reading as a class, selecting a section of dialogue which is collectively parsed using Max Stafford-Clark's refinement of this process,[8] finding the right transitive verb for each line, the more concrete the better: push, prod, poke, sting, slash and so on. These actions are related to the overall objective of the character in the scene, and their super-objective for the play; any change in objective is marked by a new unit of action, with a title given that pins down its function. Then the verbs are externalized, leading to a violent stylization of the scene and revealing the line as the end-point of an inexpressible desire. The action is finally buried, but made subtly apparent in the performance of the language.

Emotion memory

This aspect of the System is the most controversial and, in the classroom, most risky; but it is central to an authentic actor-centred theatre. It is worth taking time to demonstrate the hypothesis, advanced by the French psychologist Ribot,[9] on which the technique is based – that the human organism carries traces of all its sensory experiences, which can be reawakened through closely evoking the conditions of the original experience in the memory. Students pair off and observe each other in the process of recalling three diametrically opposed situations and attendant emotions (e.g. fear, joy, rage); the observing student scrutinizes the face of the one who recollects and through noting the focus of the eyes or subtle inner signs tries to match the emotion to its outward, subtle manifestations. When this is discussed the majority of observers are correct in matching emotion to physical symptom, which helps establish the power of precise recollection as a means of reinvoking physical/affective states.

Stanislavski aimed for greater precision in emotional expression through actors consciously utilizing their own experiences to achieve the requisite empathy for their character's predicament, even if through analogy. An exercise that helps clarify this need for precision is an improvisation on 'the lost object', which demonstrates the shift from 'acting in general' to 'acting in particular'; the class play out a moment of realization following the loss of an unspecified object, and the subsequent search; coming out of the exercise they discuss its limitations – the vagueness and generality of their 'searching' is noted. The emotion is then built up through a series of 'pre-textual' scenes wherein the lost object is imagined, the scene of its arrival into their possession enacted, and its normal setting shaped in their imagination. The loss scene is replayed with a new clarity and conviction.

Applying this to the text is again partial, given the age of the students and the time restrictions of lessons. Their own plotting and tracking of the emotions in a scene or speech, linked to the work previously done on objectives is useful – then, alone, they can work on externalizing the feelings in the scene, acting them out on a neutral chair which serves as the embodiment of the person or force behind the sentiments. Thus they work on 'mapping' the movement of that impulse visually and viscerally, anticipating Stanislavski's later work on the Method of Physical Action (MOPA).[10]

Tempo-rhythm/Method of Physical Action

Observing Stanislavski's schema, the rehearsal process moves from psycho-technique to physicalization and attentiveness to externals. The MOPA reverses these priorities late in his writings, but was always implicit in his concern with rhythm in vocal and movement work. This area of the System receives less stress than it ought often with disastrous effects such as that American heresy the 'Method' and its products, repeatedly dubbed 'private acting' by Arthur Miller. Tempo-rhythm is usefully explored through walking, getting students to formulate calibrations of energy and pace from 'one', absolute inertia, to 'ten', hysterical panic. Then they determine their character's scale, and link it to moments in the text. When rehearsing a scene, tempos can be externally tapped out, as if by metronomes, modified as the action dictates. By temporary stylizing the tempo of the scene its logic emerges; this excessive clarity can then be effaced.

Space precludes the other work that might emerge from such a process of rehearsal; assessment can be in essay form, unifying the research on the career with the concepts filtered through the students' experience of them. It is important to accept that not all the techniques will achieve their desired ends and to be honest that any enactment of Stanislavski's ideas is already a version of them and not the unmediated practice of the man himself.

CAREERS: BERTOLT BRECHT

Work on concepts will be at the core of the study; however, only by considering the circumstances that gave rise to such aesthetic alignments will their rationale become clear. With Stanislavski, his innovations need relating to what precedes him, the fin-de-siècle reinvention of the theatre as art form and the revolutionary impact of an Ibsen or Chekhov on questions of acting or mise-en-scène. Equally, Artaud's extremities need rooting in the convulsions of European culture after the First World War, the antecedents for his ideas in Symbolism and his own psychic disturbances.

These observations are further amplified when tackling Brecht, whose attempt to reconnect theatre to the struggles of his times renders his concepts opaque without reference to social and political realities. Seeking a way into these complexities that does not flatten the students (or teacher) is difficult.

However, the judicious use of the familiar drama-in-education tool of teacher-in-role offers a point of entry – in this case the role being the different incarnations of Brecht himself. For a successful session it is important that the students are briefed as to the specifics of their encounter with your version of Brecht – the young Augsburg nihilist of 1922, philandering and ambitious, sensing Germany's apocalypse, drawn from his diaries; 1929 – the steadfast communist, intensifying his understanding of Epic theatre as a tool in the class struggle, creating *Lehrstuck*, moving into working-class venues, collaborating with Eisler; 1939 – the exile in Finland, observing war's onset, working on his great parable plays and a more supple, ironic mode of theatre; 1949 – directing in Berlin, founding his ensemble, clarifying his theories on acting and the role of socialist theatre. Brief question and answer sessions with follow-up research, even creative writing or improvisation, will make apparent the transformations within his career, whetting the students' appetite for more knowledge. This can be accompanied with staging extracts from plays that correspond to each section of his career, noting continuities and discontinuities throughout.

As regards concepts, Brecht is even less easy to translate into clear-cut classroom techniques given that he never documented a comprehensive systemic practical exploration of what his scattered aesthetic proclamations meant in practice (except usefully at the end of his essay 'The street scene').[11] So, again, addressing him practically often involves a good deal of extrapolation, drawing conclusions from the patterns of action in the plays and the scattered preferences made evident in Brecht's rehearsal practice (vividly documented by John Fuegi).[12] Ways into the Epic mode of theatre are therefore speculative but hopefully heuristic, but examining his practice in the following ways can help reinforce the linkage between career and concept.

Montage and irony

The notion of montage, a term included in Brecht's infamous list of techniques that Epic theatre employs in contradistinction to 'Dramatic' or Aristotelian theatre (reproduced in his notes on Mahagonny in Willett's edition *Brecht on Theatre*[13]) is a good starting point. Equally it is something that has permeated popular culture through the influential films of Brecht's cinematic apostolic successor, Jean-Luc Godard: see his *Alphaville* (1965) for example where music and image are often in counterpoint, where text ruptures the scene and where the performances are rooted in pastiche and a 'presentational' mode of action. Selective viewing of these films, combined with simple exercises that involve staging scenes in a manner that contradicts their apparent tenor reinforces such observations. This can lead into an interesting consideration of Brecht's A-effekts[14] and love of contradiction, for example, the opening scene of *The Threepenny Opera* or the *Ballad of Human Kindness* with their tonal dissonances; the mock grandeur of the verse in *Arturo Ui* or the playing of justice by Azdak in the *Caucasian Chalk Circle*.

To politicize this concept, students can be asked to shape a Boal-like image of a form[15] of injustice or oppression that they oppose, with the poster-like clarity that Brecht asks from the Gest[16] of the actor – the class tries to interpret it, with lucidity as a criterion for evaluation. The next stage is for the student to find a slogan that stands in tension with the image, creating an ironic distance that makes us re-view it, e.g. one student imaging a 'battery hen' apparently peering through wire, simply asked, 'Which comes first – the chicken or the egg?', a brilliant 'alienation' of both image and proverb. The students then move into groups in order to turn their images into 'dynamic machines' à la Boal, kinetic enactments of the oppression, against which they juxtapose a song which 'ironizes' the action, such as the hymn *We Plough the Fields and Scatter* set against the inhumane regimentations of an agri-business farm. Analysing the often devastating impact of such tableaux vivante we talk about the effect of distancing such uses of montage have, possibly relating it to the use of song in Brecht's plays (e.g. *The Ballad of the Soldier* in scene 2 of *Mother Courage* set against the looming fate of Swiss Cheese).

Epic form

The notion of a wide-ranging episodic narrative that moves forward through time, often unified through theme rather than 'dramatic unities', is a keystone of Brecht's dramaturgy, but which has its roots in previous Expressionist theatre, and particularly the notion of the Stationen-Drama,[17] evident in the plays of a Toller or Kaiser[18] and apparent in the structure of early Brecht pieces such as *Baal* (1922) and *Mann ist Mann* (1926). Students can explore through images this method of storytelling themselves, e.g. creating six tableaux dramatizing the 'Student's Tale', each working as an exemplary 'way-station' illustrating the students interaction with an oppressive social institution (the Family, the Peer Group, etc.). The clarity of stage images arising from this leads us into a discussion of Brecht's contentions about blocking as the sources of social meaning and the *gestus*. The tableaux can be developed into mime scenes that each are focused on a telling social action that unlocks the political meaning of the narrative – the family eating supper noisily until the entrance of the father, the students unified outside the school and then in competition within. In each case social meaning and external precision is emphasized over internal or psychological concerns.

This piece can be developed further by adding in A-effekts – sudden interruptions of factual text, ironic songs, scenes played two ways, direct addresses to audience and so on. As part of the analysis of his aesthetic development, this would tie in well with considering his early career and the cultural landscape of Expressionism. Such exercises help build bridges between the exploration of Brecht's career and the concepts within it, illuminating the study of his texts and carrying over into the students' own creative work.

CREATION: ARTAUD

The climax of studying each practitioner will be a sustained piece of performance work. For Stanislavski this would be the staging of a text;

however, with Brecht and Artaud, the devising of a piece inspired by the concepts explored during the course is a potent way of assessing their absorption. With Brecht it is a way of linking in the political intentions that give his plays such urgency with the students own concerns, with the formal devices rather than the political content prescribed, such as A-effekts, direct address, irony, montage and gestic acting. In the case of Artaud, outcomes will be even more unpredictable. Of all the three practitioners he is the most impressionistic and elusive when devising a practical aesthetic. Not only are his writings fragmentary and baroque, but also his practice is only intermittently documented and falls short of the expectations raised by his prose. This, therefore, is a licence for experimentation – the sort Joseph Chaikin pioneered in his 'Open Theatre'.[19]

Consequently this process comes late in the course, when the students feel assured of what constitutes theatre, thereby acting as a challenge and a provocation to them. Relating it back to the 'oeuvre', such as it is, will be about noting where the spirit rather than the letter of his theories has been observed.

Surrealist principles of creation

Clearly Surrealism was largely a movement in the visual arts, and is only one aspect of the type of theatre that Artaud dreamed of creating. Yet it forms one of the few models which the students can grasp and use practically, in its concern with gaining access to the id and building an irrational, profoundly subversive art with which to amaze the bourgeoisie. For the students it is about relearning the need for spontaneity and danger, relishing chance over pre-determination and the safety of the script, liberating improvisation from the soapy conventionality. This can be demonstrated initially by writing tasks through 'automatic writing', a process deployed by the Surrealist group to create material that bypasses the censors of the ego and super-ego. Students write down whatever comes into their head while collectively counting aloud to 100, then formally read out their 'findings' as if lecturers, valuing the random much as the Surrealists did in their dream workshops.

This process can be made more theatrical by creating instant performances using an exercise created by Performance Artists' *The People Show*[20] the class write a series of random actions as stage directions, precisely but impersonally described on paper, ripped into strips and placed in four piles on the floor at the front of a performance space. Four volunteers leave the room and are briefed that they will re-enter, seat themselves in four provided chairs to the rear of the space and, without any consultation pick up one of the pieces of paper and perform the action therein as many times as they feel is appropriate, not interacting with their partners but aware of them. Music is added in, either played on a piano by a student facing away from the space or on CD. The performers signal the end of the piece by all sitting on the four chairs to the rear. The result is often hilarious, a piece of instant choreography whose only meaning is imposed by the audience, pure non-verbal theatre analogous to what Artaud celebrated in his writings on the Balinese dancers and the type of anarchic comedy he admired in the Marx Brothers' films.[21]

Physical improvisations

This work alludes to the type of theatre implicit in Artaud's essay 'Affective athleticism' and his celebration of Jean-Louis Barrault's performance of *Autour d'une Mère*, but also tries to respond to the type of performance figured forth in his notion of cruelty and the manifestos.[22] Breathing is a good place to start, with the class exploring different intensities, noting how it creates transformations in their organisms – shallow panicky breathing, slow deep breathing, vibrato breathing, aggressive breathing – then creating sound-collages built out of breath: the narrative of a river's journey to the sea, a condensed biography (here Beckett's notorious *Breath*[23] can be referred to) and so on. Giving the students abstract images that they can enact through breathing works as well to increase their ability to communicate physically. This leads on to screaming work, taking as its premise Artaud's dictum that 'no one knows how to scream any more, particularly actors'.[24] Finding a scale of screams and creating musique concrete through screams alone is fun but exhausting and necessarily short lived.

The next step is to play with words as things, addressing his desire for incantatory language, giving to words 'the significance they have in dreams'[25] – students pick words which, as in a Grotowski workshop,[26] are repeated until they become physical presences, broken into syllables, letters, unlearned, projected like arrows, excreted like globules of oil. This can lead to non-verbal whole-class improvisations, where through sound and gesture impossible stories are created – the birth of the universe, plate tectonics – narratives with non-human scales, created together without discussion or a sense of audience. Afterwards the students reflect on how they opened themselves up to the other performers, how they found themselves utilizing their bodies in novel ways and how they created a non-intellectual yet at the same time imaginary theatre by such means. Following this with staging Artaud's text *A Spurt of Blood*[27] is valuable, with action such as the collapsing of the heavens and a scale that moves from cosmic tumult to the descent of a scarab beetle played 'with nauseating slowness'.

Brook/Marowitz

A more coherent practice is documented by David Williams, who records the work of Peter Brook and Charles Marowitz during their 'Cruelty' season at the London Academy of Music and Dramatic Art (LAMDA), with records of their exercises to achieve 'discontinuity' in performance.[28] While these have a questionable link to Artaud's specific work they offer another interpretation. One such workshop called 'Essences' is a good model for creating non-naturalistic, physicalized theatre; the students devise a brief, somewhat melodramatic scene, the more banal the better (a husband discovers his wife with a lover, a drunken child returns home to a confrontation with anguished parents, and so on). They then divide it into sections, in which each character has only one word through which to express their action or intervention. This version then becomes completely non-verbal: they have to find a rhythm, a sound, a gesture only with which to communicate; thus the action is stripped to a universal core and what it loses in narrative clarity it gains in theatrical impact. Ted Hughes' onomatopoeic language for Brook's *Orghast* might be invoked at this point.[29]

Devising from scratch

This will be a very different process from the work the students may have carried out with Brecht, and that is all to the good. Kick-starting it with fragments of a text is useful if heretical, but then Artaud often worked with or around plays, despite his injunctions against 'masterpieces'; a good example is Heiner Müller's *Hamletmachine*, six pages long, staged by Robert Wilson, its language raw and poetic, its action baffling in the extremes it demands.[30] Therefore it is ideal for this work. A page or less often suffices to push the students into action, although equally useful are texts such as *Ubu Rex* or *The Cenci*,[31] which have immediate application to his ideas. The terms for the performance are as follows:

- Space is a participant: the students will find a non-theatrical environment in which to work or rethink their usual performance spaces.
- The rituals of performance will be reinvented; often the piece will be geared to a small invited audience, whose normal impulses and actions will be short-circuited by it.
- What language there is will not be linked to character or take the form of dialogue.
- Theatrical elements will be meaningful in themselves; e.g. if light is used it will not be to illustrate but to act on the audience; similarly soundtracks will be released from their normal functions.
- The work will be intense – not necessarily shocking but certainly risky – obviously health and safety and local college cultural norms will be relevant here!

The outcome is nearly always thrilling work, with rehearsal time being used for experiment and strategy, rather than polishing and psychological exploration.

CONCLUSION

The discussion above is rooted in a very particular experience of teaching and one that did not always achieve the ends attached to it in this chapter; each lesson and attempt at sharing such ideas with a fresh group of students will necessitate a modification of the ideas, new versions, possibly new orthodoxies. Teachers also need no reminders that the suspiciously neat ideas I have formulated above are the hard-won outcomes of the intermittent chaos of teaching during the 1990s and therefore are to be approached with caution. However, what I feel can be confidently stated is that, after practical and intellectual encounters with these practitioners, allowing for inevitable resistances, confusions, loyalties and so on, the students always emerge intellectually and creatively supple, more literate about theatre and excited about learning in order to create, rather than relying solely on their own experiential repertoire. Certainly they are well prepared for the sorts of experiences and issues awaiting them on higher education courses in this area, if they seek further progression, not only in terms of knowledge but also in the manner in which they have learned. However, more importantly, they find themselves extended in their creativity through encountering the work of those who came before them.

NOTES

1 Styan, J.L. (1981) *Modern Drama in Theory and Practice*, vols 1–3: *Realism and Naturalism, Symbolism and Surrealism* and *Epic and Expressionist Theatre* (Cambridge: Cambridge University Press).
2 For an accessible introductory description of these productions see Styan, J.L. (1981) *Modern Drama in Theory and Practice: Realism and Naturalism, vol. 1* (Cambridge: Cambridge University Press), pp. 70–80.
3 See Churchill, C. (1990) *Plays Two* (London: Methuen).
4 The 'magic if' is central to Stanislavski's method. In this, actors are asked to explore how they would feel in a particular (or given) circumstance, and to apply this insight to acting a role. The concept is explained in detail in Stanislavski, K. (1937) *op cit.*, pp. 244–51.
5 Mike Alfred's technique of questioning was revealed in a workshop with Cambridge Theatre Company, 1994.
6 Stanislavski, K. (1980) *My Life in Art* (London: Methuen); Benedetti, J. (1988) *Stanislavski: A Biography* (London: Methuen).
7 The 'period of study' is full explored in Stanislavski, K. (1981) *Creating a Role* (trans. E. Hapgood) (London: Methuen), pp. 3–34.
8 For a lively discussion of the rehearsal process, including ways in which Max Stafford-Clark has built on Stanislavski's work, see Stafford-Clark, M. (1997) *Letters to George* (London: Nick Hern), especially pp. 66–73.
9 Jean Benedetti gives a succinct explanation of the influence of Ribot's psychological works in Benedetti, J. (1982) *Stanislavski: An Introduction* (London: Methuen), pp. 31–2.
10 Students may find the summary of MOPA useful in Benedetti, J. (1982) *ibid.*, pp. 63–70.
11 Willett, J. (1964) 'The modern theatre is the epic theatre', in J. Willet, *Brecht on Theatre: The Development of an Aesthetic* (New York: Hill and Wang), pp. 33–42.
12 Fuegi, J. (1987) *Bertolt Brecht: Chaos According to Plan* (Cambridge: Cambridge University Press), pp. 132–86.
13 See Willett, J. (1964) *Brecht on Theatre: The Development of an Aesthetic* (New York: Hill and Wang), pp. 33–42.
14 Brecht's A-effekts is associated with a particular dramatic and performance style, in which the audience is challenged to question bourgeois ideas and values. For a fuller description see Willett, J. (1964) *ibid.*, pp. 136–40.
15 Boal is famous for his participatory political theatre, where spectators are invited to create images to explore issues of oppression. See Boal, A. (1985) *Theatre of the Oppressed* (New York: Theatre Communications Group), pp. 120–56.

16 Brecht's use of the term 'Gest' and 'gestic acting' describe an actor's definite social attitude which is demonstrated in his or her actions or words. See Willett, J. (1964) *ibid.*, pp. 178–201, and Styan, J.L. (1981), *op. cit.*, vol. 3, pp. 139–44.

17 Expressionist dramatists, particularly Toller and Kaiser, developed the idea of the Stationen-Drama, a form of morality play, made up of seven scenes or 'stations'. See Styan, J.L. (1981) *ibid.*, pp. 49–50.

18 For plays by Ernst Toller and Georg Kaiser, see Schurer, E. (ed.) (1997) *German Expressionist Plays* (London: Continuum).

19 Blumenthal, E. (1984) *Joseph Chaikin* (Cambridge: Cambridge University Press).

20 This approach to working was revealed in the workshop I participated in, *The People Show*, by the legendary Performance Artists, at the Royal Court Theatre, London, in 1996.

21 See Artaud, A. (1995) *The Theatre and its Double* (London: Calder), pp. 32–49.

22 Artaud, A. (1995) 'Affective athleticism', in A. Artaud *The Theatre and its Double* (London: Calder), pp. 88–95.

23 Beckett, S. (1984) *Breath*, in *Collected Shorter Plays of Samuel Beckett* (London: Faber & Faber), pp. 209–12.

24 Artaud, A. (1995) *op. cit.*, p. 95.

25 Artaud, A. (1995) *ibid*, p. 72.

26 Grotowski recognized the ways in which actors 'speak' through the body as well as with words. For a description of his workshop exercises, see Grotowski, J. (1968) *Towards a Poor Theatre* (London: Methuen), pp. 185–92.

27 Artaud, A. (1988) *A Spurt of Blood*, in S. Sontag (ed.) *Antonin Arnaud: Selected Writings* (Berkeley, CA: University of California Press), pp. 72–6.

28 Williams, D. (1991) *Peter Brook: A Theatrical Casebook* (London: Methuen), pp. 28–52.

29 Smith, O.C.H. (1972) *Orghast at Persepolis* (London: Eyre Methuen).

30 Muller, H. (1995) *Hamletmachine*, in *Theatremachine* (London: Faber & Faber), pp. 85–94.

31 Jarry, A. (1995) *Ubu Rex*, in *The Ubu Plays* (trans. C. Connolly and S. Watson Taylor) (London: Methuen), pp. 17–74; Artaud, A. (1969) *The Cenci* (trans. S. Watson Taylor) (London: Calder and Boyars).

Chapter 11

Languages of the Stage:
A Critical Framework for Analysing *and*
Creating Performance

Sharon Grady

[E]very reception of a work of art is both an interpretation and a performance of it, because in every reception the work takes on a fresh perspective.[1]

Learning how to interpret and analyse theatrical events is a critical component in the education of students of theatre. However, there is very little available to guide teachers who are struggling to incorporate this important element in their mandate to include all aspects of making, performing and responding in the subject of drama. How *are* teachers supposed to help students become more responsive to theatrical events? What skills do students need in order to openly receive and actively interpret a variety of performance texts as Umberto Eco suggests above?

A few authors have offered systematic ways to encourage students to observe more carefully performative events. For example, David Hornbrook outlined a modified framework for performance analysis based on semiotics, a system of knowledge that studies 'signs' and how they communicate.[2] Similarly, Dan Urian offers an exhaustive 'spectators' guide' that draws heavily from semiotics but also makes reference to aesthetic theory and theatre criticism.[3] Simon Cooper and Sally Mackey suggest a performance analysis 'web' that features a careful reading of the theatrical 'sign system' available in any given performance.[4] However, Jane Gangi has questioned the almost exclusive use of semiotics and contends that the 'watching and understanding of drama must include more than one approach' to interpretation.[5]

I would like to take up Gangi's challenge and argue that students should be given a range of interpretative tools *and* creative opportunities as a way to better understand the connection between making and responding. In this regard, the notion of interpretation and critique is seen to be inextricably linked to the act of creation. In this chapter, I propose a critical framework that encourages students to embrace a broader definition of 'performance' along with a more complex understanding of how performative events 'communicate' as a way for teachers to help their students develop critical powers *and* practical skills.

The framework I describe was initially developed for a new university level course serving incoming theatre and dance students, entitled Languages of the Stage (LOS).[6] In 1996 I taught the inaugural version of the course, which included 148 undergraduate students who were a mix of theatre and dance majors. By the end of the course, students were expected to be able to

- observe fully and precisely
- accurately identify and vividly articulate the connections between analysis and interpretation
- dynamically discuss the relationship between language, metaphor, meaning, context, and performative practice
- demonstrate a basic knowledge of the 'vocabularies' of the verbal, visual and kinaesthetic languages of the stage
- thoughtfully and creatively utilize these languages as analytical and interpretative tools for any given performative event as observers or as creators.

I have subsequently conducted workshops with teachers at the secondary level to explore how this basic framework can be introduced to advanced students as a way to broaden their understandings of how meaning is created in artistic events. In this chapter, I outline the basic LOS framework and its theoretical underpinnings. I then illustrate how this framework informed student responses to a *kathakali* dance drama and a university production of Caryl Churchill's *Vinegar Tom*. In conclusion, I discuss the outcomes and benefits of the LOS framework. In particular, I consider how this framework can help teachers introduce students to a wider variety of performative genres and aesthetic understandings.

CONFRONTING THE UNKNOWN

The main ballroom in the University of Texas Student Union is throbbing with the sound of Indian drums. An elaborately costumed *kathakali* actor with a vibrantly expressive green face stomps his feet and gestures purposefully (see Figure 11.1). Two singers emotionally render the story in a blend of Malayalam and ancient Sanskrit on the stage left side. The *chenda* drummer carefully watches the dancer's movements and punctuates his emotions and gestures while a singer with a bell-metal gong hypnotically tracks the rhythm or *tala*. Wide-eyed theatre and dance students with pens and notebooks poised occasionally shoot me troubled looks as they try to make sense of what is going on. A feast of theatrical languages is at play in this rare US tour of dance-drama by a South Indian *kathakali* troupe. When read against the ballroom's wagon wheel chandeliers and Wild West motifs of cactus and bucking broncos, the whole event seems slightly surreal. How are the students supposed to make meaning of it all?

Figure 11.1   Daksha and his wife Prasuti discuss their plans for the child they have just discovered by the river in *Daksha Yaga*

This performative event represented the first of many experiments in exploring the relationship between theory and practice through the LOS framework. Understanding the theatrical 'languages' used to communicate meanings in *any* piece of theatre is a complicated venture. When the opportunity arose, I wondered how responding to a *kathakali* dance drama as one of our first assignments might powerfully illustrate the ways in which the 'languages of the stage' operate, especially since many of the 'signs' in question (make-up, costume, hand gestures and music) were so far removed from the students' previous experiences of performance.

It was a huge risk. The week before the *kathakali* performance, I found myself huddled over my computer at 2 a.m. creating a handout entitled 'How to get the most out of your *kathakali* experience'. 'Work at remaining open,' I wrote, 'even when you can't quite follow what is going on. Constantly ask yourself questions about the performers' bodies, facial expressions, their relationship to other characters, the percussive instruments, the staging, the audience.' I began worrying that the particular cultural and theatrical codes unique to this genre would overwhelm the students. Yet, if they could focus their attention on responding to the performance's verbal, visual, and kinaesthetic elements as well as reflect on their assumptions about what 'theatre' is, we might be able to have a useful dialogue about how audiences begin to make meaning.

How did we arrive at this point? The LOS framework unfolded gradually over a series of five units. The first unit grappled with basic questions about language and alternately examined and unsettled various theories of communication. The second unit explored how self-consciously created 'sign-systems' help produce meaning in general and in performance events in particular. The third unit gave us the opportunity to consider the creative role of the audience in the meaning-making process and puzzle over why various spectators often disagree over meanings. The fourth unit challenged us to rethink and broaden our definitions of what constitutes a performative event. The fifth unit introduced students to culturally diverse understandings of performance.[7] Below is a brief overview of the five main units.

THE LOS FRAMEWORK

How does language work?

Students embarked on their LOS experience by first discussing how language works as a system of communication. However, theories concerning exactly how communication operates are highly contested. Basic communication models often depend on a linear set of sender–receiver understandings which assume that a sender's message reaches a receiver intact.[8] If this 'transmission' theory is true, then communicating should be easy and misunderstandings would never happen.

To test this theory, students were asked to literalize the transmission concept through an activity called 'Visual Telephone'. A group of ten volunteers were asked to stand in a line one behind the other. The last person in the line was given a mimed symbol by the leader and was instructed to tap the person in front of them on the shoulder who would turn, 'receive' the symbol, and then pass it on. Progressively, the symbol is passed all the way down the line until the first person in the line receives it. That person shares what they 'received' with the whole group. The leader then shows the symbol that was sent. Typically, the symbol changes significantly as it is passed down the line. Observers had many opinions about exactly where it started to change and why. This exercise served as an excellent way to demonstrate the problems with the 'transmission' model of communication and laid important ground work for future discussions about the active role of the 'receiver' in the communication process. Since this exercise focused on visual language, it also illustrated that verbal language is only one mode of communicating.

We established at the outset that performative events communicate various meanings to audiences through a variety of different 'languages' including visual languages (sets, costumes, lights, etc.), verbal/aural languages (words spoken by performers, music, etc.) and kinaesthetic languages (dynamic movement of the body, gesture, etc.). From an audience's perspective, visual and verbal languages are the primary ways of taking in information and making meaning of a performative event although other sensory and kinaesthetic considerations may come into play depending on the performance and context. Creators of performance, however, employ many language systems to realize their artistic purposes.[9] But exactly how do audiences begin to make sense of these various languages?

What's the deal with 'signs'?

In the next unit, the students were introduced to the basic element of meaning in any language system, the 'sign'. Signs are composed of two parts: a physical manifestation – such as the letters that make up the word 't-r-e-e' – and the concept that is conjured up in the mind – such as the category of plant life we know as 'tree'. Now depending on our different backgrounds, where we grew up or our relationship to nature, each of us may conjure up a different sort of tree. One may think of a massive oak while another may see a Christmas tree, while yet another may envision a tiny little cherry tree that never quite grew the way Mother wanted it to in the back garden.

Making sense of 'signs' becomes really interesting when we are confronted with several of them at the same time. Our first impulse is to conjure up meanings for the individual objects which are necessarily modified when examined in relationship to other available signs. For example, the strategic placement of an almost dead tree centre stage in Beckett's *Waiting for Godot* may at first conjure up mental images of trees in general. An audience member may think: 'That's a tree on stage. It's supposed to make me think about a real tree; but because of their words, actions, and costumes it also makes me think about hopelessness and despair and the miserable state of the human condition.' Performance events strategically take advantage of the fact that signs are not always what they initially seem to be. Instead, signs are loaded and their meanings are slippery depending on their context and relationship to other signs.

To understand more fully the relationship between signs and contexts, students created two different 'texts' by putting the physical form of a sign of their choosing in two different contexts to see what different meanings and interpretations they might conjure. Students were given several options for this exploration, including creating a two-frame drawing, painting or collage; creating a two-page 'thick' description, or showing an actual 'sign' in two different 15-second live action contexts which involved acting or dance in some way. Observers were encouraged to discuss the meanings made available in each context through careful description and analysis of the signs in question before leaping to interpretation. The student work on this project was especially strong and included a range of responses such as a blanket alternately covering a body and then holding a baby; a bible placed by a church and then by a judge, a rose placed on a grave and then given to a lover, a gun gazed at in a museum and then placed in an actor's mouth. As students viewed each other's work, they were encouraged to discuss the ways in which signs can transform and communicate in different ways depending on the other signs that make up a particular 'text'.[10]

What about all of these different interpretations?

After this exercise, students were asked to account for the fact that there were several different interpretations of the 'texts' created in the above exercise. Discussion centred on the fact that their perceptions are heavily influenced by their individual differences. Those differences include but are not limited to race, class, gender, sexual orientation and religion, as well as subculture affiliation, cognitive style, tolerance of ambiguity and interests. Students were asked to consider these possible 'identity markers' and reflect in their journals on how their own affiliations and abilities might affect their responses to performative work.[11]

Students also puzzled over the fact that there are often shared interpretations of events which prompted a discussion of the signs or codes that have specific meanings for members of specific groups. Shared meanings are often culturally or contextually generated. Many performative events include specific cultural and theatrical codes that need to be learned. Cultural codes are the general guidelines that govern how a society operates and include a variety of facets such as language, dress, manners, the arts, social strata, and education. Knowledge of these codes affects the extent to which an audience member is able to fully interpret a particular kind of cultural performance. Likewise, particular theatrical events may contain their own codes and accepted conventions such as the Christmas pantomime. The willing suspension of disbelief, the use of a curtain, and the understanding that the audience watches silently are all theatrical codes that govern much of Western performance. It was agreed that this represented a rather limited view of what constitutes theatre, which led us to explore how we define 'performance'.[12]

So, what is performance?

In this unit, we began to broaden our understandings of what constitutes performance. Are the Tony Awards, which mark excellence in live theatre with an emphasis on Broadway, a kind of performance? Do the rituals involved in the Mexican observance of the *Day of the Dead (Dia de los Muertos)* qualify as a performative event? Could the opening ceremony of the 1996 Olympic Games held in Atlanta, Georgia, be considered performative? What about the 1996 Democratic Convention – a political gathering of delegates from the 50 US states – is that a performative event? What about a football game that features a half-time show?

These questions excited a good deal of discussion as we pondered what makes something a performative event. Theatre historian Oscar Brockett states simply that the basic element of theatre is 'someone performing something for someone else'.[13] Performance theorist Richard Schechner asserts that a central component of performance is the notion of 'restored behaviour' – meaning that there is a rehearsed or planned quality to performance events.[14] Given these definitions, the scope of what can be considered a performative event suddenly multiplies.

For Schechner, theatre is only one node or segment on a continuum of performance that includes animal rituals (including humans), performances in everyday life (greetings, family scenes, professional roles, etc.), play, sports, theatre, dance, ceremonies, rites and politics.[15] On closer examination, he posits that there are several things these performances share:

- a special ordering of time
- a special value attached to objects
- non-productivity in terms of goods
- agreed upon rules
- often occurring in special places that are set aside or constructed for specific performance activities.[16]

As students closely examined and compared events that were not 'traditionally' or 'immediately' thought of as performance, they were encouraged to try to identify these five areas in more detail.

Instead of defaulting to various historical accounts of the origin of theatre and dance, the LOS framework embraces a theory of performance that views theatre, dance and music as part of a holistic continuum with broader connections to ritual, play, games, politics, and sports. This expansive definition led us to challenge our received Eurocentric understandings of performance genres.

What about other understandings of performance?

In the final unit, students were asked to consider how Eurocentric definitions of what constitutes art often limit an understanding of the role and place of performance in an intercultural world. Students were encouraged to look beyond their culturally determined lenses of artistic 'acceptability' and be open to the range of cultural expression represented on the stages of the world. By viewing slides and video clips of *kathakali, noh, kabuki, butoh* and African dance, students began to actively identify how the 'languages of the stage' operated in each form. Instead of fetishizing the foreign 'other' through 'cultural tourism' or strip-mining various cultural traditions or genres for their exotic flavour (as Peter Brook has been accused of), students were encouraged to better understand different culturally situated codes and contexts of the performances in question.

In any performance, narratives, codes and conventions easily read by those enculturated to them may be opaque to those not so enculturated. As students became more interested in learning and 'trying on' other culturally specific performance forms, we discussed how we might be able to honour and blend genres respectfully. We continually asked how we might develop strategies for presentation and representation which engage an audience in the examination of 'difference' without stereotyping, essentializing, romanticizing the 'other'? Sita Brahmachari argues that to mitigate cultural tourism, teachers need to avoid treating other cultural genres as decorative 'exotica' but instead practise an interculturalism that is a 'dialectic of exchanges of civilities between cultures'.[17]

Following Oscar Brockett's advice to critics, students were encouraged to develop the following qualities: a sensitivity to feelings, images, and ideas; an openness to becoming as well acquainted as possible with a wide range of performance events; a willingness to explore various texts and production processes; tolerance for innovation and unknown cultural forms; an awareness of prejudices and values; greater clarity when expressing opinions and judgements.[18] These issues were addressed throughout the course by the students, who kept detailed and focused journals.

This intensive introduction was difficult yet rewarding in terms of student outcomes which are outlined below. However, the vexing problem of what to have students read was never completely solved. At this time, there is no single text that comprehensively deals with the issues outlined in the above framework. Finding ways to make these complex ideas understandable and accessible is desperately needed for the future education of students of performance.

APPLYING THE FRAMEWORK

Throughout the course, students were encouraged to apply the framework to a variety of performance events including a *kathakali* performance by the Kerala Kalamandalum Troupe from India, *Animal Magnetism* performed by Mabou Mines, university productions of *The Killing Game* by Ionesco, *Vinegar Tom* by Caryl Churchill, a theatre for youth performance of *In My Grandmother's Purse* by Lisa Bass, and a new musical entitled *Branson or Bust* by Chan Chandler and Steve Adams as well as Pina Bausch's new dance/theatre piece *Nur Du*. A review of two performance experiences, one at the beginning of the course and one at the end of the course, illuminates how this framework helped students progress in their own understandings of how performative events make 'meaning'. The following overview of a *kathakali* performance and a college production of *Vinegar Tom* demonstrates how the theoretical framework helped students to carefully analyse these performances and formulate their responses. Subsequent active learning strategies gave them the opportunity to apply their responses to their own creative work.

Preparing for a *kathakali* experience

Kathakali is an elaborate form of dance drama from Kerala, South India. Performers enact stories from the Hindu epics through the use of intricate costumes, stylized face make-up and complex hand gestures (*mudras*). The 'text' is provided by singers as the dancers enact parables in which gods, demons, heroes, and villains battle over issues such as honour and duty. *Kathakali* as a performative genre has had a profound influence on Western theatre theorists and practitioners such as Jerzy Grotowski, Richard Schechner and Ariane Mnouchkine. We were extremely fortunate to see premier *kathakali* artists from the Kerala Kalamandalam performing on this special North American tour.

Students were initially introduced to *kathakali* through lecture materials that included music, slides and video. They were also asked to read a chapter about *kathakali* from *Indian Theatre* by Farley Richmond, Darius Swann and Phillip Zarrilli.[19] Because this was the first time many of the students had encountered any non-Western theatre forms, time was spent discussing specific cultural and theatrical codes and how the aesthetic experience is conceived in Indian theatre. According to the *Natyashastra* (the Indian book of aesthetic theory equivalent in importance to Aristotle's *Poetics*), the experience of the spectator at a performance is similar to tasting and eating fine foods. The performers should enact and literalize the various *bhavas* (feelings or emotional states) of their characters so completely that the audience should be able to 'taste' those sentiments – that is, the corresponding emotional states are evoked in the spectator.

This is done through the actor's acting ability or *abhinaya*, which literally means 'coming toward'. The idea is that the actor literally brings a performance to the spectators. Students were charged with identifying ways in which *kathakali* performers 'brought' their characters and the story to the audience. They were also charged with watching for the nine sentiments or emotional states (*bhavas*) the actors evoke in Indian performance which include love, anger, sorrow, fear, mirth, heroic energy, disgust, surprise and peace.

Students were then introduced to the specific performance codes governing *kathakali* including an overview of the specific make-up types (for example, a green face indicates a king, heroic or divine character; a red beard indicates an extremely evil character); conventions (such as men playing female roles) and use of codified gestures, simple props that transform (a wooden stool can be a throne, tree, extension of the body and so on) and music. They were also given a synopsis of the play they would see, *Daksha Yaga*, adapted from David Bolland's *A Guide to Kathakali*.[20] The central action in the play revolves around Daksha, a demi-god who is the son of Brahma the creator, and his wife, Prasuti, who adopt a child they discover in a conch shell by the river. They name the child Sati and later agree for her to marry the god Siva. After the marriage, Daksha treats Siva with contempt. On an auspicious occasion Daksha performs a *yaga*, a sacrificial fire, but declares that it will not honour Siva. Sati returns to witness the *yaga* and see her family but Daksha rebukes her and sends her away. Angered, Sati returns to Siva and insists that Daksha be punished. Siva sends two demons to destroy Daksha. Just as they are about to behead him, Brahma intervenes and asks Siva to forgive Daksha. Siva relents but replaces Daksha's head with the head of the first available thing, which is a goat. A poignant scene of repentance ends the play as Daksha is forgiven by Siva.

To help frame their experience, students were given a question guide based on several discussion topics developed throughout the LOS framework. This discussion guide included the following sets of questions to aid students in identifying the sign-systems in which meanings were being made available to them:

Performers

What can you say about each performer's
- Body position: stance, weight distribution, shape?
- Gesture: use of hands, fingers, position of arms?
- Facial expression: use of eyes, facial muscles, mouth?
- Movement: speed, use of body parts, locus of initiation of movement, quality of movement?
- Make-up: colour, accessories, hair, framing?
- Interactions: with other characters? Focus?

Setting

What can you say about the following:
- Space: framing of stage area, audience area?
- Set: What constitutes the set? How is the curtain used?
- How does the stool transform? How is the lamp integrated?
- Costumes: colour, shape, accessories, layers, nails, bells?
- Props: look and function of miscellaneous props?
- Lighting: use of lighting?

Music/sound

What can you say about
- Rhythm?
- Intensity?
- Pitch?
- Orderliness?
- Tone?
- Speed?
- Shape?

Audience

What can you say about
- Audience interactions?
- Noise?
- Reactions?
- Engagement?

Framing

What can you say about framing strategies:
- Before the event: public publicity, in class discussion/or readings?
- At the event: lobby displays? Introductory remarks? Programme?

Responding to the *kathakali* experience

At the performance, it was clear that some students were extremely frustrated over the fact that the performance was not easily or readily accessible to them. In an attempt to disarm any potential hostility, I began the next class session with a quote about negative reactions to encounters with new work. An overhead projection with background music from a *kathakali* play greeted the students as they filed into the classroom the next day: 'New ideas can be threatening, and they often provoke a negative reaction' the overhead stated. 'For example, when Stravinsky first presented his *Rite of Spring* ballet with its unusual harmonies and "primitive" rhythms, he was met with a rioting audience'. We discussed initial responses to Samuel Beckett's *Waiting for Godot* and the fact that audiences complained bitterly because there was no overt plot and, therefore, no real point! We also briefly touched on the confused responses to Ionesco's *Bald Soprano* when it first premiered. I asked students to consider these issues and to address them in their journals by grappling with the following questions: Why do people often react negatively to new ideas or forms? What can artists do about it? What advice would you give an audience seeing a new form for the first time?

After extensive discussion about their responses to the *kathakali* experience and an opportunity to talk to one of the *kathakali* performers in class, I asked the students to use their insights as the basis of an adaptation assignment. After choosing one scene from *Daksha Yaga*, each student was charged with identifying the major emotions portrayed in the scene, and creating a realistic treatment of the scene. For example, one scene that resonated for many students was Sati's return to her father's house for the *yaga* and her confusion and anger over how her father treated her. How parents sometimes deal with their adult children – many of whom are still treated as if they were children – became a focus point in several of their soap opera-style adaptations. Overall, their treatments brought together what they observed in the performance (including the performers' interactions, emotions displayed, gestures and musical accompaniment) as well as their own interpretation and analysis. An important goal for this assignment was to raise issues about how one goes about translating one culturally based form of dance or drama into another form. As our discussions developed, we began considering the role of context in the process. By examining a clip of Peter Brook's *Mahabharata* and the strong critique levelled at his perceived cultural piracy, we were able to explore fully the benefits and costs of intercultural translation.

By combining a careful theoretical framework with an active learning strategy that asked students to apply their observations and impressions in a performative mode, students were able to begin their journey toward developing their skills as careful observers, respondents, *and* creators of work with an expanded aesthetic and performative vocabulary.

Preparing for *Vinegar Tom*

Vinegar Tom was the last performative event that the students were required to see. This early play by Caryl Churchill tells the story of two farm women who are named as witches by a man they have spurned sexually. The play explores the connection between fear of female sexuality and witch-hysteria in the seventeenth century and raises provocative questions about contemporary gender relations (see Figure 11.2).

To prepare for the performance, we first looked at the social and political context out of which this play emerged. Two lecture sessions along with background readings and an exploration of several websites on Churchill and British feminist theatre provided a useful grounding. After situating the play historically, we then invited the director to discuss her concept of the play along with the design team who related how their visual and aural elements responded to the director's concept. We also asked the director about acting choices and style. Additionally, several of the actors visited the class and discussed how the historical subject matter resonated for them in a contemporary context. Armed with this information and their basic LOS framework, the students attended the performance and recorded their responses in their journals.

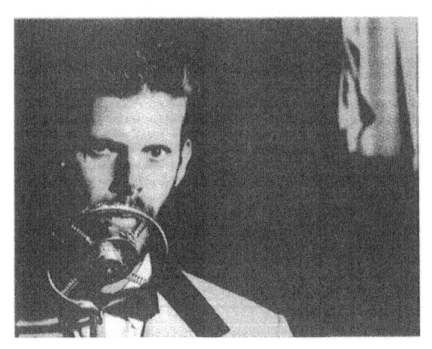

Figure 11.2   Sprenda, a professor of theology, sings a satiric commentary about the evils of women at the conclusion of *Vinegar Tom*

Responding to *Vinegar Tom*

As with all our other discussions of performance, students commented extensively on the specific sign-systems in play (the setting, performers, aural dimensions, audience, framing) as well as the text itself. Students were then charged with creating a performative response to the issues and themes in *Vinegar Tom*. Students worked in groups of five to create collectively a three-minute performative event using the various languages of the stage we explored in the class over the semester. Groups shared their performances during the large group lecture sessions as part of a four-day Festival of Performance. Because of limited time, students realized they had to be very focused and organized. Throughout the process they were encouraged to explore how best to use the resources of the group. Although all group members were expected to serve as performers in some way, students were also asked to divide up production-oriented responsibilities such as stage management, direction, design, technical elements, scripting and choreography.

Audience members were expected to write notes and in-depth commentary in their journals on a minimum of three performances each day of the festival and address several questions, including what did the piece appear to be saying? What were the specific languages of the stage used and how did those languages interact? How successful was the performance piece? What leads you to this conclusion? Each performance group was also required to hand in a prompt book that included a detailed list of job assignments; a list of props, costumes, etc.; a script, scenario or summary of performance; blocking or notation; a statement of purpose specifically situating the intent of the performance as a response to *Vinegar Tom*.

These performances were striking in their varied subject matter, styles of performance and use of LOS. Music, dance, colour and attention to the audience's experience marked a radical departure from ordinary college student performance fare that often features bawdy comedy or hopeless fervent realism (pathos). I submit that exposure to alternate aesthetic systems early in the course coupled with close analysis and interpretation of a variety of performance events helped students create sophisticated and intelligent mini-performances. Many students embraced the opportunity to make strong statements. For example, in her journal entry about her group's performance one student asserted that 'women need to try to reveal what a powerful presence they are. 'In my life', she continued, 'I'm trying to face those things that challenge me, that scare me, that inspire me – they are often times one and the same'. LOS gave her a format through which to make the connection between responding to a moving theatrical event and creating her own.

Outcomes and assessment

The overall aim of the LOS framework is to make explicit the symbiotic nature of theory and practice. In the examples offered, students not only carefully observed a variety of performative events and developed their descriptive, analytical and interpretative skills, but also continued to analyse their responses through a variety of performative exercises. These exercises were designed to reinforce the notion that the Languages of the Stage under consideration are not just for the spectator but can be usefully and self-consciously employed by creators of performance.

Another area of significant student growth had to do with a greater appreciation of the role of the critic. Students were better able to identify the difference between criticism that 'finds fault with' and criticism that 'analyses and evaluates' what was attempted, how it was attempted, and comments on the success of the attempt. By paying close attention to the basic sign-systems – performer, setting, aural (music/sound), audience, framing – as well as to the script (or other written textual materials), students were encouraged to consider the role of the critic as a productive member of the meaning-making process for performative events. Dance critic Rachel Kaplan usefully refigures this role as one of 'advocacy criticism' that demands 'conscious observation' as well as a conscious understanding of one's membership in a community of artists and meaning makers.[21]

A third benefit of this approach is that it provides a way for teachers to discuss systematically a variety of aesthetic and performative events by offering a user-friendly way to approach performance genres that may be unfamiliar. Sita Brahmachari advocates using intercultural source materials for studying and making student work, combined with an understanding of the cultural base and significance of those materials. Further, Brahmachari suggests that the exploration of different aesthetic approaches, such as the *Natyashástra*, can help students understand more about the source cultures of the various performative events under consideration so students can respond in more informed ways. She urges teachers to introduce students to the stages of the world by exploring various categories of performative work from other cultures, including ritual, classical, devotional, folk/popular and modern as one way to expand beyond the Western-based naturalism that is firmly embedded in most secondary drama and theatre curricula.[22] As was illustrated in the *kathakali* example, this framework can provide teachers with a tangible 'way in' to what is often perceived as a daunting undertaking.

The LOS framework provides a valuable way to challenge conservative assumptions about theatre and performance, including the prevalent assumption that making theatre has nothing to do with responding to performative events. As informed respondents, students were able to take their new-found critical awareness into their creative process. While self-consciously manipulating a variety of sign-systems and the languages of the stage, they demonstrated their understanding that theatre-making is not a one-way transmissive system but rather a joint venture with spectators who are situated yet who may share some similar cultural experiences. In addition, the LOS framework can provide a way to expose students of theatre to a variety of cultural performances. By actively combining theory with practice, students can become more sophisticated viewers and participants in the performative process. By employing this 'thick' theoretical framework along with active responsive strategies, teachers can graphically illustrate the relationship between making, performing, and responding in their classrooms. This critical awareness can help our students become the thinking practitioners of tomorrow.

NOTES

1 Eco, U. (1979) *The Role of the Reader: Explorations in the Semiotics of Texts* (Bloomington, IN: Indiana University Press), p. 49.
2 Hornbrook, D. (1998) *Education in Dramatic Art* (2nd edn) (London: Routledge), pp. 152–3.
3 Urian, D. (1998) 'On being an audience: a spectator's guide', in D. Hornbrook (ed.) *On the Subject of Drama* (London: Routledge), pp. 133–50.
4 Cooper, S. and Mackey, S. (1995) *Theatre Studies: An Approach for Advanced Level* (Cheltenham: Stanley Thornes), pp. 153–62.
5 Gangi, J.M. (1998) 'Making sense of drama in an electronic age', in D. Hornbrook (ed.) *op. cit.*, p. 163.
6 I would like to acknowledge the input of several of my colleagues at the University of Texas toward the final conceptualization of this course including Ann Daly, Richard Isackes and Suzan Zeder. Their insights and challenges were invaluable during our initial LOS Task Force discussions.
7 Although some of the LOS units may seem basic to the experienced practitioner or theorist, I found that practical explorations of the various theories introduced in each unit often resulted in a more integrated understanding of complex ideas in an accessible and palatable way. In subsequent endnotes, I have listed key references for readers who might like to pursue these specific theoretical areas in more depth.
8 We focused primarily on the basic Shannon–Weaver model of communication. What is generally overlooked when citing this model of the 'transmissive' process of communication is the fact that the two Bell Telephone engineers who developed the theory were trying to increase the degree of efficiency with which signals travel through telephone lines. (See Shannon, C. and Weaver, W. (1959) *The Mathematical Theory of Communication* (Chicago: University of Illinois) for more information.) The exclusive use of their model as a metaphor for how communication 'works' ignores the complexities of human interaction.
9 Whitmore, J. (1994) *Directing Postmodern Theatre* (Ann Arbor, MI: University of Michigan Press) offers an expanded examination of these 'languages'. He includes an interesting graph to help viewers and creators tract the degree to which these languages are in play in any given performance (p. 13).
10 For more information on the use of semiotics in theatre, see Aston, E. and Savona, G. (1991) *Theatre as Sign-System: A Semiotics of Text and Performance* (London: Routledge); Carlson, M. (1990) *Theatre Semiotics: Signs of Life* (Bloomington, IN: Indiana University Press); DeMarinis, M. (1993) *The Semiotics of Performance* (trans. A. O'Healy) (Bloomington, IN: Indiana University Press).
11 Reader-response and reception theories help to understand the dynamic relationship that exists between a viewer or reader and a text. See Holub, R. (1984) *Reception Theory* (London: Methuen) and Naumann, M. (1976) 'Literary production and reception'. *New Literary History*, **8**(1), 107–26.
12 See Whitmore, J. (1994) *op. cit.* for a further discussion of cultural and theatrical codes (p. 8).
13 Brockett, O. (1992) *The Essential Theatre* (6th edn) (Fort Worth, TX: Harcourt Brace), p. 6.
14 Schechner, R. (1985) *Between Theater and Anthropology* (Philadelphia, PA: University of Pennsylvania Press), p. 35.
15 Borrowing Richard Schechner's use of a fan as a metaphor and model for conceptualizing the relationship between different kinds of performative events, 'performance' can be seen as a term that encompasses a variety of activity.

Additionally, Schechner sees theatre, dance, and music as inseparable entities. He goes on to illustrate a more inclusive understanding of performance by webbing the dynamic interactions between each sector or node on the continuum. See Schechner, R. (1988) *Performance Theory* (London: Routledge), pp. xii–xv.

16 Schechner, R. (1988) *op. cit.*, p. 6.
17 Brahmachari, S. (1998) 'Stages of the world', in D. Hornbrook (ed.) *op. cit.*, p. 23.
18 Brockett, O. (1992) *op. cit.*, p. 35.
19 Zarrilli, P. (1990) 'Kathakali', in F. Richmond, D. Swann and P. Zarrilli (eds) *Indian Theatre: Traditions of Performance* (Honolulu, HI: University of Hawaii Press), pp. 315–57.
20 Bolland, D. (1988) *A Guide to Kathakali* (2nd edn) (New Delhi: National Book Trust), pp. 127–9.
21 Kaplan, R. (1991) 'Why I write criticism'. *Contact Quarterly*, **16**(1), p. 36.
22 See Brahmachari, S. (1998) *op. cit.*, pp. 18–35.

Conclusion: Changing Cultural Landscapes

Helen Nicholson

All books about the teaching of drama inevitably reflect contemporary educational concerns, and this one is no exception. In recent years, aware of the opportunities presented by living in an increasingly globalized society, drama educationalists have become concerned with how drama might reflect the dynamic cultural landscapes in which young people live. In this social climate, many drama teachers have reconsidered their customary commitment to equality, and have considered how to include a wider diversity of voices and experiences in drama education. Similarly, there have been debates about the relationship between equality and dramatic literacies, about ensuring that students learn how to use the crafts, conventions and languages of drama to explore ideas and communicate with others, thus enabling them to become active participants in constantly changing artistic and social worlds.

The approaches to teaching drama contained in this book articulate and explore many issues which seem particularly relevant at the beginning of a new century. Both drama and education come out of a historical period, what Raymond Williams used to call a structure of feeling.[1] Indeed, educational practices change quickly over time, both as a response to new social circumstances, and as an idealistic reaction against previous educational theories and ideas. But, in thinking about the changing cultural landscapes of drama and of education, it is often useful to look back, to build on what is valuable from the past, and decide what might be comfortably left behind.

Throughout the twentieth century, drama education sustained and developed sophisticated teaching methodologies and, in different guises, maintained a strong commitment to democratic learning practices. This legacy, derived from progressive education, is now often taken for granted by contemporary drama teachers. Notwithstanding many legitimate criticisms about the unevenness of progressive education, those who developed their theories and methodologies in drama education during this period taught us to value the insights of all students; contemporary ways of working which aim to encourage thoughtful participation in drama by creating stimulating learning environments remain indebted to this inheritance. Interestingly, educational innovations in the 1960s and 1970s coincided with a movement which sought to introduce greater democratic working practices in radical theatre, which have now been similarly integrated into the mainstream.[2] As educational practices evolve and change, it is important to remember that drama education grew up at a moment in history which turned the optimistic values of equality and social justice into a practical pedagogy, and that the egalitarian values of the period have continued to endure, in various forms, ever since.

The triangulation between the culture of education, theatre practices and drama education has led to new developments and approaches to contemporary drama teaching. At this moment in time, one of the issues which is discussed both implicitly and explicitly by many of the contributors to this book is how drama education might sustain its traditional commitment to equality, and also look forward to the future by taking account of the different experiences and expectations that students bring to the classroom. How an inclusive, and fully differentiated, drama curriculum might be achieved is contested terrain, and rightly so; the balance between equality and difference in a hectic classroom is extremely difficult to achieve, but always worth the pursuit.

EXPANDING CULTURAL HORIZONS

At times in the history of drama education, there has been an ambivalent relationship between educationalists, the academy and the theatre. In part, this is due to how the term 'culture' was most commonly defined, as the representation of the 'best' of humanity.[3] This idea, when combined with the modernist assumption that the arts are inherently redemptive and transformative, suggested that great works of art would educate and 'perfect' the individual and thus lead to a more civilized society. Critics of this way of thinking have suggested that this description of culture and the arts is necessarily conservative, leading to a perception of the academy an elitist institution, interested in perpetuating its own particular judgements of taste, and to the idea that theatre exists solely as a means of entertaining middle-class audiences.

Although this version of theatre and the academy continues to be a recognizable stereotype, it ignores the fact that both theatre practitioners and members of the academy may challenge established values and beliefs as well as uphold them. Perhaps most significantly, a much wider description of culture has now gained currency. Raymond Williams offered a 'social' definition of culture, which is used to describe the values, arts, behaviour and assumptions implicit in a particular way of life.[4] In this context, drama and theatre are not thought to offer a model of human nature to which all be expected to might aspire, but are symbolic of the values of a particular culture, at a particular moment in time. This expanded description of culture, brought about by the effects of globalization, has made Western thinkers increasingly aware that their own values and assumptions are culture bound and derive, as Williams suggests, from a specific context. In turn, this way of thinking has led to a reconsideration of the role and significance of the interpreter in drama practice and criticism, and an acknowledgement of the diverse functions and descriptions of drama and theatre in a plurality of cultures and societies.

Since it has become generally accepted that all cultural practices, including drama, are not universal and ahistorical but contingent on time and locality, it has been recognized that no culture is internally coherent, and that values and traditions change over time. James Clifford makes this point clearly, linking drama, identity and culture:

> Twentieth Century identities no longer presuppose continuous cultures of traditions. Everywhere individuals and groups improvise local performances from (re)collected pasts, drawing on foreign media, symbols and languages.[5]

Drama, performance and the various practices of theatre all have a particular part to play in creating identities, in challenging or affirming values and cultural traditions. David Edgar, writing about British theatre, points out that it is the 'question of belonging' which holds particular significance for contemporary drama:

> How communities of difference relate not just within themselves but also between each other in an increasingly globalised but also fractured world is the major human question we'll confront in the next century. Because it is essentially a cultural question, ... the question of belonging will inevitably foreground the arts, and particularly the narrative arts, as people seek ever desperately to construct, deconstruct and reassemble stories that make sense of the world.[6]

Drama and theatre so often raise questions about what this 'sense' might mean at a particular moment in time, whose values it might hold, and to whom it might belong, that it enables students to reach understandings about their own values and those of others. It is, however, an understanding that is inevitably embodied, provisional, dependent on context, contingent on temporal experiences. And this process may be disturbing as well as consoling.

If, therefore, students are to expand their cultural horizons, they will become involved in interpreting and making dramatic meanings with an awareness of their own assumptions, and the contexts and social purposes of drama. As such, progression in drama does not require, on the one hand, increasingly disinterested judgement of taste about canonical works of dramatic literature nor, on the other, overly mechanistic training in acting or related theatre skills. It involves students in a more complex interweaving of dramatic texts, practices and experiences.[7]

EMBODIED UNDERSTANDING

As drama has developed as an area of study and practice, the equation between theoretical knowledge about drama and practical involvement in the work has become increasingly balanced. Unlike many other areas of the 11–18 curriculum, progression in drama does not require students to move from the physical to the inert, from active involvement to critical judgement, from practice to abstract thought. Furthermore, in common with other arts subjects such as the visual arts, music and dance, students do not have to give up their own creative work as they get older, as if creativity were something that gets in the way of more serious forms of learning. This may be obvious, but it is crucial; it is not possible to make crude distinctions between learning about art and learning about life when students are actively engaged in their own creative work as thinking practitioners.

The integration between the study and practice of drama, which is a major component of drama education, has now permeated the academy. Lesley Wade Soule, writing about her work in a university drama department, focuses on the interrelationship between the physical and the cognitive in drama practice:

> It is my premise that for theatrical theory to be fully productive it should be organically linked with the physical practices of performance. There is a kind of theoretical understanding in theatre-making which can be explored only through using the body (including the voice) in space ... In theatre, as in life, physical and intellectual skills are inseparable.[8]

Seen in this light, the body is not an instrument of the mind nor secondary to it; it is central to the development of understanding and very literally how we interact with, and experience, the world. In drama, where students are given the opportunity to discover how drama works by experimenting physically, new ideas might be evolved and challenged. An embodied pedagogy, therefore, productively combines theory with practice as an affective, creative and intellectual process of speculation, and invention within the form itself.

Reaching an 'embodied understanding' of different theories, histories and practices of drama is, however, no more free from partisanship than any other cultural practice. Indeed, the political visibility of the body, when combined with an expanded description of culture, has had a marked impact on contemporary academic and theatre practices. Students following courses in drama in higher education are now just as likely to be to follow courses in popular theatre or the dramaturgy of protest as the study and performance of scripted plays, and they may participate in street theatre, carnival, community drama and Theatre in Education. As such, progression in drama cannot be regarded in term of a hierarchy of dramatic forms, from, for example, improvisation to the production of canonical plays. As the academy now rightly recognizes, all dramatic forms are worthy of critical and creative interrogation, and have their own particular histories, traditions and practices.

From the point of view of drama education, therefore, one of the ways of ensuring progression in the 11–18 age range is to encourage students to revisit aspects of drama practice with increasing understanding of the cultural assumptions and theories which inform them. In practice, an expanded description of culture does not mean that students move from spontaneous improvisation to rehearsed performances as they progress, nor from popular culture to the literary tradition, nor from practice to theory. Rather, different aspects of drama might be woven into a spiral curriculum in which the creative and the critical, theory and practice, spontaneity and rehearsal are continually interlinked.

NEW POSSIBILITIES AND UNEXPECTED GIFTS

At the centre of drama education lies the premise that students are not passive recipients of a culture, but active meaning makers. Building on reader-response theories, many practitioners have reconsidered how ideas and images are shaped and interpreted in dramatic form. Representing ideas in drama is, moreover, a practical and physical process which unites aesthetic engagement with craft, wherein the visual, aural and kinaesthetic languages of drama are combined in visible and tangible ways to create and communicate meanings.

In this collection of writings, teachers of drama articulate many different ways in which they encourage students to manipulate, shape, revise and reorder dramatic form and content. Within a changing cultural landscape, they demonstrate how the languages of drama, and the technologies and crafts associated with them, can become creative and intellectual tools. Drama is a fluid, dialogic and ephemeral art form, involving interaction between participants, but it is the languages of drama, including those associated with new technologies, which enable the physical creation of emotional and conceptual meanings in space and time. New digital technologies, for example, not only have the potential to become creative means of communication in themselves, but also in the drama classroom can provide a link between thought and practice by capturing and framing dramatic moments. Such ways of working, which focus on the crafts of drama as well as the content, draw attention to the complex ways in which dramatic narratives are symbolized in dramatic form.

For teachers working in drama education, this collection perhaps raises as many questions as it answers. As theatre practitioners and drama teachers experiment with new forms of artistic representation, issues are raised about what might be included in the curriculum, and what might be left out. The practicalities of teaching, the requirements of assessment and attention to progression mean that curriculum design is always a process of selection, in which choices and compromises are inevitably made. But to make meanings intelligible, to challenge ideas and communicate feelings young people need language, including the physical and gestural languages of drama. Drama is a *particular* form of artistic representation which is, in Madelaine Grumet's words, 'an exploration and a performance of understanding'.[9]

One of the qualities of drama, to adapt the words recalled by Jennifer Simons, is that it is as an 'unexpected gift', in which students find new possibilities and new ways of representing and interpreting their worlds. It is this engagement in drama, when combined with an understanding of craft and context, which actively invites students to explore the ambiguities, pleasures, unease and contradictions which contemporary living entails.

NOTES

1 See Williams, R. (1992) *The Long Revolution* (London: Hogarth Press), pp. 48–71 for a discussion of the concept 'structure of feeling'.
2 I am thinking here of the work of theatre practitioners in Britain such as Joan Littlewood, whose work aimed to develop collaborative ways of working, and the work of Dorothy Heathcote and Gavin Bolton in drama education.
3 Matthew Arnold, writing in the 1860s, was particularly concerned to apply this description of culture to education. See Collini, S. (ed.) (1993) *Arnold: Culture and Anarchy and Other Writings* (Cambridge: Cambridge University Press).
4 See Williams, R. (1982) *Culture and Society* (London: Hogarth Press), pp. xiii–xx.
5 Clifford, J. (1988) *The Predicament of Culture* (Cambridge, MA: Harvard University Press), p. 14.
6 Edgar, D. (ed.) (1999) *State of Play: Playwrights on Playwriting* (London: Faber & Faber), pp. 33–4.
7 As elsewhere in this book, I am using the word 'texts' in its broadest sense, including live drama as well as scripted or performance texts.
8 Wade Soule, L. (1998) 'Performing identities', in C. McCullough (ed.) *Theatre Praxis* (London: Macmillan), p. 39.
9 Grumet, M. (1998) 'Research conversations: visible pedagogies/generous pedagogies', in J. Saxton and C. Miller (eds) *The Research of Practice the Practice of Research* (Victoria: IDEA Publications), p. 10.

Bibliography

Acosta, B. (1995) *3 Girls & Clorox* (Charlottesville, VA: New Plays).

Adams, R. (ed.) (1985) *Teaching Shakespeare* (London: Robert Royce).

Aers, L. and Wheale, N. (eds.) (1991) *Shakespeare and the Changing Curriculum* (London: Routledge).

Aldrich, P.W. (1996) 'Evaluating language arts materials', in J. Van Tassel-Baska, D.T. Johnson and L. Neal Boyce (eds) *Developing Verbal Talent* (Boston, MA: Allyn and Bacon), pp. 218–39.

Allen, B. (1991) 'A school perspective on teaching Shakespeare', in L. Aers and N. Wheale (eds) *Shakespeare and the Changing Classroom* (London: Routledge), pp. 40–57.

Anon. (1984) *Brecht for Beginners* (New York: Writers and Readers).

Aoki, E. (1993) 'Turning the page: Asian/Pacific American's children's literature', in V.J. Harris (ed.) *Teaching Multicultural Literature in Grades K-8* (Norwood, MA: Christopher-Gordon), pp. 109–35.

Artaud, A. (1969) *The Cenci* (trans. S. Watson Taylor) (London: Calder and Boyars).

Artaud, A. (1988) *A Spurt of Blood* in S. Sontag (ed.) *Antonin Artaud: Selected Writings* (Berkeley, CA: University of California Press), pp. 72–6.

Artaud, A. (1995) *The Theatre and its Double* (London: Calder).

Arts Council of Great Britain (1990) *Drama in Schools* (London: Arts Council).

Asante, K.M. (1991) 'The Afrocentric idea in education', in F.L. Hord and J.S. Lee (eds.) *I Am Because We Are: Readings in Black Philosophy* (Amherst, MA: University of Massachusetts), pp. 338–49.

Aston, E. and Savona, G. (1991) *Theatre as Sign-System: A Semiotics of Text and Performance* (London: Routledge).

Bailin, S. (1994) *Achieving Extraordinary Ends* (Norwood, NJ: Ablex).

Bailin, S. (1998) 'Creativity in context', in D. Hornbrook (ed.) *On the Subject of Drama* (London: Routledge), pp 36–50.

Beckett, S. (1984) *Breath*, in *Collected Shorter Plays of Samuel Beckett* (London: Faber & Faber).

Benedetti, J. (1982) *Stanislavski: An Introduction* (London: Methuen).

Benedetti, J. (1988) *Stanislavski: A Biography* (London: Methuen).

Bent, S. (1997) *Shelter*, in *New Connections: New Plays for Young People* (London: Faber & Faber), pp. 459–526.

Berkoff, S. (1994) *The Collected Plays* (London: Faber & Faber).

Berry, J. (1997) *Classic Poems to Read Aloud* (London: Kingfisher).

Best, D. (1980) 'The objectivity of artistic appreciation'. *British Journal of Aesthetics*, **20**(2), 115–27.

Bharucha, R. (1993) *Theatre and the World* (London: Routledge).

Blumenthal, E. (1984) *Joseph Chaikin* (Cambridge: Cambridge University Press).

Boal, A. (1985) *Theatre of the Oppressed* (trans. C.A. and M-O. Leal McBride) (New York: Theatre Communications Group).

Boal, A. (1992) *Games for Actors and Non-Actors* (London: Routledge).

Bolland, D. (1988) *A Guide to Kathakali* (2nd edn) (New Delhi: National Book Trust).

Bolton, G. (1982) 'Drama as learning, as art and as aesthetic experience', in M. Ross (ed.) *The Development of Aesthetic Experience* (Oxford: Pergamon Press), pp. 148–52.

Bolton, G. (1989) 'Drama', in D. Hargreaves (ed.) *Children and the Arts* (Milton Keynes: Open University Press) pp. 119–38.

Bond, E. (1979) *The Woman: Scenes of War and Freedom* (New York: Hill & Wang).

Bourdieu, P. (1996) *The Rules of Art* (trans. S. Emanuel) (Cambridge: Polity Press).

Boyum, J. (1985) *Double Exposure: From Fiction into Film* (New York: Penguin).

Brahmachari, S. (1998) 'Stages of the world', in D. Hornbrook (ed.) *On the Subject of Drama* (London: Routledge), pp. 18–35.

Britton, J. (1970) *Language and Learning* (London: Penguin).

Brockett, O. (1992) *The Essential Theatre* (6th edn) (Fort Worth, TX: Harcourt Brace).

Brook, P. (1968) *The Empty Space* (London: Methuen).

Brook, P. (1993) *There Are No Secrets* (London: Methuen).

Bruchac, J. (1996) *Roots of Survival* (Golden, CO: Fulcrum).

Bruner, J. (1986) *Actual Minds, Possible Worlds* (Cambridge, MA: Harvard University Press).

Bruner, J. (1996) *The Culture of Education* (Cambridge, MA: Harvard University Press).

Carlson, M. (1990) *Theatre Semiotics: Signs of Life* (Bloomington, IN: Indiana University Press).

Churchill, C. (1990) *Plays Two* (London: Methuen).

Claxton, G. (1988) 'Teaching and learning', in R. Dale, R. Ferguson and A. Robinson (eds) *Frameworks for Teaching* (London: Hodder & Stoughton), pp. 21–32.

Claxton, G. (1990) *Teaching to Learn* (London: Cassell).

Clemen, W.H. (1951) *The Development of Shakespeare's Imagery* (London: Methuen).

Clements, P. (1983) *The Improvised Play: The Work of Mike Leigh* (London: Methuen).

Clifford, J. (1988) *The Predicament of Culture* (Cambridge, MA: Harvard University Press).

Collini, S. (ed.) (1993) *Arnold: Culture and Anarchy and Other Writings* (Cambridge: Cambridge University Press).

Cooper, S. and Mackey, S. (1995) *Theatre Studies: An Approach for Advanced Level* (Cheltenham: Stanley Thornes).

Cusworth, R. and Simons, J. (1997) *Beyond the Script: Drama in the Classroom* (Sydney: PETA).

Dale, R., Fergusson, R. and Robinson, A. (eds) (1988) *Frameworks for Teaching: Readings for the Intending Secondary Teacher* (London: Hodder & Stoughton).

Delpit, L. (1995) *Other People's Children: Cultural Conflict in the Classroom* (New York: New Press).

DeMarinis, M. (1993) *The Semiotics of Performance* (trans. A. O'Healy) (Bloomington, IN: Indiana University Press).

Dent, G. (ed.) (1992) *Black Popular Culture* (Seattle, WA: Bay Press).

DfEE (1993) *The Ofsted Inspection Manual* (London: HMSO).

DfEE (1997) *The National Literacy Strategy* (London: HMSO).

Drake, N. (1997) 'Introduction' to *New Connections: New Plays for Young People* (London: Faber & Faber), pp. v–x.

Du Bois, W.E.B. (1903/1995) *The Souls of Black Folk* (New York: Penguin).

Eagleton, T. (1976) *Marxism and Literature* (London: Methuen).

Eco, U. (1979) *The Role of the Reader: Explorations in the Semiotics of Texts* (Bloomington, IN: Indiana University Press).

Edgar, D. (ed.) (1999) *State of Play: Playwrights on Playwriting* (London: Faber & Faber).

Elam, K. (1980) *The Semiotics of Theatre and Drama* (London: Methuen).

Fielding, M. (1996) 'Why and how learning styles matter: valuing difference in teachers and learners', in S. Hart (ed.) *Differentiation and the Secondary Curriculum* (London: Routledge), pp. 81–103.

Fleming, M. (1994) *Starting Drama Teaching* (London: David Fulton).

Forkbeard Fantasy (1995) *Work Ethic* (Walton on Thames: Thomas Nelson).

Friel, B. (1990) *Dancing at Lughnasa* (London: Faber & Faber).

Frowe, I. (1999) '"Sticks and Stones . . .": the power of language', in E. Bearne (ed.) *Use of Language across the Secondary Curriculum* (London: Routledge), pp. 15–25.

Fuegi, J. (1987) *Bertolt Brecht: Chaos According to Plan* (Cambridge: Cambridge University Press).

Gangi, J.M. (1998) 'Making sense of drama in an electronic age', in D. Hornbrook (ed.) *On the Subject of Drama* (London: Routledge), pp. 151–68.

Giannachi, G. and Luckhurst, M. (eds) (1999) *On Directing: Interviews with Directors* (London: Faber & Faber).

Gibson, R. (1994) 'Teaching Shakespeare in schools', in S. Brindley (ed.) *Teaching English* (Buckingham: Open University Press), pp. 140–8.

Goodman, L. (1993) *Contemporary Feminist Theatres* (London: Routledge).

Grotowski, J. (1968) *Towards a Poor Theatre* (London: Methuen).

Grumet, M. (1998) 'Research conversations: visible pedagogies/generous pedagogies', in J. Saxton and C. Miller (eds) *The Research of Practice the Practice of Research* (Victoria: IDEA Publications), pp. 7–11.

Hardy, B. (1977) 'Narrative as primary act of the mind', in M. Meek, A. Warlow and G. Barton (eds) *The Cool Web: The Pattern of Children's Reading* (London: Bodley Head), pp. 12–23.

Hargreaves, D. (1982) *The Challenge of the Comprehensive School* (London: Routledge & Kegan Paul).

Harradine, D. (1999) 'What is the new mime?' *Total Theatre* 11(1), 15–20.

Harris, V.J. (ed.) (1993) *Teaching Multicultural Literature in Grades K–8* (Norwood, MA: Christopher-Gordon).

Heathcote, D. and Bolton, G. (1997) *Drama for Learning* (Portsmouth, NH: Heinemann).

Hodgson, J. and Richards, E. (1974) *Improvisation* (London: Eyre Methuen).

Holub, R. (1984) *Reception Theory* (London: Methuen).

Hornbrook, D. (1991) *Education in Drama* (London: Falmer Press).

Hornbrook, D. (1998a) *Education in Dramatic Art* (2nd edn) (London: Routledge).

Hornbrook, D. (ed.) (1998b) *On the Subject of Drama* (London: Routledge).

Howard, R. (1984) 'A material view of tragedy', in L. Bell (ed.) *Contradictory Theatres* (Colchester: Theatre Action Press), pp. 204–9.

Hughes, J. (ed.) (1991) *Drama in Education: The State of the Art* (Sydney: Educational Drama Association).

Hunt, A. (1972) *John Ford's Cuban Missile Crisis* (London: Methuen).

Hunt, A. (1976) *Hopes for Great Happenings* (London: Methuen).

Iser, W. (1978) *The Act of Reading: A Theory of Aesthetic Response* (Baltimore, MD: Johns Hopkins University Press).

Jarry, A. (1995) *Ubu Rex*, in *The Ubu Plays* (trans. C. Connolly and S. Watson Taylor) (London: Methuen), pp. 17–74.

Jennings, C. (1989) *A Lunch Line: Contemporary Scenes for Contemporary Teens* (Charlottesville, VA: New Plays).

Johnstone, K. (1981) *Impro* (London: Methuen).

Kaplan, R. (1991) 'Why I write criticism'. *Contact Quarterly*, **16**(1), 34–41.

Kempe, A. (ed.) (1996) *Drama Education and Special Needs* (Cheltenham: Stanley Thornes).

Kempe, A. (1998) 'Scunny stuff: exploring genre and irony in special needs education'. *Drama*, **5**(2), 53–6.

Kempe, A. (1999) 'Kissing with confidence', in C. Lawrence (ed.) *The Canterbury Keynotes* (London: National Drama Publications), pp. 27–36.

Kliman, B. (1992) *Shakespeare in Performance – Macbeth* (Manchester: Manchester University Press).

Kress, G. (1995) *Writing the Future* (York: NATE).

Liles, S. and Mackey, S. (1997) 'Collaboration: devising group work', in S. Mackey (ed.) *Practical Theatre* (Cheltenham: Stanley Thornes), pp. 113–62.

Lochhead, L. (1997) *Cuba* in *New Connections: New Plays for Young People* (London: Faber & Faber), pp. 115–62.

McCullough, C. (ed.) (1998) *Theatre Praxis* (London: Macmillan).

McLaren, P. (1999) 'A pedagogy of possibility: reflecting upon Paolo Freire's politics of education'. *Educational Researcher*, **28**(2), 47–59.

Many, J. and Cox, C. (eds) (1992) *Reader Stance and Literary Understanding: Exploring the Theories, Research, and Practice* (Norwood, NJ: Ablex).

Melrose, S. (1994) *A Semiotics of the Dramatic Text* (London: Macmillan).

Merleau-Ponty, M. (1973) *The Prose of the World* (trans. J. O'Neill) (London: Heinemann).

Miller, A. (1974) 'Tragedy and the Common Man', in B.F. Dukore (ed.) *Dramatic Theory and Criticism: From Greeks to Grotowski* (New York: Holt, Rinehart & Winston), pp. 894–7.

Moore T. (ed.) (1998) *Phoenix Texts: A Window on Drama Practice in Australian Primary Schools*, NADIE Research Monograph no. 5 (Melbourne: NADIE).

Morgan, N. and Saxton, J. (1987) *Teaching Drama: A Mind of Many Wonders* (London: Hutchinson).

Morrison, T. (1992) *Playing in the Dark: Whiteness and the Literary Imagination* (New York: Random House).

Müller, H. (1995) *Theatremachine* (London: Faber & Faber).

National Curriculum Council (1990) *The Arts 5–16: Policy and Practice* (London: Oliver & Boyd).

Naumann, M. (1976) 'Literary production and reception'. *New Literary History*, **8**(1), 107–26.

Neelands, J. (1998) *Beginning Drama, 11 – 14* (London: David Fulton).

Oddey, A. (1994) *Devising Theatre* (London: Routledge).

O'Farrell, M. (1999) 'Interview with Joseph Fiennes'. *Independent on Sunday*, 17 January.

O'Neill, C. (1995) *Drama Worlds: A Framework for Process Drama* (London: Heinemann).

O'Neill, J. (ed.) (1974) *Phenomenology, Language and Sociology: Selected Essays of Maurice Merleau-Ponty* (London: Heinemann).

O'Toole, J. (1992) *The Process of Drama: Negotiating Art and Meaning* (London: Routledge).

Pammenter, D. (1993) 'Devising for TIE', in T. Jackson (ed.) *Learning through Theatre* (London: Routledge), pp. 53–70.

Parafrey, A. (1990) *Apocalyse Culture* (London: Feral House).

Pascoe, R. (1997) 'Research and the arts in schools: a two-way dialogue'. *NADIE Journal*, **21**(2), 33–48.

Phelan, P. (1993) *Unmarked: The Politics of Performance* (London: Routledge).

Redington, C. (ed.) (1987) *Six T.I.E. Programmes* (London: Methuen).

Reinelt, J.G. and Roach, J.R. (eds) (1992) *Critical Theory and Performance* (Ann Arbor, MI: University of Michigan Press).

Reynolds, P. (1985) 'An active reading of Shakespeare's stagecraft', in R. Adams (ed.) *Teaching Shakespeare* (London: Robert Royce), pp. 114–27.

Ross, M. (1984) *The Aesthetic Impulse* (Oxford: Pergamon).

Schechner, R. (1985) *Between Theater and Anthropology* (Philadelphia, PA: University of Pennsylvania Press).

Schechner, R. (1988) *Performance Theory* (London: Routledge).

Schechner, R. (1993) *The Future of Ritual: Writings on Culture and Performance* (London: Routledge).

Schurer, E. (ed.) (1997) *German Expressionist Plays* (London: Continuum).

Shaffer, P. (1973) *Equus* (London: Penguin).

Shaffer, P. (1991) *The Royal Hunt of the Sun* (London: Longman).

Shannon, C. and Weaver, W. (1959) *The Mathematical Theory of Communication* (Chicago, IL: University of Illinios).

Shiach, D. (1987) *From Page to Performance* (Cambridge: Cambridge University Press).

Slade, P. (1958) *An Introduction to Child Drama* (London: Hodder & Stoughton).

Smith, M.W. (1992) 'Submission versus control in literary transactions', in J. Many and C. Cox (eds) *Reader Stance and Literary Understanding: Exploring the Theories, Research and Practice* (Norwood, NJ: Ablex), pp. 143–61.

Smith, O.C.H. (1972) *Orghast at Persepolis* (London: Eyre Methuen).

Spady, B. (1992) *Outcomes-based Education: Australian Curriculum Studies* (Belconnen: ACT).

Stafford-Clark, M. (1997) *Letters to George* (London: Nick Hern).

Stanislavski, K. (1937) *An Actor Prepares* (London: Geoffrey).

Stanislavski, K. (1980) *My Life in Art* (London: Methuen).

Stanislavski, K. (1981) *Creating a Role* (trans. E. Hapgood) (London: Methuen).

Styan, J.L. (1981) *Modern Drama in Theory and Practice*, vols 1–3: *Naturalism and Realism, Symbolism and Surrealism* and *Epic and Expressionist Theatre* (Cambridge: Cambridge University Press).

Styan, J.L. (1984) *The State of Drama Study* (Sydney: Sydney University Press).

Taylor, D.H. (1990) *Toronto at Dreamer's Rock* (Calgary, AB: Fifth House).

Thompson, J. (1991) 'Assessing drama: allowing for meaningful interpretation', in J. Hughes (ed.) *Drama in Education: The State of the Art* (Sydney: Educational Drama Association), pp. 76–82.

Urian, D. (1998) 'On being an audience: a spectator's guide', in D. Hornbrook (ed.) *On the Subject of Drama* (London: Routledge), pp. 133–50.

Van Tassel-Baska, J., Johnson, D.T. and Neal Boyce, L. (eds) (1996) *Developing Verbal Talent* (Boston, MA: Allyn & Bacon).

Vygotsky, L. (1962) *Thought and Language* (trans. E. Hanfmann and G. Vakar) (Cambridge, MA: MIT Press).

Vygotsky, L. (1978) *Interaction between Learning and Development in Mind and Society* (Cambridge, MA: Harvard University Press).

Wade Soule, L. (1998) 'Performing identities', in C. McCullough (ed.) *Theatre Praxis* (London: Macmillan), pp. 38–61.

Walton, J.M. (ed.) (1999) *Craig on Theatre* (London: Methuen).

Way, B. (1966) *Development through Drama* (London: Longman).

Wertenbaker, T. (1998) *Our Country's Good* (London: Methuen).

Whitmore, J. (1994) *Directing Postmodern Theatre* (Ann Arbor, MI: University of Michigan Press).

Willett, J. (1964) *Brecht on Theatre: The Development of an Aesthetic* (New York: Hill & Wang).

Williams, D. (1991) *Peter Brook: A Theatrical Casebook* (London: Methuen).

Williams, R. (1982) *Culture and Society* (London: Hogarth Press).

Williams, R. (1992) *The Long Revolution* (London: Hogarth Press).

Winston, J. (1998) *Drama, Narrative and Moral Education* (London: Falmer Press).

Wittgenstein, L. (1963) *Philosophical Investigations* (Oxford: Basil Blackwell).
Wollheim, R. (1987) *Painting as an Art* (Princeton, NJ: Princeton University Press).
Wooding, B. (1997) *Multicultural Education: A Consideration of Approaches, Positive Mental Attitude Pack* (London: Theatre Centre).
Wray, D. and Lewis, M. (1997) *Extending Literacy* (London: Routledge).
Zarrilli, P. (1990) 'Kathakali', in F. Richmond, D. Swann and P. Zarrilli (eds) *Indian Theatre: Traditions of Performance* (Honolulu, HI: University of Hawaii Press), pp. 315–57.

Index

Printed in Great Britain
by Amazon

70425904R10108